I0187559

KING
OF THE
SWORDSMEN

Colonel Thomas Hoyer Monstery

KING of the SWORDSMEN

❖

Colonel Thomas Hoyer Monstery

EDITED WITH INTRODUCTION & NOTES BY

Ben Miller

HOLLYWOOD
HUDSON SOCIETY PRESS
2019

Front cover image from Col. Thomas Hoyer Monstery, *El Rubio Bravo, King of the Swordsmen: Or, the Terrible Brothers of Tabasco* (London: Aldine Publishing Co., [1893]).

Cover art and book design by Bronwyn Frazier-Miller.

Back cover/inside flap author portrait from John Joseph Flinn, *The Hand-Book of Chicago Biography* (Chicago: The Standard Guide Company, 1893).

Printed in the United States of America and the United Kingdom.

Publisher's Cataloging-in-Publication data

Monstery, Thomas Hoyer, 1824-1901.

King of the Swordsmen / Colonel Thomas Hoyer Monstery; edited with introduction & notes by Ben Miller.

pages cm.

Paperback: ISBN 978-0-9990567-4-5

Hardcover: ISBN 978-0-9990567-5-2

1. Fencing. 2. Dueling. 3. Swordplay. 4. Martial arts—History—19th century. 5. Latin America—19th century. I. Monstery, Thomas H., 1924-1901. Miller, Ben, 1977- II. Title.

FIRST EDITION

10 9 8 7 6 5 4 3 2 1

For Maestro Ramón Martínez

CONTENTS

Preface / *i*

Introduction / *v*

Maps / *cv*

Note to the Reader / *cxi*

King of the Swordsmen

I. Three to One / *1*

II. The Woman in the Case / *11*

III. The Espadachíns / *19*

IV. The Cock-Fight / *27*

V. Olaf's Story / *37*

VI. A Lesson in Killing Cows / *45*

VII. Tropical Evenings / *51*

VIII. El Sequidor / *63*

IX. Bragamonte / *71*

X. The Revolution / *77*

XI. Don Jose / *85*

XII. Padre Miguel / *95*

XIII. The Padre's Story / *103*

XIV. Setting Out / *111*

XV. The Fugitives / *119*

XVI. The Capture / *125*

XVII. Ominous Sounds / *133*

XVIII. On The Brink / *141*

XIX. The Rout / *149*

XX. The Dead Jarocho / *157*

XXI. The Jacal / *163*

XXII. The Gomez Brothers / *169*

XXIII. The Bandits / *175*

XIV. Chiapas / *181*

XXV. Jose Maria / *187*

XXVI. Mexico / *193*

XXVII. A Strange Ride / *199*

XXVIII. The General Bandit / *205*

XXIX. Don Lerdo's Letter / *211*

XXX. Conclusion / *219*

Appendix / *225*

Works Cited / *233*

Illustration Credits / *237*

About The Author / *243*

About The Editor / *244*

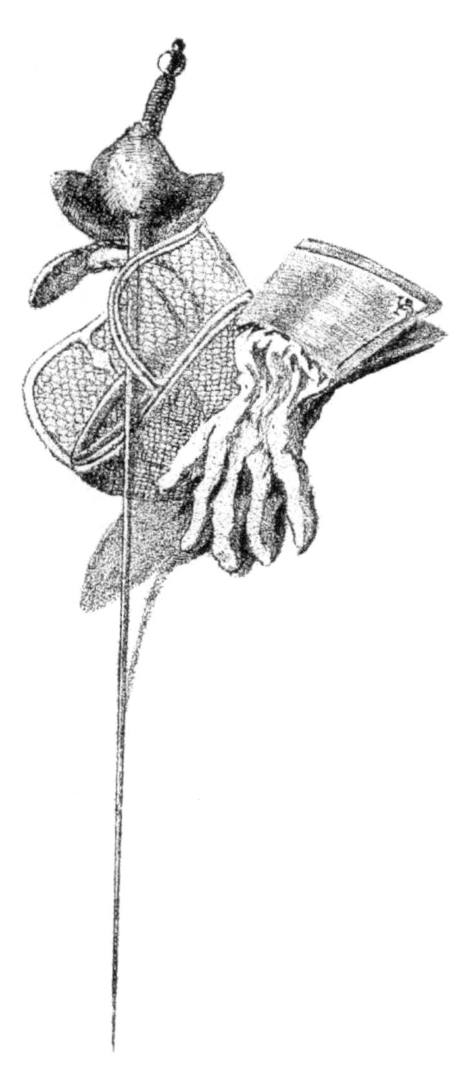

PREFACE

The idea for this book grew out of a lecture I was invited to give at the CombatCon convention in Las Vegas on August 4, 2018, entitled "Colonel Monstery and Latin America." With the growing wave of interest in the life and writings of Colonel Monstery, some readers had questioned whether his amazing, reputed adventures throughout the world could actually be true. The lecture had been an attempt to at least partially answer those questions as much as was possible, given the historical evidence available. While that event was attended by a small (yet not undistinguished) audience, the outpouring of online interest from international readers—who had been unable to attend, but were keenly intrigued by the topic—made clear the widespread desire for the material to be publicly released in another type of format. The introduction which follows this preface is essentially an expanded, more detailed version of my notes from the 2018 lecture.

In preparing this text, it became obvious that the perfect companion to the lecture notes would be Monstery's own semi-autobiographical novel, *El Rubio Bravo: King of the Swordsmen*, which detailed (in albeit altered and romanticized form) his combats, intrigues, and adventures in Spanish America. The text of that novel, presented herein, is largely based on my personal copy of the 1893 Aldine Library edition (a more elaborate version, containing a full color cover illustration), with a few added textual flourishes from the 1881 first edition.

For her assistance with research on this project, I must give immense thanks to Diane Hayes, Colonel Monstery's great great granddaughter—who, to my knowledge, has researched the Monstery family's history during the last several decades more than anyone else that I am personally aware of. Diane was absolutely instrumental in helping me delve into the Colonel's Latin American travels. In particular, I am grateful for her sharing the documents of his military service, and his case against the Mexican government, which I might otherwise have never come across, as well as for allowing me to include photographs of Thomas's wife, Carmen Xiques, and daughter, Berguita Monstery, in this book.

I would also like to thank my fencing masters, Maestro Ramón Martínez and Maestro Jeannette Acosta-Martínez, the former to whom the present volume is dedicated. In my eighteen years of martial arts experience (fourteen of which have been focused on the practice of classical and historical fencing) and historical research, I honestly believe Maestro Martínez to know more about Spanish fencing, and the history of fencing in Spanish America, than anyone I have ever encountered. Indeed, much enthusiasm and inspiration for this project can be traced to my training in Spanish saber (a historical style practiced in the Americas) under Maestro Martínez between 2005 and 2008, in which many pleasurable bouts of fencing were had with my fellow student at the time, Carl Massaro. As far as I know, Maestro Martínez was the first person to reconstruct this historical fencing method—and it is my further hope that this book can bring more attention to the swordsmanship and traditional martial arts of the Americas.

For their help in producing this book, I would also like to thank the following people:

My wife, Bronwyn Frazier-Miller, for her love and support, for her cover design, and for painstakingly restoring the many period photographs and illustrations included in the book.

Maestro Jared Kirby, who has been ever helpful in acquiring various texts and items throughout the years relating to Colonel Monstery. It was he who gave me a copy of Frederick Whittaker's 1884 biography of Monstery many years ago, at the time when I first began to uncover articles pertaining to the Colonel, and which was inspirational in leading me down the path of further research. It was also Maestro Kirby who invited me to give the lecture "Colonel Monstery and Latin America" in 2018, which gave birth to the present publication.

J. Makali Bruton, of Mexico, for generously granting permission to include his photograph of the grave and bust of General Eusebio Bracamonte, one of Colonel Monstery's nemeses.

My parents, David and Pam Miller, as well as Jack and Pam Frazier, for their support throughout these many years.

Lastly, the many readers who have brought about renewed interest in Colonel Monstery, and further attention to his amazing life.

Ben Miller
Hollywood, California
March, 2019

"If the story of his life is ever correctly written it will exceed in interest the work of the most fertile imagination."

INTRODUCTION

Thomas Hoyer Monstery was one of the most celebrated American martial arts masters of the nineteenth century. During his long life, he opened fencing academies in New York, Chicago, Baltimore, Oakland, Havana, Mexico City, and San Francisco, crossed blades with some of the greatest fencing masters of the century, and mentored Ella Hattan, popularly known as "Jaguarina," arguably one of the most accomplished swordswomen of all time. Monstery also survived participation in a vast number of duels; although it is impossible to settle on a precise number, various estimates put the figures between fifty and sixty. As a soldier and sailor, Monstery served under the flags of twelve different nations on a total three separate continents, during which time he participated in innumerable battles, conflicts, and revolutions. In 1888, a prominent Chicago journal wrote:

> There is no man living who has fought more real, hard, to-the-death duels than Colonel Monstery, the veteran disciple of the art of running one's fellow-man through the ribs. Colonel Monstery has fought duels in

> Europe, in Mexico, South and Central America, and other countries where the sword is the arbiter of the quarrel. He has pinked his man and shot his man in single combat with the same cheerful alacrity (and considerably more coolness, probably) as he has done on the open field of battle, when hot-blooded foes were spilling each other's gore by thousands. His body is a regular map of cuts and scars and blue spots where bullets have entered, yet to-day alive, strong, erect, and, despite his almost three-score years and ten, without an equal on the continent in the handling of the broadsword and rapier.[1]

Likewise, another journalist wrote that "There does not today exist between two seas a more unique character than Colonel Thomas H. Monstery."[2] After the swordsman's death, in 1901, the New York periodical *Turf, Field, and Farm* appropriately declared:

> If the story of his life is ever correctly written it will exceed in interest the work of the most fertile imagination.[3]

So extraordinary, in fact, is Monstery's life and career, that in recent years, a number of readers have speculated that certain aspects of Monstery's life were invented or concocted—that, in essence, the story of his life is simply too amazing to be believed.

In looking at the vast scope of Monstery's life and adventures—many of which took place in underdeveloped and dangerous regions of the world—it is impossible to verify everything. Much of his military service was spent among militias and revolutionary groups—rather than among regular troops—and is thus absent from official government rolls and service records. And yet, one finds that—with the exception of his age and birthplace—there are few contradictions between Monstery's own story and actual history.[4] We find, for instance, in looking at the available extant records of his travels, that he was in nearly all the places he claimed to have been when he was in them; although not *all* his travels are verifiable, we at least find very few contradictions.[5] We also find that many of Monstery's professed enemies—such as Santos Guardiola, *Señor* Galetti, Gerardo Barrios, General Bragamonte, Jesus Gonzalez Ortega, and the rival *maitre d'armes* Nicholas Poupard—were real people who actually existed in the times and places in which Monstery claimed to have encountered them. Monstery published details of his life story numerous times in the newspapers of the period, yet no one—as far as we know—ever contradicted his tales, even though there were many alive who could have done so, had Monstery's stories been false. Thus, although it is impossible to verify all the details of his life, the Colonel has, in short, given us no significant reason to doubt the bulk of them.

An examination of the full life and career of Thomas Monstery is beyond the scope of this book; those interested in a broader look at his early training, travels in Europe, duels, fencing career in America, and his writings on self-defense may be directed to the book *Self-Defense for Gentlemen and Ladies* (published in 2015 by North Atlantic Books), which includes a biography of Monstery, as well as his treatise on self-defense with the fist, foot, cane, and quarterstaff.[6]

The present text is concerned solely with Monstery's travels and adventures in Spanish America, which took place during the middle and second half of the nineteenth century.

HISTORICAL SOURCES

There are several major sources for this period of Monstery's life. The first is Monstery's 1899 biography, *The Sword Prince*, authored by Frederick Whittaker. This text, however, while informative and immensely entertaining, is also romanticized, riddled with errors, and poses obvious problems for the historian. The second source is a collection of interviews with, and letters written by, Monstery himself, published during the 1880s and 1890s in various newspapers. The third source is Monstery's petition to recover his lost Mexican treasure. These pages, which detail Monstery's military service in Spanish America, can still be found in U.S. Senate documents, as well as in truncated form in the Spanish language *Archivo del General Porfirio Díaz*.[7] Although Monstery's claim was ultimately denied, the official rejection resulted from his status as a mercenary; the truth of the story itself was not disputed at the time of his claim, and was actually verified by the testimony of several Central American witnesses as well as the Mexican government. The fourth source is a manuscript transcription of Monstery's life story, recorded during his lifetime, and passed down within the Monstery family. Although sparse in detail, this manuscript nevertheless fills in some important gaps in the early portion of Monstery's military life. The final source is a novel written by Monstery himself—which, as shall be seen, contains a mixture of both fact and fiction. For, towards the end of the 1870s, Monstery made a brief foray into writing novels for Beadle's Dime Library in New York City.

Although some modern readers might scoff at the idea of a celebrated fencing master and martial artist stooping to writing dime novels, there can be little doubt that the decision to do so was motivated by severe financial hardship. In 1879, Monstery's grand New York City fencing academy was decimated by a massive fire—not an infrequent occurrence in nineteenth century America. Three members of the Monstery family barely escaped with their lives, and his entire business—including fencing academy, boxing school, and shooting gallery—was ruined.[8] It seems no small coincidence that the very same year, Monstery's first dime novel was published. This would be followed by numerous others, which would be printed between 1879 and 1883, after which time Monstery relocated to Chicago, where he opened a new fencing academy. As his career as a master-of-arms began to flourish once again during the mid 1880s, the publication of Monstery's novels ceased—although several would be reprinted in the following decades as part of the British Aldine Library series and Beadle's Half Dime Library. Given this timeline of events, it seems extremely probable that Monstery's brief run as a novelist was sparked by the fire and the resulting financial catastrophe. However, as shall be seen, what was then Monstery's loss, is today our gain.

EL RUBIO BRAVO, KING OF THE SWORDSMEN

Monstery's first novel, published in 1879, was entitled, *Iron Wrist: the Swordmaster. A Tale of Court and Camp.* This book was the first in a series of semi-autobiographical novels chronicling and embellishing

Monstery's early adventures as an itinerant master-of-arms. The second installment of this series, published in early 1881, was entitled *The Demon Duelist, or, The League of Steel: a Story of German Student Life,* and was based on Monstery's experiences in Germany and Russia. The third part of this semi-biographical series, published in the autumn of 1881, was *El Rubio Bravo, King of the Swordsmen: Or, the Terrible Brothers of Tabasco*, and chronicled Monstery's subsequent travels in Central America.[9] Author Everett Bleiler, in his massive survey of nineteenth century genre fiction, favorably described *El Rubio Bravo* as

> harking back to the earlier tradition when the dime novel was still adult adventure fiction and had not yet degenerated into low-grade boys' stories. The story concerns an adventurer in Central America around 1860, probably with autobiographical detail...A curious work that reads (apart from occasional romantic elements) much like an authentic account by one of the early nineteenth-century travellers in Central America. Although the romance is story-book, the novel carries a quiet conviction of personality and background. It is one of the very few dime novels worth reading for their own merit.[10]

Indeed, just as Monstery was a progressive pioneer and innovator in a number of ways in his role as fencing master (for instance, in teaching self-defense to women, in his holistic approach to martial arts, and in his public support of African American martial artists)[11], this trait seems to have also extended to his fiction writing. His use in *El Rubio Bravo* of a "lost race" theme, featuring "lost cities, deep in tropical jungles, where ancient races dwelled," appears to be one of the earliest—and one that would, in the following decades, be greatly popularized by famous authors such as H. Rider Haggard, Rudyard Kipling, Arthur Conan Doyle, Edgar Rice Burroughs, Abraham Merritt, and Robert E. Howard.[12] Nevertheless, in modern times, the invention of the "lost race" or "lost world" genre has been incorrectly attributed to Haggard's *King Solomon's Mines,* published in 1885—despite the existence of Monstery's earlier novel.[13] Burroughs, at the very least, had definitely been aware of Monstery—in fact, his classic 1926 novel *The Mad King* featured a protagonist who "had been a pupil of the redoubtable Colonel Monstery, who was...'one of the thanwhomest of fencing masters.'"[14]

ENTERED AT THE POST OFFICE AT NEW YORK, N. Y., AT SECOND CLASS MAIL RATES.

Vol. XII. Published Every Week. *Beadle & Adams, Publishers,* 98 WILLIAM STREET, N. Y., September 7, 1881. Ten Cents a Copy. $5.00 a Year. No. 150

EL RUBIO BRAVO, King of the Swordsmen;

Or, THE TERRIBLE BROTHERS OF TABASCO.

BY COL. THOMAS HOYER MONSTERY,

CHAMPION-AT-ARMS OF THE TWO AMERICAS.

AUTHOR OF "IRON WRIST, THE SWORDMASTER," "THE DEMON DUELIST," "THE CZAR SPY," ETC., ETC., ETC.

"I MUST KILL THEM ALL, OR I'LL BE KILLED," MUTTERED EL RUBIO, AS HE SENT A MUSKET FLYING OUT OF THE HANDS OF DON DOMINGO.

First edition of *El Rubio Bravo* (New York: Beadle & Adams, 1881).

British edition of *El Rubio Bravo* (London: Aldine Publishing Co., [1893]).

Regarding *El Rubio Bravo*'s authorship, Bleiler notes that "it is sometimes stated that the dime novelist Frederick Whittaker wrote under Monstery's name, but the present story is different in all ways from Whittaker's work and is best ascribed to Monstery himself."[15] Indeed, Whittaker's biography of Monstery is full of errors *not* found in Monstery's own erudite writings (such as *Self-Defense for Gentlemen and Ladies*), and a careful comparison of the prose and writing styles in these various texts strongly identifies Monstery as the author of *El Rubio Bravo, King of the Swordsmen* .

There can be no doubt that the lead character of the novels, Olaf Svenson, is based on Monstery himself. In Monstery's biography, *The Sword Prince,* author Frederick Whittaker relates that *"El Rubio Bravo"* was a nickname bestowed on Monstery during his time serving as fencing master in San Salvador.[16] In the novel, Svenson describes himself as "a Norseman" and a "Danish Yankee." All other biographical details aside, the physical descriptions of Monstery and Svenson are strikingly congruent. For instance, Monstery is physically described by Whittaker in the following terms:

> He was still slender in appearance, wore his hair long; had a boyish face, and dressed in the most dandified fashion, with all the rich tastes of a Dane; but he had become known and feared as what the 'Plug Uglies' of Baltimore call a 'mighty deceivin' man.' To look at his slim, upright figure and foppish dress, you would take him for a regular milksop, only fit to swing a cane and sport an eye-glass. But when you came to measure and weigh him, you would find that it took a forty-two inch tape to go round his naked chest, that he tipped the scale at a hundred and fifty-three pounds, and was as hard as a rock all over, with the trained activity of a fighting athlete.[17]

Likewise, in the pages of *El Rubio Bravo*, the character of Olaf Svenson is almost identically described:

> He was a man about thirty, straight as an arrow, with a slim waist and an appearance of slightness that was very deceptive. Had you seen him stripped, you would have noticed a forty-inch chest, with lean, muscular arms and legs as hard as iron, and a wiry appearance indicative of unusual

> strength and activity. He stood about five feet ten, and looked taller, while his complexion and hair were remarkable among the dark, sallow men of the tropics, with their black hair and eyes. This man was a regular white blonde such as the Spaniards call a "Rubio," with fierce blue eyes and hair so light that it looked like spun flax in the sun, for he wore it long and curly...

An early likeness of Monstery, published in California during the 1860s, clearly exhibits the same "dandified" appearance, slim frame, and blonde curls.[18] If any doubt still remained that Olaf Svenson represented Monstery himself, it was dispelled in 1883, when the character appeared in print once again, this time in Monstery's novel *Fighting Tom, the Terror of the Toughs.* In this tale, set in rough-and-tumble New York City, Svenson runs a fencing and boxing academy, is introduced as the one who trained the "man who won the Canzi-Fardella duel" (something Monstery had actually done)[19], and was described in physical terms identical with Monstery: "A tall gentleman of military appearance...he was a handsome man, with long pointed mustache and beard, and wore his light-gray hair quite long, with glasses on his nose. He looked like an old soldier certainly, but the last man one would have taken for an athlete."[20]

In perusing the pages of *El Rubio Bravo, King of the Swordsmen*, one may be surprised to find a number of incidents extracted almost verbatim from Monstery's life. We also find that several of the main characters are based on people that Monstery knew personally (one being his own wife, Carmen Xiques). Despite these facts, the novel obviously integrates a great deal of fiction; there is no evidence, for instance, that Monstery was ever on the trail of a lost Aztec civilization (although he did travel near the "ancient [Mayan] city of Palenque"), and many of the events of the novel which take place in Mexico do not match up with the biographical timeline given by Monstery in later interviews and writings.

Nonetheless, the novel offers a fascinating glimpse into Monstery's views of Central America, and gives more vivid and detailed accounts of numerous incidents in his life which are known to have actually occurred.

What follows, then, is a chronicle of what is known of Monstery's real-life travels and experiences in Spanish America, and a discussion of the similarities and differences between the novel, and actual history.

* * *

We now offer a word of caution to those readers who wish to read *El Rubio Bravo: King of the Swordsmen* unspoiled—many of the twists and turns in Monstery's narrative will be revealed in the remaining pages of this introductory essay.

Reader, you have been warned! If you wish to enjoy Monstery's novel completely unspoiled, skip ahead to Chapter One, and return to this essay after you have finished reading the novel.

FIRST FORAYS INTO SPANISH AMERICA: THE MEXICAN WAR, 1846-1847

Monstery's first travels to Spanish America began at a young age, when he was still a teenager serving as a Naval cadet aboard the ship *Bellona.* During this time, he took part in a two-and-a-half year cruise in which he sailed "through Spanish America, the Indies, Brazil, and the Mediterranean." At age fifteen, he deserted from a Russian ship at London, and "got on a Spanish ship for Cadiz." Later, Spanish sailors "got him drunk and kidnapped him after a knife fight, on board the lugger *Adda de Mastora*, a slaver and pirate." While that boat was being chased by an English ship, Monstery jumped overboard, spent seven hours in the water, and was rescued by fisherman. He returned to the Danish service, and eventually commenced training at Ling's Institute of Physical Culture in Stockholm, Sweden.[21]

Despite these dangerous encounters, by all accounts, Monstery had become a firm hispanophile—that is, one who "had always been fascinated by Spaniards." According to his biography,

> This is a very common thing among Scandinavians. There seems to be some fascination which makes the fair-haired, blue-eyed children of the North admire the dark eyes and olive faces of the South, and revel in the soft liquid language, so different from their own deep-toned, guttural tongue.[22]

It may also be that Monstery was attracted to Spanish America due to his love of fencing and hand-to-hand combat; as another article about him stated,

> The Spaniard is earth's greatest enthusiast in all weapons that shine. He does not like firearms, though his personal courage compels him to face them when necessary.[23]

At age twenty-two, Monstery received word of the outbreak of the Mexican-American War. Traveling to Virginia, in the United States, he applied for a commission, but was "laughed at," and enlisted instead as a common sailor, or seaman. Assigned to the ship *Ondiaka*, Monstery took part in the bombardment of Tuxpan and Veracruz in 1847, later fought at Tabasco, and was eventually removed from active service and sent back to Portsmouth on account of sickness.[24] In his pension application to the United States government, Monstery personally related:

> I actually served sixty days with the Army or Navy of the United States in Mexico, or on the coast or frontier thereof, or en route thereto, in the war with that nation, which service was as follows: Went from the "Ondiaca" (or "Ordiaca")—to Tampico—to Lopez Islands, Sacra-fecio—Vera Cruz, Tuxpan and up a river, and sent back on account of sickness to Portsmouth Hospital...I am disabled by reason of Rupture and injuries to left side...incurred at Vera Cruz, Mexico on or about the month of March, 1847, in manner as follows: by overexertion (and) a fall while assisting in moving cannon in small boats. I was actually engaged with the enemy in the war with Mexico, to wit: in the battle of Vera Cruz in the month of March, 1847 and Tuxpan on the coast of Mexico.

Monstery further related that the *Ondiaka* was "wrecked near Tampico, commanded by (name not remembered), Col. DeBucy or DeRucy was on board with his Regiment." Monstery's claim was ultimately denied by the U.S. Government, which determined that the *Ondiaka* was not an official American military ship, but was instead "hired by the Government during the Mexican war as a Transport...[and] by the Q.M. [quarter master's] Dept."[25] Another account related by Monstery, while a member of a Mexican War veterans association, reads as follows:

> [Monstery] was refused a commission because he was not a graduate of West Point. Hearing that a Col. De Busey was raising a regiment at New Orleans he hurried down there and endeavored to get a commission, but De Busey refused him. The only chance to go to Mexico was to enlist as a common seaman on the transport on which De Busey's regiment was to be taken to the seat of war. He took the chance. To use his own words, he "was the only gentleman before the mast." On nearing the Mexican coast the vessel was wrecked near Tampico. This was the spring of 1847. They managed to make their way to Tampico, which was held by United States troops. From here they went to the Island of Lobos, and from there to Sacrificio, near Vera Cruz. Col. Monstery was wounded, but not disabled. After the fall of Vera Cruz he went to Tuxpan, was in the fight there, and from there went up the Tabasco River with the expedition against San Juan Baptista, the capital of the State of Tabasco. Soon, after the battle he was taken sick and was sent to the hospital at Portsmouth, Va., where he was kept until the close of the war.[26]

Two years following the war, in 1848, Monstery befriended the militant Cuban exile, Narciso López, an event which would have significant ramifications for the "Danish Yankee" in subsequent years, when he would be drawn into the struggle for Cuban independence.[27] Before that time, however—in less than a year—Monstery took part in his first expedition as a soldier-of-fortune, to Nicaragua.

1849: FILIBUSTERING IN NICARAGUA

At this juncture in Monstery's career, having become dissatisfied with opportunities in the American military, and perhaps hungering for adventure abroad, he became a filibuster. An explanation of this term, in

American filibusters in Nicaragua, "reposing after the battle."

the context of the nineteenth century military world, can be found in the writings of Anderson C. Quisenberry:

> What is filibustering, or who is a filibuster? Different origins and meanings have been given, but we have doubtless derived filibuster from the Spanish *filibustero*, and understand it to mean a citizen of one country who invades another, with which his own is at peace, for the purpose of subduing and occupying it. Filibustering has not always been the same, but in one form or another it may be said to have existed time out of mind.[28]

Monstery's first expedition reportedly took place in 1849. He had been in New Orleans earlier that year, and had "started to San Francisco by way of Santa Fe...Instead he reached Nicaragua." It was recounted,

> A revolution was in progress, of course, and, equally of course, [Monstery] went into it. He did not remember the names of the contestants or upon which side he fought. He says that he is satisfied, however, that he was on the side of the Liberals as opposed to the Conservatives or clergy. He is satisfied of this, because in all of the dozens of Central and South American wars in which he has been a participant he was always against the Church. Near Nicaragua one day, in a desperate fight in which he was

> doing the usual yeoman service for the patriot whose name he has forgotten, he was cracked on the head with a musket butt. When he came to, the field was deserted. He did not know which side won, and does not know now. Blood was running from his ears, and he started to discover a doctor. He did not succeed, but after a day of travel found himself in a little town on the coast. Here he met an Italian, who agreed to operate under his direction. A poignard was run through the back of Monstery's neck and a piece of linen shirt inserted, forming a sort of seton. For more than fourteen months the seton did its work of suppuration, but brain fever was averted.[29]

This episode remains one of the least well-documented episodes of Monstery's career, and it is uncertain to which conflict the account refers. The story may be pure apocrypha, or its events may have been related to a series of treaty disputes between the United States, Britain, Nicaragua, and Honduras which took place during the latter part of 1849. An 1895 interview with Monstery confirms this timeline, for in it, he states:

> I taught fencing for a time and went, in 1849, to California. From there I went to Nicaragua, ahead of Walker, but for the same purpose. I was wounded...[30]

1850-1851: WITH LOPEZ AND CUBAN EXILES

At the midpoint of the nineteenth century, the political climate in Cuba was such that its people had become increasingly dissatisfied with Spanish rule—culminating in a "strong movement for liberty in the central portion of the island" under the leadership of Narciso López, a former general of the Spanish army. However, his revolutionary plans being prematurely exposed, López was compelled to fly Cuba for his life:

> He escaped to New York, where he was joined by a great number of Cuban exiles, with whom he fomented a plan for achieving the liberty of Cuba by armed expeditions from the shores of the United States...After the detection of his plot in 1848, his estates in Cuba were confiscated by the Captain-General; but it seems that he had previously succeeded in

GENERAL NARCISO LOPEZ.

> depositing some very considerable sums of money in the New York banks, all of which were subsequently sunk in his several attempts to invade Cuba. Personally, he has been described as a fine-looking, well set-up man with a splendid head. handsome black eyes. and benevolent countenance. His manners showed that he had had the advantages of the best of breeding and association; he was distinguished by his simplicity of dress and demeanor, and was devoid of arrogance and ostentation. He was a man of the supremest courage and daring; and physically he was endowed with a capacity for the greatest hardship and endurance. Before the close of his checkered career this capacity was tested to the utmost limit and met all the calls that were made upon it.

López was just the sort of person Monstery would have liked and admired, and, by his own account, in 1848 the Dane became his "intimate" friend.[31]

After establishing himself in New York with a large following of Cuban patriots, López set to work to create an "army of invasion whose landing on Cuban shores was to be the signal for the rising of the natives." In 1849, 1850, and 1851 three expeditions were fitted out.

According to an American historian of the period, these were "movements in the interest of humanity." It was insisted,

> They were not for plunder and spoils, but for the freedom of human beings from the galling yoke of tyranny. The Spanish had first depopulated the island of Cuba with fire and sword, and then afterward so oppressed the English and French and Dutch who came into it that they were driven from the land and took to the sea as buccaneers.[32]

In America, López found many sympathetic soldiers and would-be adventurers lining up to join his revolution:

> The American people had become interested in the project of freeing Cuba, by whatever honorable means, and openly sympathized with it in every section of the country, more particularly in the South and West, where many gallant and daring men of high social position felt their souls in arms and eager for the fray. It is needless to say that the project attracted not only lovers of liberty for liberty's sake, but also lovers of adventure for adventure's sake, and lovers of money for the sake of the money there was supposed to be in it.[33]

It was in this climate that Thomas Hoyer Monstery found himself. He soon became swept up in the wave of enthusiasm and lust for adventure. According to his biography:

> [Monstery] had, as a cadet and in Mexico, acquired quite a knowledge of Spanish, and had always been fascinated by Spaniards, which was perhaps the reason that he made the acquaintance of the unfortunate Lopez about this time, and became crazy for Cuban independence. All his friends were Spaniards or Cubans; and he was full of the romance of the Spanish character...For more than a year Monstery kept Spanish company, at first because the Spaniards were the only people he met who could fence, and, after a while, because of the Spanish beauties he met.[34]

López soon enlisted a force of around fifteen hundred men, whom he attempted to get off as a joint expedition from New York and New Orleans.[35] Monstery, who had been living and working in Baltimore, related that in 1850, he "tired of [selling] cigars, had money, tried to raise volunteers, went to New Orleans."[36] Although Lopez spearheaded several incursions between 1848 and 1851, according to several accounts written by Monstery, the majority of his involvement occurred in 1851, thus firmly placing the Dane as a potential member of the final, ill-fated Bahía Honda Expedition. As Monstery later recounted, "After drifting around, I took part in the insurrection in Cuba in 1851."[37]

During the month of July, 1851, López's unorganized recruits were given the word to assemble quietly in New Orleans, where they were secretly organized into companies and regiments, the officers of which were regularly commissioned. Their object was to free Cuba from the tyranny of Spain, and either form a republic of their own or annex the island to the United States. In addition to their American and Cuban-exile soldiers, the expeditionary force included hundreds of "refugee patriots," or former revolutionaries, from Germany, Hungary, Poland, and Ireland.[38]

The expedition left New Orleans at daybreak on the morning of Sunday, August 3, 1851, in the steamer *Pampero*. About two o'clock on the morning of the twelfth of August, Lopez's army—just four hundred and fifty-three strong—disembarked upon the shores of Cuba, approximately twelve miles west of Bahía Honda, and fifty miles from Havana. The men were armed with condemned muskets, and had no rifles; but many of them had revolvers and knives of their own.[39]

At first, López's troops impressively battled through the country against overwhelming odds, defeating "the Spaniards in every engagement, notwithstanding their largely superior numbers."[40] The revolutionaries, however, had expected the local Cubans to rise up and join their ranks; instead, "the Creoles appear to have everywhere opposed their liberators with the utmost hostility."[41] Within days, after a series of vicious battles with local and Spanish troops in which the invading forces became divided, López's army was routed in the village of Las Pozas by Spanish troops. The first fifty-one men captured from López's army—including forty Americans, four Irishmen, two Cubans, two Hungarians, one Italian, one Scotchman, and one Filipino—were swiftly executed by firing squad, and the vast majority of the others were taken prisoner and sentenced to hard labor in quicksilver mines.[42] López himself was executed publicly in Havana on September 1. Before his death, he shouted defiantly, "My death will not change the destiny of Cuba!"

A brush with death in America, however, saved Monstery from this fate. On May 3, 1851, just a few months prior to the planned expedition, the Dane suffered an assassination attempt by three knife-wielding members of the Spanish secret service led by a man named Jose Jesus de Gomez. Monstery only barely escaped with his life by expertly using his cane in self-defense, as he later recounted:

> I found I had got three stabs altogether, the last two in the forearm, and, I think, all given by the same man in my first confusion and surprise, before I recovered my presence of mind and used my stick...My principal assailant was arrested, and I recovered in two months' time, but I carry the scars today, the largest of all being of that first stab where Gomez splintered the bone of my arm.[43]

It was undoubtedly this incident to which Monstery referred, when, in an 1895 letter to an old Cuban revolutionary comrade, he mentioned being López's "companion in 1851, fighting for the Cuban cause, for which cause I carry four wounds."[44] Monstery noted that these injuries rendered him bed-ridden for more than six weeks, and that they thus "saved him from joining Lopez and the garrote."[45]

Later, in his writings on self-defense, Monstery makes brief reference to the time when he was "quite intimate with poor Lopez, who was executed in Cuba for attempted insurrection."[46]

1851: MARRIAGE TO CARMEN XIQUES

During the other half of 1851 Monstery lived in Baltimore, where he set up a cigar store, boxing school, and fencing academy.[47] Even more momentously, earlier that year, he had fallen "over head and ears" in love:

> He had acquired plenty of money in his new trade, when he met a lovely Spanish girl, whom we will call only by her Christian name, which is very pretty. Her name was Carmen, which the Spaniards are apt to soften into

Carmen Xiques. Photograph courtesy of Diane Hayes.

> Carmelita, and with Carmelita Monstery fell over head and ears in love, much to the satisfaction of the lady...[48]

Carmen Xiques had been born in 1831 in Cuba. She was the daughter of Joseph Xiques and Gertruda Romero, and her paternal grandfather, Juan, had reportedly hailed from Catalonia, Spain. Carmen was described as "beautiful...with a regular Spanish face," a "high-spirited, quick-tempered little creature," and, "like all Spanish women, very proud of her pretty little feet."[49] When Monstery suffered the attack by members of the Spanish secret service, it was Carmen who nursed him back to health.

By all accounts, Thomas and Carmen's relationship was tempestuous. According to their great great granddaughter, Diane Hayes,

> We believe Thomas was married to Carmen in 1851 in Philadelphia, but have no record of the marriage. I do have a copy of their divorce, however, in I think [1855]. In spite of that (and the fact that I haven't found any mention that they remarried), they ended up back together and had several children born to them in the 1860s (some, including my great-grandfather, were born in California).[50]

Carmen was clearly the basis for Olaf Svenson's love interest, "Carmelita," in *El Rubio Bravo: King of the Swordsmen.* However, contrary to the timeline presented in that story, it is clear that Monstery and Carmen had already been married years before the events of the novel began.

A vivid illustration of Carmen's fiery personality can be seen in an incident that occurred in 1853, and which is recounted in Monstery's biography. Carmen was described as "perfectly devoid of fear and [could be] wild with anger."[51] When she was insulted by a member of the infamous Baltimore gang, the Plug Uglies, Carmen threatened the aggressor, insisting that her husband would kill him. Monstery soon confronted the man, a fight ensued, and the Dane knocked the gang-member senseless with a storm of fisticuffs. It was later related in court:

> [The aggressor, Wills] asked her where she lived, and she answered him and then started home. He followed her first to her boarding house on Second street, and thence to the store of her husband on North street...She then said that Wills had followed and insulted her, and turning to him told him he was "no gentleman," when he struck her in the face. Her husband interfered, and the affray terminated in Wills being considerably injured. The court acquitted Monstery and his wife...[52]

Still dissatisfied with this outcome, Carmen was said to have complained, tearfully: "If my husband had been a Spaniard, he would have killed him. Oh, why did I marry a man like you?" Monstery, however, "only laughed at her. It was not his nature to bear malice."[53] Later, when an entire gang of vengeful Plug Uglies came to Monstery's shop to steal cigars, Carmen stood up to them once again, insisting that they "leave them alone." According to Whittaker, "It was only a pretty little Spanish girl that said it, but she had a dangerous look about her, and they hesitated." At that instant, Monstery entered the shop with two revolvers cocked and aimed, and the men were pacified.[54]

1854: COLOMBIA

In later interviews, Monstery relates that years after his involvement with López, he "took part in a war in the United States of Colombia," under the general and future dictator, José María Melo. Along with his reputed service in Nicaragua, this remains some of Monstery's least well-documented wartime escapades. However, the timeline presented by Monstery closely coincides with historical events in Colombia that took place in 1854. Just years prior, New Grenada had approved a bill freeing the country's slaves, prompting the country's slave-owners to rebel against the liberal government. President José Hilario López made Melo the general of the government army, and Melo—finding wide acceptance among the troops—soon defeated the forces of the slave-owners. In 1854, with the support the country's Democratic Societies (a coalition of artisans and liberals), Melo assumed power as the head of state. However, he would be toppled the same year, and his soldiers and artisans viciously repressed. A journalist who had interviewed Monstery related:

> José María Melo was dictator, and Monstery fought for him because he was a Liberal. The Liberals were scattered and the heads of Melo and his new friend rolled loosely upon their shoulders. Disguised, they made their way to the coast. There Monstery smuggled Melo on board a British vessel which put to sea. For himself, he found a vessel sailing northward. Nursing two sabre slashes, one on the head, the other on the arm, he reached New York eventually.[55]

Monstery would reunite with Melo for additional adventures, though not for an interlude of several years.

1855-1858: SPAIN AND CUBA

The next year, after a brief sojourn in the United States, Monstery traveled to Denmark, France, Germany, Italy, Russia, and Spain. This voyage may have occurred as a result of his 1855 divorce from Carmen, or the trip itself may have been the cause of the breach in their relationship. The *New York Daily Tribune* of June 25, 1855 noted the recent arrival in the city of the "brig S. B. Hill, from Trinidad fr Cuba" bearing "Mrs. Monstery and two children, Mrs. and Miss Xiques." The official decree of divorce between Thomas and Carmen was published later that year, in the *Baltimore Sun,* on October 9, 1855. It would not, however, be the end of their passionate and stormy relationship.

During his time in Europe, Monstery learned a special system of bayonet fencing that would earn him fencing laurels, as well as much-needed employment. In his manuscript, Monstery refers to this method as the "Nachtegall system"—a reference to Vivat Victorius Fridericus Franciscus "Franz" Nachtegall, a man regarded as the founder of physical culture in Denmark.[56] Monstery would describe this system, which he later modified (and subsequently called his own) as follows:

> The French parry a bayonet thrust with the stock and barrel of the musket, using the arms to hold it out. The bayonet points up or down in parrying, and has to make a wide sweep to come back to a return point. This sort of motion is exactly opposite to the rules of fencing with the foil or sword, where the principle is to keep the point always ready to thrust, and to make the motions as small as possible from parry to thrust.
>
> The Monstery system of bayonet fencing is quite different. The bayonet is always kept pointing straight at the enemy, and the butt of the piece is kept on the thigh, the parries being made by small motions, in which bayonet crosses bayonet. Thus the whole strength of the body is thrown into the parry, instead of merely the force of the arms.
>
> The consequence is that a man using the Monstery system will whirl his opponent half around at every parry and be able to run him through before he can recover his balance, if he fence on the French system.[57]

In Copenhagen, in 1855, Monstery reportedly "saved the life of the Spanish Charge d'Affaires, who sent him to Madrid."[58] Being asked for further evidence of his skill, Monstery issued a challenge to any man "who fancied himself clever with any weapon." He fought with sabers, rapiers, broadswords, foils, bayonets, knives and lances.[59] Three months later, in 1855, he was offered the post of Instructor of Arms in Cuba, with the rank of major and $200 dollars per month from the Spanish government. He related, "I entered the Spanish service as instructor general of fencing and swordsmanship...I was then sent to Cuba as instructor of the Spanish forces."[60]

According to Monstery, he then "landed at Puerto Principe with seventy ounces of gold in his pockets and his credentials." As he entered the door of the Governor's palace to present his papers,

> He saw a long table piled high with glittering pieces, and behind the gold was a man was dealing monte. It was a feast-time and the custom in Cuba then to run a monte game at the entrance to the palace. Monstery walked to a table and bet his seventy ounces on the queen. He lost, and a moment afterward entered the Governor's presence penniless save for the diamonds he wore. After some months in Puerto Principe he was transferred to Havana, then one of the gayest capitals in the world. It was a life of labor with the sword, gambling, hard drinking, love-making and duelling.[61]

In 1856, while waiting at a hotel in Neuvitas, Cuba, Monstery took part in a public assault-at-arms with the administrator, del Duana.[62] From there, he took a steamer to Havana.

In the Cuban capitol, Monstery set up his own fencing school, and attracted a number of pupils. Although no Cuban print sources could be found attesting to the existence of Monstery's school, an article published nearly two decades later, in a New York journal, cites an illustrious Cuban fencer who testified to the Colonel's former presence there.[63]

Monstery related that in Havana, he found another "flourishing fencing-school" called the *Circolo de Tiradores*, or Circle of Fencers, headed by one "Senor Galetti."[64] As the record shows, this individual was Don Juan Galletti, a seminal figure in the history of fencing in Cuba. A native of Bologna, Italy, Galletti had arrived in Havana in December 1833, where he established his *Academia de Esgrima*, and was reportedly "one of the first to give fencing lessons in Havana."[65] The "Circle of Fencers" referred to by Monstery was undoubtedly the *Sala de Armas Blancas del Circolo de la Habana*, of which Galletti was director.[66] According to Frederick Whittaker, a great rivalry sprang up between Galletti and Monstery, which "spread to the pupils of both." A "grand public match" was thus arranged between the two fencing masters, on which very heavy bets were laid by rival supporters.[67] Monstery himself related:

> Soon after I arrived in Havana I arranged to meet Senor Galletti, the finest swordsman on the island, but I was stricken with the yellow-fever. Thousands of ounces of gold had been wagered on the result, and the friends of Galletti, as I learned later, hired a doctor to cut the tendon of my sword arm under pretense of bleeding me. I was between life, and death for six weeks, and for a time it looked as if my arm would be useless, but I managed with care to pull through all right.[68]

Monstery was forced to withdraw from the contest, and spend many months in self-imposed exercise and physical therapy in order to recover the use of his arm.[69] He reportedly "sat for hours at a table, holding the fingers in his left hand, and worked it back and forth. He would wake in the night, turn on his side and exercise it. In six months the arm was as good as ever."[70] This was in the year 1857.[71]

1858: HONDURAS

Around this same time, in 1858, Monstery received word that William Walker, a well-known American filibuster, had made an armed expedition to Honduras. This occurred as the result of a dispute arising over the possession of the nearby Bay Islands, on which there had been a historical presence of English settlers since the mid eighteenth century, and which had been proclaimed a British possession. In 1859, however, England, under a great deal of pressure from the United States, agreed to surrender the Bay Islands and the Mosquito Coast of both Honduras and Nicaragua. Many of the English settlers disagreed with this resolution, and sought the help of Walker (who had previously seized and lost control of Nicaragua) to put pressure on the British government to retain

William Walker

possession of the islands. Walker agreed, and made haste to the coastal city of Trujillo, Honduras, accompanied by one hundred men.

Upon hearing this news, Monstery, still in Cuba, joined up with a party of men under a German referred to as Baron Carl "Von Wetholz" (or "von Weitholz"), who planned to follow Walker's lead and make his own expedition to Honduras.[72] Additional historical information regarding this German individual has not, unfortunately, been forthcoming. Just before this time, Monstery had evidently reunited with his wife Carmen—albeit briefly—for in his manuscript, he declares that he "left wife at Puerto Principe in 1858 and started for Honduras with Baron Carl Von Wetholz, excited by squier's accounts of country to help Walker..."[73] Another account, published decades later, explained:

> Having nothing to do in Cuba, [Monstery] listened to Baron Carl von Wetholz, a German of education and bravery, who assured him that the people of Honduras were ripe for revolution, needed only a leader, and pined for annexation to the United States. At the head of fifty-four men, well armed, they landed at Truxillo.[74]

Unbeknownst to these men, however, the first expedition had already failed. Walker had been seized by Captain Nowell Salmon of the British Royal Navy—who, viewing the American as a threat to the British-Honduran agreement, promptly turned him over to Honduran authorities. Walker was eventually prosecuted, sentenced to death, and executed by firing squad on September 12, 1860.

After disembarking from their ship in Honduras, things did not go as planned for Monstery and Von Wetholz's party of oblivious adventurers. Monstery recounted:

> I began to smell a mouse. The boats which had brought us, however, had set sail immediately. We could not escape to sea, and it was best to make a bad bargain as good as possible. I found a deserted castle on a hill and housed the men in it. Next morning we were summoned to surrender by a large force of sandalled ragamuffins, headed by a magnificently caparisoned Spanish officer. I went out to talk to them and assured them that we were a party of peaceful miners, come to the country to prospect for gold, of which we had heard much. That tale was received with credulity, so far as my companions were concerned. They were ordered to get out of the country, and they got out with speed. My trunks were broken open, however, and therein they found my commission from the

The execution of William Walker.

The fort at Trujillo, where Monstery was imprisoned.

> Spanish Government and other papers, showing my military character. The officer's name was Valdarama and he put me in jail until he could hear from President Guardiola, surnamed the Butcher, who was at Tegucigalpa.

Though Monstery was now a prisoner, an accident of fate would incite an attack which would give rise to what was reportedly one of his most impressive martial feats:

> I was allowed to exercise in a paved court, and at the doorway opening into this court from the street a single soldier stood guard. I approached him too closely one day and he attempted to bayonet me. I had no idea of escape, but was forced to defend myself. I took his musket from him and stunned him with my fist. At that moment eight others, armed with muskets and bayonets, sprang out of the guardhouse and attacked me. Then followed one of the fights of my life. I demonstrated there that Dumas's back-to-the-wall heroes were frauds. I would have been stuck like a pig but for the fact that I had a space in which to maneuver. They knew nothing, of course, of scientific bayonet play, and their weapons fortunately were unloaded. I had pinked two of them, broken the bayonets of three, and was nearly fainting from exhaustion when I heard a stern command behind me: "Halt!" My opponents dropped their weapons. Turning I saw [Commandant] Valdarama, who was standing in the

The guardhouse at the Trujillo fort.

> doorway, an interested spectator of the bout from its beginning. He approached me and looked me over.
>
> "My God," he said. "Can a man learn to do that?" I told him that a sure-enough man could. He gave me my liberty at once and in return I gave him instruction.[75]

Although it is impossible to verify this story from sources other than Monstery himself, an examination of contemporary photographs of the fortress at Trujillo reveals a structure that closely matches Monstery's description. Visible still are the main gate, the prison yard, and the guardhouse—all mentioned in Monstery's account. Looking at these photos, one can put images to the Colonel's words and imagine him maneuvering to defend himself against multiple attackers. Whatever the precise truth of the story he related, Monstery had clearly visited the actual fortress, or had spoken with someone who was intimately familiar with it, as detailed physical descriptions of the structure do not seem to exist in the available literature of the period. According to Monstery, things went well after his promotion from prisoner to instructor, for he recounted: "in a little while I was as happy as ever, the friend of all of the leading citizens of the town and making much money from my pupils."[76]

JOSÉ SANTOS GUARDIOLA

Now enters into Monstery's life the man who would be cast as the villain of his novel—the president of Honduras, José Santos Guardiola. He is a figure spoken of glowingly in modern histories of Honduras; a man responsible for reforming and liberalizing the country. To this day, some of Honduras's most opulent buildings are named after him.

In contrast to these modern depictions, Monstery's extremely negative characterization of Guardiola—the man he referred to as "The Butcher"—echoes sentiments expressed by other Americans and Englishmen of the period. The following (albeit rife with prejudice) is merely one example:

> Guardiola is a dark-colored *mestizo*, stout-built, and rather corpulent, his face expressing his fiendish temper; but well liked by the soldiers, whom he indulges in every way. To his habits of intoxication may be added every species of vice which can be named among the vicious inhabitants of Central America; and frequently, in his drunken fits, he orders people to be shot who have in nothing offended him, while at all times the most trifling expression, incautiously uttered, is sufficient to cause the babbler to be shot without mercy. In private life he is as brutal as can well be imagined. In all the towns through which he passes, he makes a habit of calling in the best looking women he can see, and, after subjecting them to infamous treatment, he drives them forth with the most insulting epithets; yet he is certainly the best and most successful general of any now existing, and, probably, of any who have appeared in Central America. Like Marius, the Roman leader, his brutal manners serve to terrify the enemy; hence, while the arrival of Cabanas and most of the other leaders is looked upon without fear by the people of the contending States, the bare mention of the name of Guardiola is sufficient to make the inhabitants fly to the woods, leaving every thing behind them.[77]

SANTOS GUARDIOLA.

Other contemporaries referred to "the dreaded Guardiola" whose "wild hordes" were "little else than robbers,"[78] while others spoke of the man who, "by his unparalleled cruelties to young and old, men and women alike, acquired the dread name of 'The Tiger of Honduras.'"[79] Likewise, in his reminiscences of the war in Nicaragua, Charles Doubleday recounted that "Guardiola had a reputation for cruelty similar to that of Mendez, being surnamed the 'Butcher,' as he usually slaughtered his prisoners."[80]

Monstery's first encounter with Guardiola was precipitated by a "gently worded request" from the president that the fencing master make his appearance at Tegucigalpa, the Honduran capitol. Monstery recounted,

> I did not understand then that the commands of this strange and ferocious man were all put in the form of a soft request and I paid no attention to it, being well satisfied with Truxillo. In a month's time I learned from American Consul Purdot, with whose family I was intimate, that I was to be arrested and shot by command of the Butcher. I decided to take the bull

by the horns, and, loading my belongings into four narrow trunks, designed to be carried muleback, I set out for Tegucigalpa. I reached there early in the evening. There was a banquet at the President's palace, and I presented myself, travel stained as I was. Guardiola was a Mestizo Indian. He scowled at me and said:

"You have decided, have you, to grant our simple request? That is a good thing for you. Have some wine."

I drank with him and next day was made instructor to his miserable unpaid and half-clad troops.[81]

DUELS AND CONTESTS WITH *ESPADACHÍNS*

Now an instructor for the Honduran military, and serving under the watchful eye of a fearsome tyrant, Monstery nevertheless found that his skills were high in demand—even more so then they had been in Spain and Cuba. According to his biographer,

> He had struck the right chord at last. The Spanish-Americans are enthusiastic on the subject of swordsmanship, and care very little about firearms. The reason is simple. Modern firearms are made by expensive machinery and require special cartridges, which are not made in Central America. They have to be imported, and the people are dependent on the United States for their supplies. Consequently they are scarce. But swords, pikes, lances and daggers can be made anywhere, and the Spanish-Americans are never happy unless they are fighting.
>
> So they use their own weapons for their own fights, and practice fencing all the time in their own rough and ready fashion. Every village has its own local celebrity as a swordsman, and at the country fairs these men—called *spadachins*—come in from all sides to challenge each other, carrying their long swords and a bundle of sticks.[82]

Although the Spanish term *espadachín* denotes, quite simply, a swordsman, in the context of the period it more often referred to a sort of "gladiator" or sword-wielding bravo. By all accounts, Monstery came into frequent contact with such individuals during his travels in Central America. An echo of such accounts can be found in the works of Costa Rican writer and politician, Ricardo Fernández Guardia. Writing during the mid nineteenth century (about the same time that Monstery was in Central America), Guardia wrote:

> My fellow countrymen...will not take it ill that I reveal one of their small defects, if indeed it is a defect to be somewhat of a braggart. Still, why deny it? The Alajuelan* is boastful, and it is not displeasing to him in case of need to make a bold threat.
>
> During the first presidency of Dr. Castro, whom they declared deposed by a daring act of rebellion, there was a time when they made valor a profession...I say, then, that at that time, now long past, all the men in Alajuela were given to deeds of daring and were also more or less skilled in the use of weapons. The gentlemen of the city devoted themselves enthusiastically to the management of the *guacalona*†, the men of the neighboring villages to that of the *Cutacha*‡ and the *realera*∞.
>
> From this love for arms, quarrels arose between one and another, occasioned by local rivalries. Still, as their rancors were not deep and the combatants were more desirous of showing their skill than of doing injury, they generally contented themselves with giving each other a few strokes with the flat of the sword without greater damage.

Following this account, Guardia proceeds to relate a story of an *espadachín* named "Don Telesforo," described as "a man of mature age, although still agile and vigorous, who passed as an adept in the management of arms and as being experienced in all kinds of adventures." Guardia recounts an incident when, in order to prove his prowess and establish his reputation as a swordsman, the Don

> sallied forth from his house, *guacalona* in hand, and went to place himself in the most frequented street in front of an adobe wall of no great height. There he planted himself in the middle of the road, and after passing the *tizona* [blade] several times along the ground as though to sharpen it, he roared in a stentorian voice:
>
> "Let no one pass this way!"

---

* *Alajuelan:* a native of Alajuela, the second-largest city in Costa Rica.

† *guacalona:* a basket-hilted sword.

‡ *cutacha:* a kind of *machete.*

∞ *realera:* a long machete.

Immediately the movement of traffic stopped, while the people, some curious, others frightened, commenced to form in groups on all sides to see how the matter was going to end.

"Let no one pass this way!" shouted Don Telesforo, flourishing his sword. "And if any one wants to pass, let him come on. Here I wait him with point, edge and *guacal* *.[83]

As is evident from Guardia's writings, the *espadachíns* mentioned and described by Monstery were a very real phenomenon in Central America during the nineteenth century. Returning to Monstery's own experience, his biographer noted that after his appointment by Guardiola, the Danish yankee "found no trouble in getting up a match with the best *spadachins* of the country."[84] It seems that his status as the top fencing master in the country was resented by jealous local *bravos*, for Monstery himself recounted:

In Tegucigalpa I was forced to make my footing good by fighting the Honduran champion. I have forgotten his name, if I ever knew it. I remember only that he was an enormous fellow, six feet six inches high, and insisted upon using a pair of tremendously long Toledo blades which belonged to him. The fight occurred in the plaza and was witnessed by 20,000 people. As I was held to be a representative of Spain, the Spanish merchants of the town bet 8,000 copper dollars on my success. These dollars were worth twelve and one-half cents each in gold. They subsequently dropped to eight cents, and the entire issue was bought up by an English syndicate, which rehabilitated the currency and made something like sixty percent on its investment. The Honduran's merit as a swordsman consisted almost wholly in strength. I disarmed him three times, making no attempt to injure him. From the thousands of his fellow countrymen fell on him a storm of appeal: "Kill him! Kill him!" He was a giant country yokel and very naive.

"Yes," he said, standing with outstretched hands when disarmed for the third time. "I would kill him, but he keeps knocking my sword out of my fist." That caused a general laugh and my backers took down the money.[85]

---

* *Guacal:* a name formerly given to the basket hilt of a sword, on account of its resemblance to the cups and bowls made from the gourds that grow on the tree of that name.

According to his biographer, Monstery "easily" defeated the champion, and "made two thousand dollars in the match, American money." For a time, Monstery was considered the "pride of Telucigalpa," but was forced to enter into yet another martial contest of a much different nature.[86]

BULLFIGHTING

According to Monstery, the following incident occurred subsequent to his fight with the *espadachín:*

> One night at a banquet we were all heated with wine. Several of the Honduran gentlemen, having found out that I was an American, began casting slurs upon this country, which in those times occupied a low place in the estimation of other countries. I told them that it ill became Hondurans to say [such] things, as their nation amounted to nothing at all whatever: that they were imitators of the Spanish and that even in their bullfights they sawed off the horns of their victims. They replied that the American did not live who dared enter the arena against a bull of temper and horns.
>
> Being full of wine myself and pot-valiant, I responded that I dared. The upshot of it was that a bet was made that I would not enter the arena a week from [that] date against a bull of their selection. I knew nothing in the world of bullfighting, and when I waked the next morning I was a sorry man. I could not back out, however.
>
> I went to a friend, an American doctor named Wells, who had found his way to that far country, and told him my troubles. He suggested that we buy a bull and practice the matador death stroke. Bulls were $2 each, and we bought five. Going to the suburbs we tied them, and I slew them with the straight downward thrust I had seen in the ring. In each case we cut the animal open after it fell and traced the course of the sword blade. The last bull dropped as if struck by lightning, and I found that my point had severed the cervical vertebrae just in front of the shoulder top.[87]

Six days later, Monstery "went into the arena" before a vast crowd. He described the bull his Honduran friends had "furnished for his undoing" as a "wonder," relating:

> He was of immense size, a dark dun in color, utterly wild, and his horns had not been cut. On the contrary, their points had been filed to a needle keenness. Furthermore, he was what is known as a *ruscador*, or follower: that is, he was not to be diverted from his charge, but followed straight after the object upon which he had set his red vision. The picadores, or horsemen, and the banderillos, who throw the tiny barbed flags, deserted me after the first charge and I was obliged to enter the ring alone. Being a matador, I was on foot.
>
> Six times the bull chased me over the palings, and the last time I fell in the lap of my friend Wells, who was by no means sober. He had a six-shooter in each hand and swore that he would empty every chamber into the Hondurans if I were killed. In civilization Americans don't give a damn for one another, but in the wild places they stick together like brothers. It is very good in those places to have a friend like Wells.[88]

Monstery's friend, Wells, would serve as the basis for Dr. Charles Brown in the fencing master's later novel, *El Rubio Bravo.* However, unlike the real-life Wells, the Dr. Brown of the novel is described as an Englishman and a pugilist. As Monstery was known to have been acquainted with several English boxers throughout his career, it seems probable that Brown was thus a composite character of both the American-born Wells and at least one or more English pugilists personally known to Monstery. A highly likely candidate is William Miller, a boxer and wrestling champion born in Cheshire, England (and later a resident of Australia), who participated in a number of Assaults of Arms with the Colonel, during which he demonstrated wrestling, pugilism, and single-stick, and who served as Monstery's second in a high-profile sword contest with rival fencing master Regis Senac.

We now return to Monstery's bullfight, the end of which he described as follows:

> I reentered the ring for the seventh time, determined to die in my tracks before I would give another inch before the enraged animal. I had been already called a coward twenty thousand times and it angered me. As the bull came on, with head not a foot from the ground, I leaned forward and lunged with all my force. I did not know enough to leap to one side nor to withdraw my sword as the matadores sometimes do. The enormous brute

Monstery's friend, the English pugilist William Miller, who may have served as the partial basis for Dr. Charley Brown.

> stopped in his tracks, shivered and fell like some great tree. I still clung to my sword handle and was pulled to my knees. I did not hear a whisper of the wild shouts that rent the air, but when I rose I did hear a rapid fusilade. Looking to my left, I saw Wells dancing about his box on one leg, screaming at the top of his voice and working his six-shooters brilliantly straight up into the air.[89]

The real-life Wells, unfortunately, did not meet with the happy ending that Dr. Brown enjoyed in the novel. Alcoholism was Wells's undoing, as Monstery grimly related: "He was a good fellow and brave. He died of *delirium tremens*, cursing America, the land that gave him birth."[90]

After his victory over the bull, Monstery became a popular local hero. However, he made the mistake of "dancing too often with Mrs. Guardiola," the wife of the "Butcher," and was promptly sent by the

President to the jungle to fight Cardenas, a revolutionist, in the hopes that he would be killed. Monstery was defeated, taken prisoner, and tied to a tree for eventual "torture." Fortunately, Monstery had noticed that one of his captors, named Miguel, was a former valet to Dr. Wells. During an unobserved moment, Monstery spoke with Miguel and struck a bargain: he would give the valet his diamond studs in return for secretly cutting his bonds that night. Miguel was true to his word, but Monstery's escape was detected and an alarm raised. Under gunfire from approximately fifty soldiers, the Danish Yankee ran three hundred yards to a "wide stream, plunged into it, and was swept over a waterfall." He made his way through the foam at the bottom and floated quietly for a mile or two. Gaining the further bank, he struck out through the forest in the direction of the El Salvador line, knowing that he would be killed for sure if he returned to Honduras.[91]

EL SALVADOR

Penniless, alone, on foot, and "dressed in rags," Monstery "traversed the wild wilderness" towards the town of San Miguel, in eastern El Salvador.[92] After weeks of incredible hardship, he reached the city, and, "the veriest vagabond in appearance," presented himself to Señor Antonio Blanco, a Spanish merchant of wealth and breeding. The Dane merely introduced himself as "Tomas Munstery, the *maitre d'armes.*" His fame, according to his own account, "had gone through all of the Central American republics," and he was welcomed. Blanco gave a dinner in his honor that night to sixteen other merchants, and each of them placed on the table an ounce of gold for the adventurer. Monstery recalled: "In the morning I was a loafer, and at night I was a cavalier."[93]

In the city, Monstery "flourished" as the only master-of-arms in the city, "giving lessons at sixteen gold ounces a course—equal to about $180 —with the first cavaliers contending for places under his tuition."[94]

From San Miguel, however, Monstery was soon again "obliged to flee, on account of the enmity of the governor, who was jealous of his popularity." He traveled further west, to the capital city of San Salvador, where "he was welcomed with open arms and made colonel and Instructor-at-Arms." Thus, once more began "the old life of sword instruction, swordplay, gold, gaming, and love."[95] It was here, according to Monstery's biographer, where he acquired the *nom de guerre* by which he was afterwards known in Central America: *El Rubio Bravo*—the "Brave Blonde."[96]

Importantly, we now enter the moment in Monstery's story in which his adventures can be verified, or at least somewhat supported, by the official testimony of others. In a deposition given years later to the Mexican government, an ex-soldier named Pedro Pacheco, born in San Salvador, recounted that he "first became acquainted with Thomas [Monstery] in San Salvador, Central Am., where he (Thomas) held the position of Colonel of Cavalry & Chief Military Instructor, under the Presidency of Gerardo Varios [Barrios]."[97] Yet another soldier, Ignacio Quiroga, formerly of Costa Rica, also "first became acquainted with Thomas in San Salvador, when Thomas was Colen [Col.] of Cavalry and Chief military instructor under command of Gen. Mella [Melo]."[98]

JOSÉ MARÍA MELO

It was here, in San Salvador, that Monstery reunited with his old friend and comrade, who would soon play a pivotal role in his adventures: the "liberal" former dictator, José María Melo, whom Monstery had "last seen disguised as a servant making his way to sea on a British ship after their defeat in Colombia."[99] A comparison of Monstery's biographical writings about this period with *El Rubio Bravo* makes clear that Melo was the basis for the novel's character Don Jose Ramirez. According to the Colonel's biography, Melo was "the one honest and brave Spaniard in all [Monstery's] experience...and to whom he was very closely attached by ties of affection." It further relates,

> Jose Maria Melo, like [Monstery], was a *Rubio*—a fair-hair—descended from the pure Gothic stock, without any Moorish crosses, and brave to a fault. He was a cavalier in the true sense, chivalrous, generous, and kind-hearted, and never went back on a friend in need...Yet such is Mexican

> misrule, Melo was a partisan officer, now on one side, now another, and living off the country.[100]

Contrast this now with the introduction of Don Jose Ramirez in the novel:

> "He is a *rubio* like yourself, general [Ramirez]."
>
> Indeed the general, though evidently of pure Spanish blood, had fair hair and blue eyes.[101]

José María Melo

Just like the historical Melo, Don Ramirez switches sides, and allegiances, to the countries he serves. Also, just as Monstery kept Melo's lance as a keepsake, so the fictional Olaf Svenson receives Don Ramirez's lance as a gift.[102] The travels of the fictional duo also closely mirror those of the real-life pair.

Monstery and Melo must have reunited toward the end of 1858, or the beginning of 1859. In the Colonel's own words: "I then...entered the service of Gen. Melo at the capital."[103] Another source elaborates:

> Melo was high in place in San Salvador, and the two men swore a blood brotherhood. One feature of their compact was that the survivor of the twain should carry news of the other's death to relatives in person, no matter where they might be or how far the travel. Melo was a Venezuelan, an accomplished soldier, a man of high literary attainments and an adept in statecraft. Monstery has as a memento of him only his lance, which he saw gallantly borne on fifty fields.[104]

Salvadorean histories confirm that Melo was indeed stationed in San Salvador during this period, when Monstery claimed to have joined up with him.[105]

A DUEL IN SAN SALVADOR

According to an interview with Monstery, he and Melo "became such a power in San Salvador that they excited the alarm of Gerardo Barrios, the President."[106] Barrios, a former general, had first proclaimed himself President on March 12, 1859—which, given the previous and subsequently known timeline of Monstery's travels, means that Monstery and Melo must have entered San Salvador around March of that year, or shortly thereafter.

During his time in Central America, Monstery reportedly engaged in a large number of duels. Frederick Whittaker, in speaking of his life during this period, noted that

> In Spanish America, a man has to be ready to defend himself at all times, and an American has to look as sharp for his life against knife and sword as a miner in the fighting West has to watch for the pistols of the desperadoes that infest the mining towns.[107]

It was during his interlude in San Salvador when Monstery would engage in a combat which would serve as one of the most descriptive episodes of his biography. In later accounts, the Colonel's antagonist is simply referred to as "General Bragamonte." Frederick Whittaker related:

> Bragamonte was a general in rank, but noted chiefly as the most dangerous duelist in Spanish America. He was said to have killed more than fifty people at different times and always at unfair advantage, but claimed to be the most skillful swordsman living.[108]

A studious review of Monstery's journey, and a comparison of it with the historical timeline, identifies this individual as General Eusebio Bracamonte, who served directly under President Gerardo Barrios during the same period of time in which Monstery was stationed in the country. That the name differs by a single letter from the one specified in Whittaker's biography is not at all surprising, as the text is full of such misspellings. In an article published in Chicago, 1887, Monstery's antagonist is referred to as "General Brocomonte" of "San Salvador."[109] Braca-

President Gerardo Barrios

monte is described in Salvadoran history texts as Barrios's "most trusted officer," and the governor and commander of San Vicente.[110] Whittaker related that "the general was a hero, but [Monstery's] arrival put Bragamonte in the position of second best, which he could not bear."[111]

A newspaper account (derived from a personal interview with Monstery) explained how the Danish Yankee came to first meet Bracamonte, and eventually fight a duel with him:

> In 1858, when the soldiers of San Salvador were engaged in cutting the throats of the soldiers of Guatemala, the San Salvador forces received an unexpected reinforcement—a certain General Bragamonte coming over from the Guatemalans and bringing his entire command with him. There was a nasty story afloat to the effect that Bragamonte, in order to effect this move, brought about the assassination in cold blood of all the officers under him who remained loyal to Guatemala. It was the story, which was well authenticated, that gave rise to Colonel Monstery's duel, as will be seen presently.

> When President Barrios...acquired supremacy in San Salvador, this General Bragamonte was made military commander of the Province of La Union. He did not owe his good fortune to any love that Barrios bore him, but his great popularity with the half-rebel people rendered it necessary that some distinction should be given him. While he was Governor of La Union a grand military review took place at the capital, and, of course, every civil and military officer of the administration was present. To Colonel Monstery, as chief of cavalry, was allotted the task of inviting General Bragamonte to a great banquet that was to be given in the evening after the review. Colonel Monstery, of course, had to obey orders, but he bore the man such a hatred on account of his murderous record that he revolted against the task. He got out of it neatly, however, by taking an orderly with him and dictating the invitation to him in the presence of General Bragamonte, for repetition to the latter. The general was not slow to perceive Monstery's sentiments, and when the two met at the banquet, some hours later, they glared at each other like tigers about to spring.[112]

In his biography of the Colonel, Frederick Whittaker explained that Bracamonte "did not dare to insult and challenge Monstery openly at first, but pretended great courtesy when he met him one night at [the] great banquet held in a ruined convent, remnant of the old Spanish dominion."[113] But that was about to change, thanks to the Dane's boldness, keen sense of justice, and devil-may-care attitude. According to the 1888 article:

> When the feasting was over and *cigarros* in full blaze, Colonel Monstery was called on for a toast. He responded promptly, and with his goblet raised high in the air, ordered the company to drink to the health of a true soldier, who lived and fought and died for honor and his country, but to drink death to the traitor—here he glared straight at Bragamonte—who would sell his country and assassinate his fellow men for the purpose of furthering his own successes.[114]

The general became quietly furious. Whittaker's account explained what happened next:

> Monstery...was not surprised when in the course of the banquet General Bragamonte told him he had something very particular and private to say

to him, and begged him to accompany him out into the dark shadow of the cloisters, where they might be undisturbed.

El Rubio Bravo looked at the sinister dark face, read treachery there, and remembered [assassin] Jose Jesus Gomez, and replied, coldly:

"We have nothing to discuss, senor, that we cannot speak of here in the light. I don't love darkness."

Bragamonte frowned.

"Senor, what do you mean? I tell you I have important private business, on which I must consult you."

"And I say, senor, that if it is so private that it cannot be discussed here, you can come to my quarters in daylight. I will not go with you to-night."

Bragamonte drew himself up, and frowned savagely. He had a fierce, cruel face, was a large man, and most men would have quailed before him, but *El Rubio Bravo* merely smiled in a derisive way, watching him keenly for fear of treachery, and Bragamonte finally turned away, muttering under his black mustache something the other could not catch.

When Monstery rejoined his friends one of them told him he had done right. It was Bragamonte's plan to entice him into the dark, draw him into conversation, and then, on the pretext of a sudden quarrel, draw on him and stab him, as he had done before with others. He never fought fairly unless he knew he could beat his opponent easily.

Monstery went home, escorted by a party of friends, and had forgotten all about Bragamonte next morning, when he was suddenly wakened by a loud voice at the door threatening his orderly, and the next moment in strode the valiant Bragamonte, sword in hand, growling:

"You insulted me last night; now get up and fight!"

But Monstery had acquired the habit of never going to bed without a pistol under his pillow, and the brave general, who had come to stab him, suddenly recoiled before the muzzle of a Colt's navy revolver, while *El Rubio Bravo* said, coolly:

"Get out of my room, and you shall have all the fight you want."

And he looked so menacing that the brave Bragamonte beat a retreat to the plaza outside, where he raved up and down, swearing and shouting, trying his best to get up a mob feeling against the American, while our hero hastily dressed.

The fact was, Bragamonte had gone too far to retreat. He had come expecting to stab an unarmed man on the pretext of a quarrel, counting on the surprise and confusion of a man just roused from sleep to enable him to pass it off as a duel. He had thought Monstery would jump out of bed and rush for a sword, so as to give him an excuse to say he acted in self-defense. The pistol had quite upset his plans, and his reputation as a duelist was at stake. If he ran now, every one would despise him; he would be mobbed and killed by his numerous enemies. It was quite necessary to keep on blustering, in the hope that national feeling might come to his aid, and Monstery might be mobbed.

Our hero, however, gave him no time to work on the people, for he had slipped on his trousers and boots, and ran out with his sword before the valiant Bragamonte had ceased his vaporings. Then it was too late to retreat, and Bragamonte had to fight, out in the open plaza, before all the people.

To do him justice, he fought well in his desperation. His style was that of the Spaniards inherited from the Moors, of making wide, sweeping cuts, and trusting to agility rather than parries to escape return blows. He sprung forward like a tiger, cutting high and low with all his force, and shouting savagely at every cut, while the American stood cool at every turn. Bragamonte even cut at the ground, and one vicious slash grazed Monstery's foot, cut through the boot, and slightly wounded his great toe, though he did not feel it at the time. But at last Bragamonte wearied, and *El Rubio Bravo* became the assailant in turn, cutting lightly and cautiously and always on guard.

At length Bragamonte tried his last secret trick, which would have puzzled any merely school fencer. Monstery made a light cut at his arm, outside, and Bragamonte threw up his own sword to bind his enemy's blade there, quick as a flash threw forward his left foot and clutched for Monstery's sword-wrist with his left hand.

It was the end of the duel.

Quicker than even the Spaniard, the American threw forward his own left foot, drawing back his sword out of danger, and in an instant had reversed the trick. Bragamonte's sword-wrist was in his grasp, and he plunged his own blade deep into the Spaniard's vitals, so that the point came out behind Bragamonte's back, and the hilt struck his breast.

With a howl of pain the would-be assassin dropped helpless to the earth, and *El Rubio Bravo* plucked out his sword, once more the victor.

Bragamonte had fought his last duel, and, although he survived the wound, he never shone as a swordsman again.[115]

Burial monument and bust of General Eusebio Bracamonte. Courtesy of J. Makali Bruton.

Following this duel, Monstery was arrested and "almost convicted of attempted murder," with "Bragamonte declaring that he had made a peaceful morning call and that the Colonel had rushed out and stabbed him." In the nick of time, however, "some officers, who had seen Bragamonte standing at Monstery's door with his drawn sword in his hand, and afterward watched the fight, offered their testimony, and Monstery was acquitted."[116]

Although Monstery would soon leave the country, General Eusebio Bracamonte would remain there until his death. In 1863, during an invasion by Guatemala, the general was sent by Barrios to crush a number of uprisings by rural native militias. After executing numerous prisoners, and "committing excesses and violations of various types," Bracamonte led his troops to victory during the spring and summer of 1863. He was later killed during the Siege of San Salvador on October 20, 1863.[117] An account originating from Monstery confirmed that his antagonist, "Bragamonte," afterward "became a good soldier, fighting gallantly for Barrios until captured by the enemy and shot."[118] Barrios himself was deposed as President and attempted to flee from El Salvador, but was arrested and executed. The lavish grave of General Eusebio Bracamonte, complete with monument and bust, can still be seen in San Salvador today. A less flattering monument to the general survives in Monstery's novel, *El Rubio Bravo, King of the Swordsmen,* wherein he serves as the basis for one of the villainous "terrible brothers of Tabasco."

COSTA RICA and GUATEMALA

Monstery, fortunately, had left the country before these calamities occurred. According to the timeline given by the Colonel, his departure must have been sometime shortly after his duel with Bracamonte in 1859, when he and Melo "excited the alarm" of President Barrios and were forced to flee.[119] In an 1887 article, a "Mexican gentleman" residing in Chicago claimed that Monstery engaged in a fencing contest in San Salvador, following his duel with Bracamonte. He stated:

> In the same year and same place [Monstery] met the famous swordsman Augenont, who had acquired a great reputation in Peru, and who, having heard of [General Bracamonte's] defeat, made a special trip to San Salvador to contest for the championship honors. Augenont was willing to wager a large amount of money on the result. A Belgian by birth, he stood 7 feet high and had been employed for some time as an instructor in the French army. He fell an easy victim to the Colonel, however, who defeated him with all weapons, relieving him at the same time of a large sum of money.[120]

As no other reference to this contest, or to Augenont, could be found, it is not known whether the incident actually occurred, or is merely apocryphal.

Whittaker's biography relates that from San Salvador, Monstery and Melo escaped the country together and traveled to several "Central American republics where he remained till the year 1859, moving north at each successive revolution..."[121] This however, was not completely true, as Monstery's journey had involved at least one detour south: to Costa Rica. In an interview with the *New York Sun,* Monstery gave further details of this period:

> To quiet [President Barrios] and give him time to think better of them[selves] they took some soldiers and went into Costa Rica, where President [Juan Rafael] Mora was combating a full-grown revolution. They were beaten.

This firmly places Monstery and Melo in Costa Rica during the summer of 1859. On August 14 of that year, a coup headed by a politically conservative coffee baron named José María Montealegre forced President Mora to abandon power and go into exile in San Salvador. Later, in 1860, Mora would launch an expedition to reclaim power, but would be "captured and shot" by firing squad. Monstery's own account continues:

> Melo and Monstery got back to San Salvador, after a hard chase, with little glory and a new assortment of wounds. Two weeks afterward they were notified by friends that [President] Barrios had condemned them to death. They mounted their horses at 1 o'clock on a moonless night and rode hard for the Guatemalan frontier. They were pursued, but got across the line in

> safety. Here and there they picked up a man-at-arms until they had twelve in their train. With this trifling force they made their way across Guatemala into the state of Chiapas, Mexico.[122]

In an interview with the *Utica Globe,* Monstery stated: "I made my way with 13 men to Mexico after many adventures and skirmishes."[123] Monstery's biography also relates that, along with Melo, he journeyed north "till he came to the Mexican State of Chiapas."[124]

ADVENTURES IN MEXICO
1859-1860

In Mexico, Monstery would engage in what would become his best-documented Spanish American exploits, thanks to Mexican newspaper accounts, as well as court records still extant in both United States and Mexican archives. Monstery himself recounted that, upon his arrival in Mexico, "I was made military instructor general, with the rank of chief of cavalry."[125] This fact was verified by the Mexican government in later years, when it declared:

> The petitioner [Thomas H. Monstery]...was a military officer, to wit, a colonel of cavalry, in the State of Chiapas, as appears by a certificate of judicial authorities of that state, filed by petitioner in the case...[126]

As military instructor under Melo, Monstery entered Mexico during a time of extreme chaos known as the War of Reform, a three-year civil war that began during the Second Federal Republic of Mexico. Monstery's biography explained:

> Mexico is not a single state, but, like our Union, a confederation of states, with a central government. Unlike our Union, however, the different states are allowed to have troops of their own, not militia, and are very frequently at war with each other. The consequence is a series of petty revolutions, which will probably never subside till this power is taken away as it is in our United States...At the time Monstery met Melo, war had existed for a long time between the states of Chiapas and Tabasco, and

Miguel Miramón

> the two friends went into it on behalf of Chiapas. They prospered greatly, and Monstery became famous for the manner in which he trained a body of Indian pikemen, who conquered everything before them.[127]

Monstery related that he "soon engaged with [President Benito] Juarez and the liberals against Miramon and the church party."[128] The aforementioned individual, Miguel Miramón, was a Mexican general who served as anti-constitutional interim conservative President of Mexico in opposition to the constitutional president, Benito Juárez of the Liberal Party. Miramón was a staunch conservative, a supporter of monarchy, aristocracy and religious privileges for the Catholic Church. An interview with Monstery further related:

> Mexico was in the throes of a tremendous conflict between the Liberals and Conservatives, and for the time being the Conservatives were the underdogs. Melo and Monstery's band of twelve had met many parties of them, fleeing into Guatemala, and, as they were headed the other way, their Liberal tendencies were apparent, and many handsome fights resulted. In Chiapas the pair were welcomed by the Liberals and from Mexico City, Melo received a commission as commanding General of Chiapas, and he made Monstery his chief of cavalry. Then began a long war against Miramon, the Conservative leader.[129]

Monstery's military nemesis in Mexico, however, was not Miramón, but Jesús González Ortega, a soldier and Mexican politician. Ortega had served as governor of Zacatecas, and had previously participated next to Benito Juarez in the War of Reform and during the French intervention in Mexico. In an interview with Monstery, it was explained how Ortega switched sides to become their implacable enemy:

> There was a man named Ortega who had been the Chiapas Governor of Customs and whose peculations had run into the millions. He had been dismissed from office by the central Liberal Government and in revenge joined Miramon. He was a soldier and a valiant captain, as well as a thief, and one of the most murderous leaders in the history of that land of murder. His hundreds of followers were distinguished by a white cross worn on the left shoulder, and where the white crosses rode there death and ruin were most plentiful. Against this General Monstery and Melo were specially pitted. The American had at his command 331 cavalrymen, each of whom was trained to the nine and a master of his weapons. He had in addition a force of 2,000 infantrymen, who were of little value to him, as Ortega adopted the guerrilla style of warfare. For months clash after clash strewed the Mexican soil with corpses. Ortega had amassed a large part of his plunder from churches. It consisted of gold pieces, and jewels stamped from chalices by his boot-heels. This treasure he had secreted in the mountains and it became Monstery's chief task to discover the hiding place. This he accomplished at last by means of spies and he moved on the rocky stronghold. Ortega was defeated and the treasure was captured, but the white cross bandit escaped with most of his men.[130]

Disaster, however, was soon to follow. Five days after his escape from Melo, on June 1, 1860, Ortega "defeated him, took Melo prisoner and

Jesús González Ortega

executed him."[131] Today, the site of Melo's assassination and burial can still be seen in Juncanú, Chiapas, México. A lengthy article on Monstery explained what happened following the death of Melo:

> Thirst for vengeance then took possession of Monstery and he resumed the pursuit with added zest. The last battle between the two occurred upon an elevated plateau, thick with chaparral. One side of it sloped down to the country beneath. Ortega had been driven to the top and made his stand there. Monstery sent his men into the engagement and, with a few chosen troops, placed himself to one side of the slope and remained hidden in the trees, knowing that his foeman would endeavor to escape by that exit, and determined to cut him down with his own hand. When the battle had been in progress for an hour and the advancing tide of shouts showed that the Liberals were winning, Monstery saw a small detachment of cavalrymen, headed by an officer and bearing the white crosses on their shoulders, break through the edge of the chaparral and start at a hand gallop

down the slope. Convinced that it was his enemy at last rushing to destruction, Monstery gave the word of command, dropped the reins, struck his spurs home and dashed from his ambuscade to intercept the flight. For some reason his men did not follow him and he found himself facing a party of nine, headed by a young officer who was not Ortega. There was no time to rectify the mistake. Instantly the contending parties, ten to one, were deep in strife.

ONE AGAINST TEN.

Though it happened forty years ago, the old soldier of fortune cannot mention this affray without deep excitement. He rises from his chair and recounts its various phases with flashing eyes. He emptied three saddles with his revolvers before they closed in on him, and a fourth man fell before a thrust of his lance. The attacking party threw themselves from their horses, and one of them stabbed his horse in the chest, piercing its heart. The animal fell, pinning its rider under it, and for a moment he lay at the mercy of his enemies. In five seconds twenty blows fell on him. He was freed by the death struggles of his steed and hobbled to his feet. His left knee had been broken by the fall, and he stood on one leg, like a stork. His lance, too, had been smashed, but he still held to the business end of it. As one of the white cross men turned to flee Monstery levelled this broken bit of lance like a javelin and sent it through him, at a distance of five yards, with such force that the spearhead projected a foot beyond the breast. The man fell upon his face, gasping. Balancing himself on one foot and partly braced by the dead body of his horse, against which he leaned, the master of arms drew the rapier, which had never failed him, and engaged his five adversaries. The young officer was first to fall before a [thrust] that caught him on the throat. A trooper who sprang in with clubbed musket was struck with such violence that the hilt thumped against his breast bone. As he fell the sword snapped. The other three leaped back out of reach of the terrible American and began reloading their muskets, intending to finish him at leisure. At this juncture some of Monstery's victorious riders broke from the chaparral in pursuit of stragglers, and his assailants fled. The warrior did not see them. He had fainted. He does not know now what became of the men who were with him when he made his charge alone, nor why they deserted him. In this fight he had been struck in the chest by a spent ball, and was coughing blood. His sword hand was wounded. His left knee was broken. His brother officer, Melo, was dead. Ortega, for the twentieth time, had escaped. He decided to give up the pursuit.[132]

CHIAPAS.

Una fuerza pronunciada contra los constitucionalistas, batió el 1.° de Junio á otra fuerza de estos situada en la hacienda de Yuncaná inmediata á la frontera de Guatemala, y le hizo algunos muertos, incluso su gefe, el llamado general D. José María Melo.

El *Progreso* asegura que la fuerza pronunciada contra la constitucion de 1857 en Chiapas, pertenece á Guatemala. ¡Es su manía vieja!

Mexican report of Melo's death, in *La Sociedad*, July 15, 1860

In later years, Monstery recounted that "while lying bleeding on the ground an attempt was made by one of the other side to stab him to death, but he warded the blow off with his right hand which now bears the scar of the knife-cut received at the time."[133] In another interview, Monstery related that this "hot fight" occurred "during the winter of 1859-60," and that "a young boy and myself were the only survivors of our party and we were wounded."[134]

THE STORY OF A TREASURE

Despite suffering these massive losses, Monstery was still in possession of Ortega's treasure. His account of the subsequent journey related:

> From Ortega's treasure [Monstery] had paid his soldiers liberally and had for his own portion nearly $400,000 in gold and jewels. It was put into mule trunks, bound on the backs of Indian bearers and, himself seated in a chair strapped to a man's back, he took up his march for the Atlantic coast, hoping to find in one of the sea towns a competent physician. Near the ancient city of Palenque it became necessary to cross a lake in a canoe. Knowing that the frail craft would not bear the weight of the men and all of the metal, he separated the gold from the jewels, put it into four trunks, and, making a diagram of the place, buried it. The fifth trunk, containing gold and diamonds, was placed in a canoe. Among these jewels was the diadem of an Archbishop, stolen from some wealthy church by Ortega.

Contrary to his custom, that bandit had not broken it to pieces. It was of massive gold, spangled with diamonds, sapphires and rubies, and was valued at $63,000.

At the frontier city of Petucalco [Pichucalco], ruled by a Governor and patrolled by a commander of his own appointing, Monstery stopped to rest. The Governor's name was Martinez: the military commander was Pancho Flores. Martinez gave a banquet, which Monstery attended. When he returned to his quarters he found that the back door had been broken open with a bayonet, while his dozen sentries stood about the front door, and his jewel trunk abstracted. He remained in [Pichucalco] three weeks, endeavoring to trace his property. He did find a Sergeant who told how he and companions had forced the door, acting under the command of Flores, and of how they had borne the trunk into the hills, where Flores broke it open and buried the treasure in places known only to himself, while they stood guard along the pathways.

"It was the rainy season," says Monstery, "and the mountain torrents were bankfull. I found the trunk as the Sergeant had said. The few papers still in it had been beaten to mush by the falling water, but in the middle of the mass lay an open daguerreotype uninjured, and out of it smiled at me the face of my wife. The jewels, of course, were gone, and among papers which Flores had abstracted was the diagram, showing the location of my buried trunks of gold. They are there yet, I make no doubt. No man can find them. I could not find them myself should I make the effort. That lake rises once each year and overflows the spot where they are hidden, and doubtless they are now under twenty feet of deposit."[135]

Receiving compensation for this lost treasure would become a lifelong obsession for Monstery. Seven years following the original events, in 1867, he journeyed again to Mexico City to "secure indemnity for the injuries done to his person and property," but was repeatedly denied in his attempts to obtain an interview. In 1869, after an American-Mexican commission had been set up to adjudicate claims by citizens of one nation against the other, Monstery filed a case against the Mexican government. His petition included additional details which were not related previously. It reads, in part:

In the year 1860, General Melo was taken prisoner by the revolutionary forces under command of General Juan Ortega, and executed, your memorialist being in ill-health, converted all of his property and means into money, jewelry, and diamonds, and prepared to leave the country, and started for Vera Cruz, and on his route, stopped at the village of Pichucalco, in the latter part of the month of July, 1860, a fair being held at the time, on invitation of Francisco Flores, Commandante, to spend a few days there to witness the fair, and also to give him and some of his officers, lessons in fencing and the sword exercise.

Your memorialist further states, that Commandante Flores assigned him quarters in a building occupied as a garrison by his troops, and knowing that he had a large amount of money and jewelry in his possession and valuable baggage, detailed soldiers from his troops to act as sentinels, and guard his rooms day and night.

That on the evening of the fourth of August, 1860, the Prefect of Pichaculco, Senor Castillo, invited your memorialist to a dinner and entertainment to be given at his house that night, and that on the morning of the fifth of August, 1860, when he returned to his quarters, he found the back door of the same broken open, and his trunk with all of his contents missing.

Your memorialist further represents, that at the time his trunk was taken away by the Mexican soldiers, under Commandante Flores, it contained one thousand Mexican gold ounces and thirty-five thousand dollars worth of diamonds, among which were three diamonds of the value of twenty thousand dollars, and other valuable and costly jewelry, and also clothing, family papers, certificates of service, military manuscripts of great value to your memorialist.

Your memorialist further represents, that upon the discovery of the loss of his trunk and contents as aforesaid, he gave notice immediately of the same to Commandante Francisco Flores and to the Alcalde, who were reluctant to take action in the premises. Several days after the robbery of your memorialist's quarters, a soldier by the name of Martinez, under the command of Flores, and who had been detailed by him on guard duty at his quarters, confessed to a full knowledge of the robbery and made a statement of the facts and circumstances under oath before Alcalde Hernandez, which is made a part of this memorial, and is as follows:

"That on or about the fourth of August, 1860, he was ordered by Commandante Francisco Flores to station himself at a certain place fully armed, and he was at the place at 12 o'clock at night, the time fixed by Flores for him to be there, when Flores came up to him and ordered him

> to follow. They went to the rear of the quarters occupied by your memorialist, and Flores then ordered him to break open a door leading into another apartment, and there they found the trunk, and carried it out to a place some distance from the quarters, across the river and in the bushes; that Flores then ordered him off to some distance, and Martinez, the witness, saw him strike a light, and force open the trunk with a bayonet, and load himself with the contents, but not being able to take all at one time, ordered him to stand guard, and shortly afterwards Flores retruned and carried off the balance of the contents of the trunk; and that he was then ordered by Flores back to his quarters, and to say nothing of the robbery or he would have him shot, and that this threat of Flores had prevented him from making the statement before."
>
> On this sworn statement of Martinez, Commandante Flores was arrested and charged with the robbery of your memorialist's trunk, etc., as will appear by the certificate of Policarpio Hernandez, Judge of First Instance of the Department of Pichucalco, State of Chiapas, hereto annexed and marked "A."[136]

What Monstery did not mention in this petition, and what only appeared later in his biography, was that "the wily commandante [Flores] soon effected his release by dividing his plunder with the judges."[137]

In the pursuit of his claim, Monstery secured additional testimony from four witnesses, including former soldiers who had served under him. Pedro Pacheco claimed to have seen Monstery at Pichucalco, where "he & others were engaged by Thomas to go to Vera Cruz to join the Mexican Army under General Juarez." Pacheco verified the story of the robbery and stated that he had seen "the empty trunk brought back by soldiers to the office of the Alcalde...Estimates the property value to be between forty & fifty thousand dollars."[138] Antonio Zema of Los Angeles, formerly of Tabasco, Mexico, attested to the story of the robbery and claimed that Monstery had lost "not less than twenty thousand dollars in Mexican gold & silver coin."[139] Another witness, Ignacio Quiroga, a Costa Rican who had been "engaged by Thomas to go with him to Vera Cruz to join the liberal Army of Mexico under command of President Juarez," claimed to have been in Pichucalco with Monstery while the latter was "giving instruction in fencing," and further verified the story of the robbery. He related: "During month of July 1860,

[Quiroga] frequently met with Thomas (at the fair)...Saw Thomas in possession of large sum of money & jewelry & heard of robbery of all his property."[140]

Throughout the course of his case, numerous witnesses—as well as findings by the Mexican government itself—largely verified Monstery's story. However, instead of disputing the account of what had happened, the Mexican Republic moved to reject Monstery's claim on the grounds that Flores's crime was "a private robbery, and not an act of the 'authorities of the Mexican Republic'"—while at the same time admitting that "the alleged robber or robbers [was] a fellow-officer and soldier." The defense for the Mexican government stated that Monstery's claim was "by its nature outside of the Convention," since "no Government is responsible in damages for private wrongs perpetrated by an officer, military or civil." The Mexican Republic also moved to dismiss the case on the grounds that Monstery "held the rank of colonel of cavalry in that state [Chiapas]. The effect of this is to make him a citizen of the [Mexican] Republic." Thus, as a citizen of Mexico and not the United States, Monstery was ineligible to make a claim through the Commission. This was, of course, in spite of Monstery's sworn statement that he was "a citizen of the United States of America at the time his claim had its origin," and that he had "never taken the oath of allegiance to Mexico, or any foreign government."[141]

Of this high-profile decision, the *Chicago Tribune* stated that "the behavior of the commission upon the claim of Colonel Monstery was in the highest degree reprehensible," and noted that "every claim has been rejected which has been considered up to the present time." The editors elaborated:

> [The commission] simply said, you have no claim before us, as you represent it, for when you were robbed, no matter whether you were robbed or not, you did not fill the character of an American citizen. By the laws of the Mexican Republic, and by the admitted theory of the United States, you were then a Mexican citizen...the commission disallows your claim because you do not appear in your proper character.
>
> The decision of this claim has been written by Mr. Wadsworth, in a handsome and learned judicial paper. It cites the maxim of Jefferson, that

> whoever pays taxes and fights must vote; and it builds up, through the practice and authority of the United States upon the right of expatriation, a clear statement that this claimant was not an American. The lawyers of this chevalier had anticipated no such inquiry...[142]

The irony of the commission's decision was not lost on the editors of Mexico City's journal, *The Two Republics*, which opined in March of 1871:

> Thomas Hoyer Monstery, the distinguished fencing master, is well known to the citizens of this Capital...In the course of the examination the fact was developed that Thomas had served the government of Mexico, in a military capacity, and the court decided for having been guilty of such an indiscretion, that he forfeited all claim upon the American government or its protection.
>
> This is the law as settled in the Mixed Commission, and its promulgation should serve as a caution to all misguided foreigners who stray over into Mexico; if they do not want to be robbed and mistreated with impunity they must not serve the country. If they do render service and are mistreated they cannot look to their governments for protection.[143]

Despite the commission's decision, in subsequent decades, Monstery would make repeated attempts to obtain compensation for his lost treasure—even up until the last few years of his life. As to the fate of his great malefactor, Commandante Flores, Monstery related the following story:

> Twenty-five years ago while in San Francisco and giving sword lessons to [Daniel E.] Bandmann, the actor, he told me that his brother, a civil engineer, had met a man of my name and military rank in Bolivia. As Bolivia is the only South American republic I have never visited, I thought this singular. I met Bandmann's brother, and he described the Col. Monstery he had seen down there. Instantly I recognized Pancho Flores, who had fled from [Pichucalco] years before. He had ascertained from my papers that I had never been in Bolivia, so he made for that country. He not only took my gold and jewels and papers, but he took my name, and as he was a fairly expert swordsman, though not by any means a phenomenon, I do not doubt that he made the title good against such fighters as he could meet there."[144]

RETURN TO CENTRAL AMERICA: 1867

Following the loss of his Mexican treasure in 1860, Monstery "was compelled to leave the country with what he had left."[145] He started from the mouth of the Grijalva river in the schooner Tallahassee, "intending to sail to Veracruz and there join the liberal party of Mexico, but storms that could not be successfully contended against drifted the vessel off her course." A landing was instead made on the coast of Texas, "just about the time the agitation was beginning over the [American] civil war question." From there, Monstery journeyed to "New Orleans just at the beginning of the exciting winter of 1860."[146] He was at once "importuned to join the Southern Confederacy which was then being formed," but, being an ardent Unionist, declined. Monstery searched for his wife, for "he had heard that a child had been born to him shortly after his separation from Carmelita." His biography relates:

> He had hoped to come back with a fortune, but luck was against him in that line. He had several thousand dollars worth of diamonds left, and he sold these and went to the West Indies to find Carmelita. At Puerto Principe [Camagüey, Cuba] he found she had gone after him, hearing of him in Central America, and at last they met in the island of Curacoa, where he saw his child for the first time.

Now reunited, the Monstery family embarked in a steamer toward Vera Cruz, Mexico, but encountered a severe storm at sea, almost wrecking their ship, and tragically causing the death of their infant child.[147] Crossing through Panama, Monstery and his remaining family made for "the port of Acapulco where an attempt was made to reach Mexico City to join the liberal forces, but the road was blocked by General Cobos and Regara, all his horses captured and himself forced to abandon the trip."[148] In disappointment, Monstery, along with his family, journeyed to California with his remaining seven thousand dollars.[149]

In San Francisco, Monstery served as fencing master at the noted Olympic Club, and ran several private *salles des armes* of his own. His first extant fencing advertisement in the city dates from April, 1861, when "Col. T. H. Monstery, Late of the Mexican Army," offered to "give lessons with the Foil or Small-Sword, Cavalry and Infantry Broad Swords, Fencing with the Bayonet, Lance, Dagger, and other offensive and defensive arts."[150] According to Monstery, "Here I stayed for five years before I started on the warpath again."[151] While living in California, several children were born to Thomas and Carmelita Monstery.[152]

In August of 1867, Monstery declared his intention to leave San Francisco for Central America.[153] The next month, as reported in the newspapers, "Col. T. H. Monstery, wife and two children" sailed for San Juan del Sur (in Southwest Nicaragua), on the steamship "Moses Taylor."[154] Frederick Whittaker claimed that "from California [Monstery] went to South America...and fenced through his old ground in Guatemala, Honduras, and other places, till he went through Peru."[155] This, however, may be pure apocrypha, as no known extant records attest to Monstery visiting these countries during this period. Ship passenger records show that the Monstery family sailed from Nicaragua on the Steamer *Santiago de Cuba*, arriving in New York on Oct 8, 1867.[156]

According to Whittaker, after visiting New York, and before the close of the year, Monstery set sail to Cuba to challenge his old nemesis, Don Juan Galletti of the *Sala de Armas Blancas del Circolo de la Habana.* This time, however, the Italian was found to be "pacific...Galetti would not fence on the plea that he was getting old."[157] Although this particular incident cannot be verified, the next episode described by Whittaker can be. According to this account, Monstery journeyed once again to Mexico, where he would challenge other fencing masters to various contests of arms, and fight a series of duels—at least one of which would result in a fatality.[158]

FENCING MASTER IN MEXICO CITY: 1868

Although the precise date of his arrival in Mexico is not known, Monstery had become well-established in the nation's capital by mid-February of 1868, when he began advertising his *Academia de Esgrima,* located above the famous Cafe Concordia, offering lessons in a variety of weapons such as the sword, knife, bayonet, as well as in boxing.[159] Little

Academia de Esgrima.

El ceronel Tomas H. Monstery últimamento profesor de la Academia militar de West-Point (E. U.), se ofrece à los cuerpos militares, colegios, y al público en general para dar lecciones en

FLORETE,
ESPADA,
SABLE DE INFANTERIA,
ID. DE CABALLERIA,
ESGRIMA DE BAYONETA,
JUEGO DE PUÑAL Y BOX.

Sala de Armas, esquina de las calles de San Jo-é el Real núm. 1 y 2.ª de Plateros, arriba del Café de la Concordia.
Asalto de Esgrima todos los domingos de diez á una.

3s—2

Advertisement in *El Monitor Republicano* February 15, 1868

more than two weeks later, the following announcement appeared among the pages of the *Mexican Standard:*

> COL. MONSTERY.—Gave an entertainment at his rooms over the "Concordia" yesterday morning in which he exhibited the use of the foil, sword, knife, bayonet, and gloves. His past experience in the profession to which he has devoted himself, and his splendid success at his rooms on the occasion referred to, especially recommend him to the public; should the present Congress establish a military academy, we believe that no better selection could be made than that of Col. Monstery as Professor of this department, to which he is so eminently situated. Officers of the army and private individuals who desire to become accomplished in the sword or bayonet exercise or in the art of "self defence" are sufficiently guaranteed in securing the professional services of the Colonel, not only by his reputation in the United States, but by his merits as shown yesterday at his rooms before the great number of gentlemen who visited them.

Monstery's popularity in Mexico City incurred the resentment of Nicolas Poupard, another local fencing master with his own *salle d'armes.* A native of France, Poupard had previously immigrated to Mexico, where he became a disciple of Maestro Roman Punzalan Zapata, a master of the Spanish school of fencing, *La Verdadera Destreza.* In 1865, Poupard was publicly advertising lessons in the metropolis for "Esgrima y Espadon."[160] According to the Mexican journal, *El Monitor Republicano,* by 1868, Poupard had become "the most famous fencing master in Mexico."[161] Other histories of fencing in Mexico note that Poupard had participated in numerous duels and *rencontres* "without receiving a single injury," and had thus manifested "the superiority of the school of fencing of Maestro Poupard."[162]

In Monstery's biography, Poupard is described as "a burly, black-bearded Frenchman with bully written in every line of his face, a thorough French *maite d'armes.*" The first meeting between Poupard and Monstery was described as follows:

> The Frenchman tried to cow [Monstery] at once in shaking hands by squeezing with all his force, glaring at him with a fierce smile as much as to say:
>
> "So you are the little man that dares to think of fighting *me*, are you?"
>
> Like many another before and since, he was deceived by our hero's pleasant face, his exquisite Spanish politeness, and his pleasant smile. This line just suited Monstery. He could squeeze as hard as any man and he smiled up at Poupard with a bland sarcasm that irritated the Frenchman as he said:
>
> "Aha! you are a gladiator I perceive. I love to meet them and beat them."
>
> Then changing like lightning to one of his most savage scowls he flung off the Frenchman's grasp, growling:
>
> "Let go my hand!"
>
> Poupard had tried the bluff game and Monstery had gone over him. After that the Frenchman was civil and he soon developed a sort of puzzled fear of this fierce blue-eyed man, who was so deceiving in his appearance. There was no getting out of the public match, however, which was of the kind which Monstery favored most.

A contest was arranged, with the two fencing masters agreeing to fence with the foils, saber, rapier, dagger, and bayonet—the man making the most points to be declared champion of Mexico.[163]

This match took place on Sunday, March 1, when a large crowd, including many Mexican army officers, numerous gentlemen "of distinction", and five noted Mexican fencing masters, packed Monstery's fencing academy on the second floor above the Cafe Concordia. According to Whittaker, "the French backed Poupard and most of the

Maitre d'Armes Nicolas Poupard

Mexicans with all of the Americans backed Monstery." Feeling ran high, he related, "for the French were much hated in Mexico." The contest proceeded as follows:

> The foils were first on the programme and Poupard made a furious lunge to pierce the American's guard by main force at the first pass. A shout of rapturious applause burst forth from the crowd as Monstery with one of his sharp parries struck the foil from Poupard's hand and disarmed him at the first thrust.
>
> "Where's Poupard's iron wrist?" shouted an exulting American. "Do your best, colonel! We're looking at you."
>
> Deeply mortified Poupard picked up his foil and came on guard again. He attributed the disarm to an accident.

This time he feinted for an opening, and a sharp rally followed in which our hero pinked him twice, for it is in the confusion of a rally that Monstery is at his best, as active as a cat.

In the third pass Poupard, in spite of his vaunted strong wrist, was disarmed a second time and the Mexicans yelled themselves hoarse over Monstery.

By the rules of the assault nine passes were to be made, thrusts and disarms to count each one point. At the expiration of the nine, Poupard had been disarmed three times, had only got in his point twice, and Monstery was declared victor at foils.

The people were delighted and expected still more fun with the other weapons. But Poupard had one good quality: he knew when he had enough. He had been beaten at his national weapon and had no confidence in his ability to reverse the issue with anything else. He gave up the contest in despair.[164]

In the following March 7 issue of *The Two Republics,* it was reported that Monstery "had a formal trial of skill with Monsieur Poupard, a professor of fencing, and the Colonel was victorious, having twice disarmed his antagonist, and delivered four hits in succession at the outset."[165]

Following the publication of this report, Poupard wrote to the editors of *El Monitor Republicano,* complaining that the account in *The Two Republics* was unfair, and had been written by friends of Monstery.[166] However, a much lengthier and more detailed account of the event, published in Spanish in *El Monitor Republicano,* offers what appears to be generous treatment of Poupard, while also testifying to Monstery's superior skill and victory. Following is a full English translation of that article:

ASSAULT-OF-ARMS BETWEEN PROFESSORS.— During the week, before Sunday 1 of the present, it was said, that by desire of certain authorities, an assault-of-arms was going to take place, between Colonel Monstery, the famous professor and fencer of the United States, and Mr. Poupard, the most famous professor in Mexico.

On Sunday, March 1, by invitation, we attended the room of Colonel Monstery, at the Calle de San José del Real no. 1. Upon entering we found the room full of gentlemen, and among them many of distinction. At half past eleven, Mr. Poupard arrived, and was cordially received by the colonel, and invited to begin the assault.

The colonel then said that the principal object of his coming to Mexico was to restore his health, which was not yet in good condition. But that nevertheless, he wanted to give an assault with the following weapons:

1. Foil.
2. Infantry saber.
3. Sword.
4. Mounted saber.
5. Dagger play.
6. Dagger versus foil and saber.
7. Bayonet fencing.
8. Saber on foot versus bayonet.
9. Mounted saber versus bayonet.
10. Boxing.

After this explanation, the colonel greeted his adversary and the audience, and began with the salute or the postures (which is the introduction of fencing.) After putting on the masks, they began the assault, the result of which was victory for the Colonel, as the first four thrusts with two disarmaments were in favor of the colonel.

What was strange for those who knew Mr. Poupard were the two disarmaments, because of the great fame of the strength of his wrist.

The colonel then invited Mr. Poupard to enlist for the saber assault; but the latter refused, as did the other fencing masters, of whom there were five—and among them, Mr. Martel, the oldest one in Mexico—perhaps for the consideration of not exhausting the colonel, and since the assault should mainly be with Mr. Poupard. Mr. Becker, formerly captain in the service of the General-State of General Leyva, accepted and showed considerable skill in the handling of the saber; but the colonel overcame him by his superior skill. As he also did in No. 3, with the sword. In No. 4, saber as mounted. In No. 5, dagger play, the colonel said that he felt very good, and desired to try the skill of Mr. Poupard, or of any other person, in fencing with the dagger, because the colonel had never found another competent person for said weapon. But as there was no one who acceded to this wish, it went unnoticed and without effect.

However, the colonel had a desire to prove his skill against Mr. Poupard while using that weapon, and offered to fence with the dagger against Mr.

> Poupard's foil, which the latter also refused, as with the other times that he was invited.
>
> Captain Becker agreed to fence, and was conquered by the colonel with the latter's dagger against his foil, and with the dagger against his sword, but the captain managed to touch the colonel twice in the arm in the final interplay, difficult for the colonel.
>
> The 7th combat arrived; the colonel announced to Mr. Poupard that it was the time for the fencing of the bayonet, and that being the weapon with which the French had achieved so much glory, he hoped that he would distinguish himself; but Mr. Poupard did not feel eager to win these laurels. Captain Becker showed his knowledge in this weapon; but the colonel used the said weapon [bayonet] with the same skill as he had with the foil; because his quick attacks and ripostes against the plastron did not give his adversary the opportunity to touch him, and left no doubt as to the fame that the colonel has in the United States for the simplicity and effectiveness of his system in said art.
>
> 8. The Colonel proposed the opposition of the bayonet against his saber, but as no one accepted, this was passed over.
>
> 9. Mounted saber defense by the colonel, against bayonet, in which the difficult play was defending while being elevated. He showed that, although it was very difficult to defeat the infantryman while wielding so short a weapon, he still defended himself and showed that the cavalry had a defense against the bayonet, which is the most fearsome weapon.
>
> 10. Boxing. Mr. Valdez, a disciple of the colonel, gave as much credit to his professor as to himself, and it is believed that if Mr. Valdez takes another ten lessons in addition to those he has already taken, he will be a formidable combatant in that art.[167]

This last-mentioned bout, between Monstery and Sr. Valdez, a Mexican subcabinet minister, won acclaim in local newspapers. "As boxing is not the peculiar amusement of Mexicans," wrote one reporter, "his acceptance of the challenge produced as much surprise as his performance elicited admiration." Spectators reported that Valdez "took good positions, eyed his adversary and threw out, and altogether handled his gloves to the great satisfaction of his friends."[168] For his triumph over Poupard, as well as his others in Spanish America, Monstery would go on to claim the fencing championship "of the Two Americas."

DUELS IN MEXICO

After defeating Poupard, Monstery remained in Mexico for several months, attempting to popularize his *salle d'armes,* however, "the country was still too unsettled to make it pay, and he never could get on with the Mexicans." According to Frederick Whittaker, "they hated the Americans then, in 1868, about as badly as they did the French and tried to fasten quarrels upon them or kill them by treachery whenever they could. Monstery's life soon became a succession of affairs with Mexican officers, quarrels forced on him by their rancorous hatred..."[169]

Of these duels, a number of accounts survive. The most lethal was reported by Monstery himself, in an interview given late in life. He recalled, "May 23, 1868, I was forced into a duel which caused me to kill my opponent, and I had to retire precipitately."[170]

Aside from this particular combat, however (and at least one other that took place in Europe), Monstery claimed that none of his other duels ended in a fatality. An entertaining example of one such affair took place in Mexico, and was recounted in detail among the pages of Monstery's biography:

> [Monstery] was introduced one night by a friend to a Mexican colonel, a tall, black-bearded fellow, with a ferocious face, who only scowled at him and refused his proffered hand.
>
> Monstery pretended not to notice it, on account of his friends, and went on with his conversation with the rest as if nothing had happened. He could not keep peace, however, for the Mexican constantly interrupted him and contradicted him so rudely that our hero at last said gently:
>
> "*Senor coronel,* it seems to me that you have some antipathy to me—"
>
> "Antipathy—!" cried the Mexican, with a savage curse. "You are a cowardly—"
>
> A foul word escaped his lips and the next moment down he went under one of Monstery's terrible right-handers, with his cheek cut open. In a moment the friends and bystanders came between the two men, and the Mexican foaming with fury was taken off one way, Monstery another, while preliminaries were hastily arranged for a duel at sunrise of the next day.

Nothing but blood would satisfy the Mexican colonel, whose seconds met one of Monstery's friends, and it was arranged that they should fight with navy revolvers, beginning at ten paces, both parties to be at liberty to advance and fire when they pleased after the word. Monstery did not want such a savage duel in which one or both was certain to be wounded; but the Mexican was inexorable and he had to yield.

Matters once arranged, the Mexican's second observed to Monstery smiling:

"Now we have made it up for you two to kill each other to-morrow there's nothing to hinder us from passing the night together like gentlemen. Have you any objection to my ordering some wine and cigars? They have them good in this hotel."

This exactly suited our hero's generous and chivalrous nature which had always been incapable of bearing malice and he consented on condition that he should be allowed to pay his share. Then the Mexican's second, Monstery, and Monstery's second sat down to make a night of it. They tried to induce the Mexican colonel to join them, but he held sullenly aloof. He was bound to have blood in the morning and nursed his hate.

The three gentlemen at the table smoked, drank and told stories till long after midnight, and the Mexican's second became fairly fascinated with our hero. He, on his part, was delighted with the other, who proved to be a gentleman of cultivation, brave, generous and amiable, and penetrated with sorrow at the duel in which two men whom he liked were about to engage.

"What a shame it is!" he exclaimed, "that two such gallant fellows as you, who ought to be friends, should shoot at each other. At least you and I, colonel, whatever the result, will be friends forever."

The hour, the stories of war, the good wine—all were in favor of the pledge, and the two men swore eternal friendship over a clasp of hands.

Suddenly the Mexican started and looked earnestly at Monstery.

"It is not possible!" he ejaculated. "Shake hands again."

Then as their hands met he uttered a cry of amazement and shouted:

"It is true. You are a brother. This duel cannot take place."

Monstery's second, an American, looked as if a thunderbolt had fallen.

"Not take place!" he echoed. "Why not? It must take place. We didn't come here to be fooled."

But to still his greater surprise, Monstery answered him, very gravely:

"No, captain, it cannot take place, if, as I apprehend, the gentleman upstairs is what I think he is."

"He is, he is!" cried the Mexican, eagerly. "He is a brother. It is impossible. You see it. It would be sacrilege. I will go get him. He must shake hands. He shall. I will not allow the duel. It is monstrous."

And away he rushed after his friend, while Captain B—, the American, sat staring at Monstery with a mixture of amazement and rage, ejaculating:

"What does this mean?"

"It means, my friend, something that you don't understand and never will till you become a Mason. The friend who has just gone upstairs gave me the grip of the Royal Arch Masons, of which I am a brother, and if the Mexican colonel is one also, it ends the affair. We *cannot* fight a brother without breaking a sacred oath."

Captain B— was thunderstruck.

"What nonsense is this? Blows have passed, and no fight! I don't understand it."

"You never will till you are a brother; then you will do as I do," replied Monstery, in a solemn tone; and just then down came the Mexican colonel and his friend.

Slowly and reluctantly, as if he hated the deed he was about to do, the Mexican came into the room, advanced step by step to Monstery, and held out his hand. He had to clinch his teeth hard to keep from breaking out, but for all that their hands met and they exchanged the secret grip.

Then, as if the words were being torn out with red-hot pincers, the Mexican said:

"Brother, forgive me."

And Monstery answered:

"I freely forgive. Forgive thou me, brother."

The Mexican bowed his head and whispered:

"I do."

He was as white as a sheet under the conflict of emotions, and soon after left the room. Monstery never met him again.

As for Captain B—, at first inclined to be furious at the interruption of the fight, he was reconciled to it at last by the assurance of his friends:

"You don't understand it now. If ever you do, you will see we could not have done anything else, for all Masons are brothers, and brothers cannot fight."[171]

Monstery's second, the "Captain B—" mentioned in this account, was undoubtedly Captain Baker (or Becker) of the United States Army, who had competed with the saber, sword, foil and bayonet against Monstery during the second half of the contest with Poupard.[172]

ONE VERSUS FOUR

In 1887, yet another exciting account of a combat involving Monstery, fought against four Mexican swordsmen simultaneously, was related by an "Old Sport" (personally known to the editors of the *Pittsburgh Dispatch*) who had supposedly befriended Monstery during his sojourn in Mexico. Although the author does not refer to Monstery by name—but instead, by the pseudonym "Tom Montvey"—a wealth of personal details in this account confirms that the subject is none other than Monstery. As dates are not given, the combat could have occurred during any of Monstery's sojourns in Mexico. Be forewarned—there are ethnic references in this account, not unusual for the period, which may be offensive to some readers:

> I had been traveling about over the world and had brought up in the City of Mexico. At that time the Mexicans had even less love for the Americans than they have now, and I had to keep my eye wide open all the time to keep from being drawn into a brawl in which the chances were I would have a knife or sword thrust between my ribs. One day I fell in with a young fellow, an American, who had been in Spain and had bested all the Spanish swordsmen of the day. He was going under the name of Tom Montvey, though that was not his proper cognomen, and a finer looking and more companionable young fellow you never saw. He spoke the Spanish language like a native, and, made up in the costume of the country, he readily passed for a Mexican. We became great friends, and he prevailed upon me to take a trip with him through the country. I found that in the little towns and villages remote from the Capital the feeling against an American was more bitter, and I would have fared badly had it not been for Tom. We stopped for a long time in the city of Guanajuato, Capital of the State of that name. There were many Spaniards and native Mexicans there who considered themselves masters of the sword, and Tom

soon had his hands full. I never saw a man with such a sword arm. His wrist was like steel, and when engaged in a combat he appeared to me more like a fiend than a human being. His great, broad chest would heave, his nostrils would expand, and his eyes glitter with a most devilish light when engaged in a contest, for he hated a Mexican, and delighted in seeing their blood upon his weapon.

Well, he conquered several of their best swordsmen and the whole country was talking of his prowess. They called him a devil, and many a gay Mexican youth would have given his entire fortune to have been able to run a sword through his heart, for the beautiful senoritas of Guanajuato were smitten with Tom's handsome figure, and to please their lovers, it became fashionable for them to promise their hand as soon as the lover should succeed in winning a victory from Tom. In this way it came about that almost every gay youth in the city cordially disliked Tom, and they hated me because I was an American, and, if I do say it myself, could handle a sword about as well as some of them. Things were getting warm, and to cap the climax, I found favor in the dark eyes of a rosy-lipped beauty, and two or three yellow-skinned youngsters who had in vain sought her smiles put up a job to shut out my light.

Tom got wind of the affair, and forewarned is forearmed. We were to attend a grand festival given by one of the nabobs of the State, whose residence and beautiful grounds were in the outskirts of the city. This was the occasion which was to be taken advantage of by four young Greasers to forever settle my chances with the sweetest little Mexican girl I ever saw. Well, we went to the fete, and I was I so taken up with the fascinating senorita that I forgot about the scheme on my life; but, thanks to ever-vigilant Tom, he was cognizant of every move made by the enemy. Of course he was the great lion of the occasion, but as everybody thought he was a Mexican it was all right.

To make a long story short, the four conspirators set upon me in a little grove near the house. The moon was shining through the branches of the trees, and; save for the shadows, it was light as day. I was taken by surprise, and never thought of a sword, but I banged the fellow a pelt in the jaw with my fist, and I laid him out. The others were making at me with drawn swords when Tom jumped in and took up the fight. Talk about sword play. I don't believe there was ever another battle like it. Tom's cuts, thrusts, and parries were so rapid that it looked as though he was using a dozen swords. Not a word was spoken, and I stood there like a jay watching the fight. I suppose I should have come to my senses had

> Tom been getting the worst of it but, as it was, I never moved until three Mexicans were stretched on the grass. The fellow that I had knocked down had disappeared.
>
> That was a sword contest that was a contest. Though it wasn't in the regular order for a stake, it would have cost us our lives had Tom lost. As it was we made a dead sneak out of the city that night, and got back to the City of Mexico as fast as we could. I would never have been here if we had remained to see the result of the fight.
>
> Well, Tom cleaned out all the best swordsmen in the country, and when he returned to the States he brought a Spanish wife with him. I hear from him occasionally now. He taught fencing for a time in New York, and is now teaching young aspirants the use of his favorite weapon in a city not far from Chicago, under an assumed name. He is an old man now, but a most remarkable one, and I would put up a large sack of dust that if he should enter into a contest he could best any swordsman in America to-day. He can give any of them pointers on their business. You couldn't get him into a fake, though; he's too fine-strung for that.[173]

Whatever the truth of the above story, Monstery's last duel in Mexico reportedly took place "after the death of the Austrian"—that is, after the death of Austrian Archduke Ferdinand Maximilian, who had been installed as emperor of Mexico by French Emperor Napoleon III, and was executed in 1867 on the orders of Mexican President Benito Juarez. Of Maximilian's death, Monstery was quoted as stating, sorrowfully:

> He was a brave man...he was murdered between two black cut-throats named Miramon and Mexia. I fought against him, yes; but it was the cause and not the man we fought. We liked him. His execution was murder.[174]

The execution of Emperor Maximilian

FENCING AND BOXING ACADEMY,

NO. 302 MONTGOMERY STREET, northeast corner of Pine, upper floor.
COL. THOS. H. MONSTERY respectfully informs his friends and the public that having returned from the Eastern States and Mexico, he is ready, at the above named rooms, to give instruction with Foils, Broadswords, Bayonets, etc. Boxing taught in twelve lessons, by a system that will give efficiency. Classes (age of pupils 10 years and upwards) attended to in Schools and Colleges in San Francisco or its vicinity. N. B.—A select assortment of Fencing Apparatus on hand for sale. fe14-1m

Advertisement for Monstery's San Francisco Academy, February, 1869

As to his final duel in Mexico, Monstery's interviewer recounted, in later years:

> It was in 1868 against Ramon Valdez, a Colonel in the Mexican Army. Valdez had made public reflections against America and Americans and the fiery fighter in fifty wars resented it with a blow. The weapons were six-shooters, distance thirty yards, advance at the word and fire at will. At the first crack of Monstery's pistol the Mexican's right arm dropped and hung to a shattered shoulder. That ended the quarrel.[175]

Monstery's fighting days in Mexico were over. On June 14, 1868, the *New York Herald* reported that the "Colonel," along with "Mrs. Monstery and family" had arrived in New York on the Steamer Virgo from Vera Cruz, Sisal, and Havana.[176] By February of 1869, he had returned to San Francisco "now wearing additional laurels since his visit to New York, Havana, and Mexico, (in each of which places he challenged the professors of arms to a trial of skill,)" and was once again teaching at the Olympic Club, as well as at his *salle d'armes*, located on the corner of Pine and Montgomery Streets.[177]

Cuban revolutionary leader Francisco Vicente Aguilera, whom Monstery claimed to have trained for a duel.

THE VIRGINIUS AFFAIR

In 1870, Monstery relocated from San Francisco to New York City. After moving his school from location to location, he finally settled at 619 Sixth Avenue.[178] The same year, he claimed to have received a visit from Salvador Cisneros Betancourt, a former Cuban revolutionary and president of the Republic of Cuba. In a letter penned to Cisneros decades later, Monstery recounted:

> I met you again in New York in 1870, when defunct Mayorga was the head of the Junta and our beloved friend Aquillara was the president of the republic. You may remember that at that time, I had a large family and that the Junta was too poor to pay anything for recruits, and hence, much as I wished to throw myself into the Cuban cause, family ties with-

> held me, but I still trained the unfortunate Virginius expedition, fitted out by Amela Villa Werda under the direction of the Junta. I also trained our dear friend Aquillara and his son for a duel since. Where is the son now—alive? It is nearly seventeen years since you and I met at no. 619 Sixth Avenue, New York, where you visited me, and the picture you gave me of yourself I still have.[179]

The above-mentioned President "Aquillara", whom Monstery claimed to have trained for a duel, was undoubtedly Francisco Vicente Aguilera, a prominent Cuban revolutionary leader who had fought with Betancourt in Cuba's Ten Years' War, and who eventually died in exile in New York in 1877. The Virginius Affair mentioned by Monstery was a diplomatic dispute that ran from October 1873 to February 1875, between the United States, the United Kingdom, and Spain (then in control of Cuba). The affair was named for the ship *Virginius,* which secretly aided the Cuban rebellion while being protected by United States naval ships. After three years of aggressive attempts by Spain to capture it, the *Virginius* was finally overtaken. Its crew members, comprised of both American and British citizens, as well as native Cubans, were sentenced to death; a total of fifty-three were later executed by firing squad, and decapitated by Spanish soldiers. Aside from the cryptic reference in the above letter, no other evidence relating to Monstery's involvement in this affair could be found, and it remains one of his most obscure and least-documented exploits.

LATER YEARS, AND FURTHER LATIN AMERICAN DOINGS

Throughout the 1870s, while residing of the United States, Monstery continued his involvement in Spanish American affairs. In 1874, a visit was paid to his New York *salle d'armes* by the Cuban general and fencing master, José Recio Betancourt, who had been a pupil of Monstery's in Havana. The journal *Turf, Field, and Farm* described their reunion:

> On Friday [Monstery] was surprised by the visit of a gentleman who had been his pupil in Cuba nineteen years ago, where the colonel was then in

> the Spanish service. Gen. Resio Betancourt has since become an expert, famous as a master-at-arms. He has taken a forward part in the present struggle for liberty in the Faithful Isle, and the chances of war brought him to Mexico, from where he has just arrived. He returns to Cuba with the first expedition, and woe to the Spaniard who meets him hand-to-hand. The General relates some amusing and highly interesting incidents which occurred during his brief sojourn in Mexico—his assaults with celebrated swordsmen there, the recognition of his thrusts and parries by his opponents as those of Col. Monstery, who had also left part of his world-wide reputation there. It was there he learned of the Colonel's whereabouts, and he came as much to try his own skill as to revive the old friendship.[180]

At an assault-of-arms that evening, the two men engaged in an exciting fencing bout:

> Col. Monstery...introduced Gen. Betancourt, and in this assault an entirely distinct school was again fully illustrated. It was *L'Espada Espagnol*—no quarter, no rule, but do the best you can, and may the best man win. Gen. Betancourt is a man of powerful build, yet withal exceedingly rapid, and at all times showing the calmness and confidence acquired by long familiarity with the sword and danger. After a little preliminary play, the General settled well into a low guard, with a pleasant, confident smile beaming through his mask, his sword-hand resting on his advanced knee, and in this *degage* position he awaited the attack of his famous adversary. It came like a pistol shot—a straight lunge; but; although nearly home, the blade of the General whizzed and curled around that of his opponent, and stopped the first attack beautifully. But this manner of defence was good for once only with the Colonel. The next time the same thrust went direct to its destination on the broad chest of the General. Thrust and parry now followed each other in confused rapidity, and when both recovered it was apparent that the work had been warm. The next attack, a furious one, attempted by the General, was avoided by the Colonel binding his opponent's weapon with a *quinte* parry; then came close work, the Colonel getting a home thrust with a turn. After about fifteen minutes of intense excitement, with the odds in favor of the Colonel, the two masters exchanged a hearty salutation, and Mr. Johnson took the General's place.[181]

Colonel Thomas H. Monstery, "Champion of the Two Americas."

Five years later, in 1879, Betancourt and Monstery again crossed blades at a "Grand Assault at Arms" at the Colonel's New York school.[182] The next year, Monstery was publicly challenged by Betancourt to a friendly contest of arms, with the stipulation that "instead of the sabre we might fence with the rapier, cut and thrust."[183] Monstery would later accept this challenge, agreeing to "his choice of the rapier."[184]

During the 1870s, Monstery's wife, Carmen, often accompanied him to fencing events. In 1876, during the Colonel's high-profile contest with rival master Regis Senac, it was noted that during the combat with broadswords,

> Mrs. Monstery, in the audience, appeared only able to follow the gyrations of these more dangerous weapons, announcing in a shrill voice the success of her husband, now and then, and encouraging him on from time to time.[185]

At another lavish Grand Assault-of-Arms, directed by Monstery himself, and exhibiting a wide range of weapons and combative styles, it was reported that "Mrs. Monstery performed very admirably on the piano."[186] This same event, which took place in 1876, also included the participation of "Spaniards," a certain "Señor Martinez," and demonstrations of "Spanish knife."[187] During the next two years, in 1877 and 1878, Monstery published his magnum opus, a lengthy series of articles on self-defense with the fist, foot, cane, and quarterstaff.[188]

In 1883, following the destruction of his New York *salle d'armes* by fire, Monstery moved to Chicago, where he opened a fencing academy and taught at a number of institutions. That May, he reportedly entertained the Mexican President, Porfirio Díaz, during the latter's visit to the lavish Palmer House.[189] During this period, and throughout the next decade, Monstery was also prominent in Mexican War veteran circles, and was mentioned in numerous articles in the local press. Although Monstery had been denied a pension by the United States government for his war service, he was an active and official member of the Mexican Veterans' Association, whose members periodically gathered for meetings at Monstery's academy. The *Chicago Tribune* enthused:

Monstery, seen at upper left in an 1896 article for the *Chicago Tribune.*

Once a month, the veterans meet at the school-of-arms of their comrade, Col. T. H. Monstery, in the Schiller Building. The surroundings here are well calculated to awaken fading memories. The walls are covered from floor to ceiling with trophies of war in many countries. There are armor and weapons brought to Central and South America, by the followers of Cortez, lances that have been bathed in blood in South American revolutions, priceless old Toledo blades, daggers, Cuban machetes, quaint old guns and pistols, and similar arms of the latest pattern, swords from every country where such weapons are made, fencing foils and masks, and military accoutrements.[190]

Additional accounts of Monstery's *salle d'armes* mention the presence of relics from his adventures in Spanish America:

> Above the rack [of foils] was a magnificent Toledo blade which, the colonel said, was his favorite, and was 500 years old...On the front wall between two windows hung a breastplate of steel, found in Central America, and undoubtedly worn by one of the Spaniards who first invaded that land.[191]

Another article noted: "Monstery has as a memento of [José María Melo] only his lance, which he saw gallantly borne on fifty fields.[192]

Although the whereabouts of these weapons (if they still exist) are not currently known, the San Jacinto Museum of History in Texas contains in its collection several specimens of Monstery's old equipment—including the 1846 belt from his Mexican War uniform, a photograph of Monstery with other Mexican War veterans, and a fraternal ribbon with a silver pin, labeled "Thos. H. Monsterry," claiming him as one of the early "California Pioneers."

In later years, Monstery became estranged from many members of his family. His wife Carmelita remained in New Jersey when Thomas had migrated west, and many of their children became scattered. One of the latter, his son Emilio, left him and "ran away to sea, where he lived the laborious life of a sailor before the mast."[193] Emilio, however, eventually reunited with his father, became expert in the use of the sword, and took part in his father's fencing events.[194] Another son, Ole, traveled the old Chisholm Trail (famous in the post-Civil War era as the main route for cattle-driving between Texas and Kansas).[195] Yet another child, his daughter and reputed "swordswoman" Berguita "Rita" Monstery, performed feats for the Orris Brothers' Mexican circus, and later returned to Cuba, where she caused both scandal and local headlines by becoming the first woman to ride a bicycle on the streets of Havana.[196]

Throughout this time, the evidence suggests that Thomas Monstery still pined for Latin America. When the former Cuban revolutionary Salvador Cisneros Betancourt appeared in Chicago, Monstery wrote him the following letter:

Thomas Monstery's daughter, Berguita, photographed in Havana, Cuba.
Image courtesy of Diane Hayes.

Excellent Sir: You can imagine how my heart beat and my eyes filled with happy tears when I saw in one of the Chicago papers your honored name and learned that you were among the living and had at last attained the honored position in the republic of dear Cuba that you so richly deserve and for which you have suffered so much...For thirteen years I have been in Chicago, still hale and hearty and following the profession of an old

Salvador Cisneros Betancourt

soldier to teach other people how to fight. I am alone in the world now, and not too old to draw a sword again in the sacred name of liberty. Too old! Indeed nothing would give me such pleasure as to change this monotonous life for one of action again.

Have you any use for me and if so how can I be of service to the glorious cause of Cuban independence, the lone star, to rise now, never to set again? Let me know, and let me know soon, when, where, and how I can serve you, and with blessings on your dear head I remain affectionately and respectfully, your friend,

THOMAS HOYER MONSTERY.[197]

Unfortunately, there seems to be no record of a response from Betancourt, or of another trip to Cuba by Monstery. He appears to have remained in Chicago, where, four years later, his lifestyle and diet at age seventy-five were described by a visiting journalist:

He is as active as a cat, as springy as a young ash, and, but for an accident which occurred two years ago, would now be as strong as a lion...He still gives fencing lessons, working for hours each day, and apparently has lost nothing of his skill or agility. There is no food which his iron stomach does not digest. After frankfurters, sauerkraut, and beer at three in the morning, he sinks into the dreamless sleep of infancy. All honors are alike to him. Weather, hot or cold, wet or dry, do not affect him. Verily, 'he who lives by the sword lives long.'[198]

RETURN TO MEXICO, AND DEATH

This robust constitution was not to last forever. In December of 1900, after taking ill, Monstery departed Chicago for Mexico City in one last attempt to both improve his health, and to again press for compensation for his stolen fortune. A lawyer named Robert Redfield had become "interested in the romantic tale" of the veteran's lost treasure, and agreed to help Monstery seek damages for its theft. Further assistance was enlisted from Republican Illinois Senator William E. Mason. Reportedly, "after securing copies of the reports an appeal was made to the Mexican government and a favorable reply received." The *Chicago Tribune* triumphantly reported that "the octogenarian athlete will go to the City of Mexico to meet his old comrade-in-arms, Porfiro Diaz, President of Mexico, and to present his claim against the Mexican government..."[199]

Monstery's journey to Mexico City took less than two weeks, and when he arrived on December 19, his return was gloriously announced in Mexican newspapers, beneath headlines such as: "A FAMOUS SOLDIER. Col. Monstery Again in Mexico After Many Years. Served the Liberals Here in Turbulous Times. A Noted Duelist." The *Mexican Herald* declared,

A celebrated personage in the history of Mexico arrived in the city yesterday in the person of Colonel Thomas H. Monstery, who has figured in the principal events that have taken place in this country since as far back as 1859.

Colonel Monstery is an American by birth...he bears the honor of being the champion swordsman of the continent and wears a medal awarded by

> the Mexican government on the 1st of March 1868 for having defeated the famous French Capt. Poupard, who was at that time instructor in fencing and foiling in the army of Mexico...when word came that the colonel was in the city, a HERALD reporter immediately called on him to get a short account of his experiences...
>
> Colonel Monstery talks of the happenings in both Europe and America of the 40's and 60's as fluently as we are used to hear the news of the last election...This is the first trip to Mexico since over thirty years ago and of course his comparisons between the times of then and now are vividly interesting. If the weather clears up today he will stay in the city of week or two; otherwise he intends going to Cuernevaca or some other milder point in order to get rid of a cold that has been troubling him ever since leaving the North.[200]

During his final time in Mexico, Monstery visited old friends and continued to pursue his financial claim—but all to no avail. A local journal reported that he had been impeded by the fact that "the papers in the case had been stolen from him by some enemy...which greatly embarrassed him in making good his claim." Monstery finally left Mexico in May, 1901, when the *Herald* reported that "Gen. Monstery, after a stay of some months in this city, departed last evening for Chicago. Gen. Monstery was a veteran of the war against the intervention and the empire."[201]

By August, he was back in Chicago.[202] One month later, in September, he publicly announced:

> NOTICE—I TAKE THE PLEASURE TO INFORM my pupils, friends, and public that I have returned from Mexico, and have established my Fencing, Boxing, and Swimming Academy at Lakeside Building, 214 Clark St., corner of Adams St., where I will be pleased to see them.
>
> COL. THOMAS H. MONSTERY.[203]

It was to be one of his last advertisements as fencing master. In less than four months, on New Year's Eve, 1901, Colonel Thomas Hoyer Monstery passed away at the Presbyterian Hospital in Chicago due to an "embolism of a throat artery."[204] The New York journal *Turf, Field, and*

The sixteenth-century Franciscan monastery at Cuernavaca, Mexico, the place where Monstery intended to regain his health.

Farm, which Monstery had often corresponded with, published the following notice:

> The death of Col. Thomas Monstery at the Presbyterian Hospital, Chicago, a few days ago, was a surprise to his family living in Jersey City. His home coming was looked forward to with interest, as he had sent no word of his sickness.
>
> The life of Col. Monstery was crowded with adventure, and some twenty-five years ago he told much of his history to the readers of the *Turf, Field and Farm*. He was [77] years old, and had participated as principal or second in 58 duels. He was one of the most expert swordsmen that ever lived, and yet his heart throbbed with kindness and a quarrel had to be forced upon him. He was of gentle birth, but loved adventure and sought it on distant fields. In moments of danger he carried himself gallantly, and seemed to bear a charmed life. He had a fencing school in Chicago at the time of his death.[205]

His passing was reported as far away as Mexico City, where the *Mexican Herald* lamented:

> Some of our readers may recall a tall, wiry, soldier-like gentleman of perfect manners, who seemed to have stepped out of one of Dumas's novels, and who was visiting this city six months ago...Colonel Monstery was what is called a "character," for he had seen many lands and fought in many wars. Personally he was the most courteous of men in that fine old-fashioned way now disappearing in the hurry of our modern times...Everyone who met Colonel Monstery during his visit to this city was impressed with his delightful courtesy, his erect and military bearing, and his manly character. Peace to his ashes! He died poor, but rich in the regards of men who could appreciate so striking a type of the old soldier.[206]

Perhaps the most poetic epitaph, however, appeared in *Everybody's Magazine*, which concluded a romantic summary of Monstery's adventures with the following passage:

> The bones of Thomas Hoyer Munster Monstery rest in Forest Home Cemetery. He was a gallant gentleman. Through what dim halls wanders that splendid spirit which so loved the sliding grind of blade on blade? Does it stop and listen with bent shadowy head to the tinkle of falling broken steel?[207]

CARMEN XIQUES MONSTERY

More than six years later, in 1908, Thomas Monstery's beloved "Carmelita" followed him to the grave. A brief notice, published in the *New York Herald*, announced:

> —On April 9, CARMEN XIQUES DE MONSTERY, wife of the late Colonel Thomas H. Monstery, aged 77 years. Interment Sunday, April 12, at two P. M. from her late residence, 17 Montgomery st., Jersey City. Puerto Principe and Cuban papers please copy.[208]

A lengthier obituary published in the *Jersey City Journal* read:

Carmen Xiques Monstery in later years. Photograph courtesy of Diane Hayes.

Carmen X. de Monstery.

Carmen Xiques de Monstery, widow of Col. T. H. Monstery, died Thursday at her home, 17 Montgomery Street, after a short illness. She was 77 years of age and is survived by two daughters. Her husband was a well known soldier of fortune and had seen service in the armies of Russia, Spain, United States and Mexico, and was at one time instructor-general in the service of the Mexican Government. His death occurred several years ago in New York. The deceased was a member of Trinity M. E. Church and was an earnest worker in church matters. Funeral arrangements will be announced later.[209]

In spite of their frequently stormy relationship, divorce, and occasional estrangement, Thomas and Carmen had nevertheless continued to reunite throughout nearly half a century—living together and having children together. Perhaps, as something of a tribute, the Colonel had also made her the heroine of his novel, *King of the Swordsmen,* wherein she serves as the love interest for his own *nom-de-guerre*, Olaf Svenson. The following letter, written by her character to his, appears among the novel's pages. Although undoubtedly a fictional composition, it offers a glimpse into Thomas's romantic view of his own wife—and an idealized version, perhaps, of their own relationship. It is a fitting epitaph for this couple, who had lived and traveled so much throughout Spanish America, and an appropriate way to close this chapter in the life of Thomas Hoyer Monstery:

> MY SOUL:—My father is determined I shall marry the infamous Guartiola, and I can only depend on your courage and address to save us both. They are hatching a plot to get rid of you. Be on your guard, and always believe in the undying love of
>
> Your own
>
> CARMELITA

NOTES

1 *Daily Inter Ocean*, July 15, 1888.

2 *Daily Inter Ocean,* November 11, 1894.

3 *Turf, Field, and Farm*, Jan. 24, 1902.

4 Monstery often claimed to have been born in Baltimore when, in fact, records show that he had been born in Copenhagen, Denmark.

5 Following are the major discrepancies in Monstery's story. He frequently claimed to be born in the United States, but was born in Denmark, a fact which he admitted in applications for U.S. naturalization. Also, Monstery's petition (possibly drawn up by his lawyers) to the Mexican American Claims Commission erroneously indicated that he had lived in Mexico throughout the 1860s, omitting his sojourn in California during those years (it is uncertain as to why Monstery would have stated this, as it could only have undermined his claim). This may have been a simplification or miscommunication by Monstery's lawyer, and does not necessarily represent an attempt to mislead the commission. Advertisements for Monstery's Mexico City fencing Academy indicate that he was "of the military academy of West Point", yet by his own admission he was not a graduate; although it is possible that he taught there in some minor capacity at some point in time, such is not mentioned in any historical source, and he is not listed as fencing instructor in any of the West Point yearbooks.

6 Thomas H. Monstery, *Self-Defense for Gentlemen and Ladies* (Berkely: North Atlantic Books, 2015).

7 *Claims on the Part of Citizens of the United States and Mexico, 44th Congress, 2d Session* (Washington: Goverment Printing Office, 1877), 36. Alberto María Carreño, *Archivo del General Porfirio Díaz, Memorias y documentos. Tomo IV* (México: Universidad Nacional Autónoma de México, Instituto de Historia/Elede, 1947), 364-367.

8 "At midnight on April 22, 1879, a fire broke out in the apartments occupied by Col. Thomas H. Monstery, at No. 619 Sixth Avenue; an alarm was sent out at once, and upon the arrival of the firemen it was found the flames had cut off all means of egress by the stairway. Robert Williams, then foreman of Hook and Ladder Company No. 4, taking in the situation at once, had ladders erected against the burning building; ascending one of them, he hastily entered the apartments, where he found three members of Colonel Monstery's family in a partial state of suffocation. Lifting up the insensible bodies of the men and women, he carried them to the window, where he was

met by members of Hook and Ladder Company No. 4, who received them, and then conveyed them safely to the street. But for the fortunate arrival of the firemen, a terrible calamity would have taken place." J. Frank Kernan, *Reminiscences of the Old Fire Laddies and Volunteer Fire Departments of New York and Brooklyn: Together with a Complete History of the Paid Departments of Both Cities* (New York: M. Crane, 1885), 590.

"At the meeting of the Board of Fire Commissioners yesterday a communication was received from Samuel Campbell, chief of the Seventh battalion, stating that during a fire at No. 619 Sixth avenue, on the morning of the 22d ult., the members of Hook and Ladder Company No. 4 rescued from suffocation the family of Colonel Thomas H. Monstery, consisting of Mrs. Monstery and her two children, aged respectively seventeen and ten years. They were confined on the second floor and were surrounded by the flames, their exit by the stairs having been cut off. Ladders were placed in position and by this means Firemen Brown and McAuliffe rescued them and conveyed them to a place of safety. The names of the brave firemen were ordered to be placed on the roll of merit." *New York Herald,* May 1, 1879.

9 *Beadle's New York Dime Library*, Vol. XII, No. 150. September 7, 1881. It should be noted that another book starring Colonel Olaf Svenson, "late Instructor-at-Arms, Spanish Army" was published just before *El Rubio Bravo*, in the summer of 1881. However, although this book features Monstery's *nom de guerre* Svenson, it does not appear to be semi-biographical, but is a sequel to *The Iron Wrist*, in which Monstery posits a fantasy scenario with Svenson returning to Russia at age fifty-six. Thus, although published *prior* to *El Rubio Bravo*, the events of the novel come *after* it chronologically. See *Beadle's New York Dime Library*, Vol. XII, No. 143. July 20, 1881.

10 Everett Franklin Bleiler, *Science-fiction, the Early Years: A Full Description of More Than 3,000 Science-fiction Stories from Earliest Times to the Appearance of the Genre Magazines in 1930: with Author, Title, and Motif Indexes* (Kent, Ohio: Kent State University Press, 1990), 512.

11 For his pioneering mentorship of female fencers, see Monstery, *Self-Defense for Gentlemen and Ladies,* 20-27. Likewise, in 1889, Monstery did something that few high-profile white American martial artists of the period were willing to do—he publicly expressed admiration for the black boxing champion Peter Jackson: "Colonel Monstery, the champion swords man of America, called at this office Monday last. The gallant Colonel, who is one of the most popular and adventurous sports men in America, is exceedingly fond of boxing and a great admirer of Peter Jackson." See *Topeka State Journal,* Sept. 23, 1889. Monstery also mentored the mixed-race actress Ada Isaacs Menken in swordsmanship. See *Daily Inter Ocean*, Oct. 29, 1893.

---

12 Randy Broecker, *Fantasy of the 20th Century: An Illustrated History* (New York: Barnes & Noble Books, 2001), 31-47.

13 "Haggard invented a new type of fantasy adventure for which the term 'the lost race novel' was later coined. Writers virtually fell over each other, following in his footsteps—as they do in the wake of every literary innovation..." Lin Carter, "Lost Races, Forgotten Cities" in H. Rider Haggard, *The People of the Mist* (New York: Ballantine, 1973). See also Robert E. Morsberger, "Afterword" in H. Rider Haggard, *King Solomon's Mines* (Pleasantville, N.Y.: The Reader's Digest, 1993); Carter F. Hanson, "Lost among white others: Late-Victorian lost race novels for boys" in *Nineteenth-Century Contexts: An Interdisciplinary Journal*, Volume 23, Issue 4 (Abingdon: Routledge, 2002), 497-527.

14 Edgar Rice Burroughs, *The Mad King* (Chicago: A.C. McClurg & Co., 1926).

15 Bleiler, 512-513.

16 "It was in San Salvador that [Monstery] acquired the name by which he was afterward known in Central America, of *El Rubio Bravo*—the Brave Blonde." Capt. Frederick Whittaker, *The Sword Prince: The Romantic Life of Col.Monstery, American Champion-at-Arms* (New York: M. J. Ivers & Co., 1884), 20.

17 Whittaker, 13.

18 Edward Jump, *San Francisco at the Fair* (California: 1864). This image was reprinted, with permission from the Bancroft Library, in Monstery's *Self-Defense for Gentlemen and Ladies,* 12. The key identifying Monstery in the image by Jump was published in *The San Francisco Newsletter*, July 20. 1916, 30.

19 Monstery, *Self-Defense for Gentlemen and Ladies,* 33-34.

20 *Fighting Tom, the Terror of the Toughs* (New York: Beadle & Adams, 1883), 5.

21 "Notes on the Life of Thomas Hoyer Monstery," a manuscript originally written during the 1870s, copied by Monstery's granddaughter Carmen Katherine Van Ness (nee Monstery), and passed down within the Monstery family. Copy of this MS courtesy of Thomas Monstery's great great granddaughter Diane Hayes.

22 Whittaker, 13.

23 H. S. Canfield, "Soldier of Fortune," in *Everybody's Magazine,* October, 1902.

24 Whittaker, and "Notes on the Life of Thomas Hoyer Monstery," MS.

25 Mexican War Pension, Act of January 29, A.D. 1887, Declaration of Survivor for Pension. Mexican War Pension, Act of January 29, 1887, Survivor's Brief. Partial transcription by Diane Hayes. Pension, Illinois,

NARA microfilm publication T317 (Washington D.C.: National Archives and Records Administration, n.d.); FHL microfilm 537,007.

26 *Chicago Daily Tribune,* February 2, 1896.

27 *Daily Inter Ocean*, October 11, 1895.

28 Anderson C. Quisenberry, *Lopez's Expeditions to Cuba, 1850 and 1851* (Louisville: John P. Morton and Co., 1906), 7.

29 *New York Sun*, April 9, 1899.

30 *Utica Saturday Globe,* August 10, 1895.

31 *Daily Inter Ocean*, Oct. 11, 1895.

32 Quisenberry, 12.

33 Ibid., 27-31

34 Whittaker, 13.

35 Quisenberry, 27-29.

36 "Notes on the Life of Thomas Hoyer Monstery," MS.

37 *Utica Saturday Globe,* August 10, 1895.

38 Quisenberry, 68-69

39 Ibid., 74, 79, 80.

40 Ibid., 102.

41 Ibid., 110.

42 Ibid., 87.

43 Monstery, *Self-Defense for Gentlemen and Ladies,* 143-144.

44 *Daily Inter Ocean*, October 11, 1895.

45 "Notes on the Life of Thomas Hoyer Monstery," MS.

46 Monstery, *Self-Defense for Gentlemen and Ladies,* 144.

47 Whittaker, 16.

48 Ibid., 13.

49 Ibid., 16.

50 E-mail from Monstery's great great granddaughter, Diane Hayes, to the editor, March 31, 2012. A record of Monstery's divorce can be found in the *Baltimore Sun*, October 9, 1855. The *California Weekly Alta* of May 11, 1867, relates that Mrs. Monstery had given birth to a son on April 30.

51 Whittaker, 16.

52 *Baltimore Sun*, February 17, 1853.

53 Whittaker, 17.

54 Ibid., 18.

55 *New York Sun*, April 9, 1899.

56 "Notes on the Life of Thomas Hoyer Monstery," MS.

57 Whittaker, 18.

58 *New York Sun*, April 9, 1899.

59 Canfield.

60 *Utica Saturday Globe*, August 10, 1895.

61 *New York Sun*, April 9, 1899.

62 *Daily Inter Ocean*, October 11, 1895.

63 *Turf, Field, and Farm*, January 16, 1874.

64 Whittaker, 18.

65 "D. Juan Galletti, who died on November 21, 1872, a native of Bologna, arrived in Havana in December 1833...He was one of the first to give fencing lessons in Havana." *Necrópolis de La Habana: historia de los cementerios de esta ciudad: con multitud de noticías interesantes* (Habana: Imprenta El Trabajo, 1875), 449. *Temas*, Issues 49-52 (Habana: Departamento de Ciencia y Técnica del Ministerio de Cultura, 2007), 27, 29. *Semana literaria, ó, Compañero de las damas, Volume 1* (Habana: M. Soler, 1847), 28. *Revista bimestre cubana*, July-October, 1910, 92. "La Esgrima en la Habana," *El Sport*, May 27, 1888. "La Esgrima en la Habana," *El Sport*, June 13, 1888.

66 *Estatutos de la sociedad de recreo titulada Circulo de la Habana* (Habana: "El Iris," 1861), 15.

67 Whittaker, 18.

68 *Utica Saturday Globe*, August 10, 1895.

69 Whittaker, 18.

70 Canfield.

71 "Notes on the Life of Thomas Hoyer Monstery," MS.

72 Whittaker, 19.

73 "Notes on the Life of Thomas Hoyer Monstery," MS.

74 *Inter Ocean from Chicago*, January 5, 1902.

75 *New York Sun*, April 9, 1899.

76 *New York Sun*, April 9, 1899.

77 Ephraim George Squier, *Honduras and Guatemala* [New York: 1854], 11.

78 Karl Ritter von Scherzer, *Travels in the Free States of Central America: Nicaragua, Honduras, Volume 2* (London: Longman, Brown, Green, Longmans, & Roberts, 1857), 87, 96.

79 James Jeffrey Roche, *The Story of the Filibusters* (London: T. F. Unwin, 1891), 80.

80 Charles William Doubleday, *Reminiscences of the Filibuster War in Nicaragua* (New York: G. P. Putnam's Sons, 1886), 156.

81 *New York Sun*, April 9, 1899.

82 Whittaker, 20.

83 Ricardo Fernández Guardia, *Cuentos Ticos: Short Stories of Costa Rica* (Cleveland: Burrows Brothers, 1904), 236-244.

84 Whittaker, 20.

85 *New York Sun*, April 9, 1899.

86 Whittaker, 20.

87 *New York Sun*, April 9, 1899.

88 Ibid.

89 Ibid.

90 Ibid.

91 Ibid.

92 Whittaker, 20.

93 *New York Sun*, April 9, 1899.

94 Whittaker, 20.

95 *New York Sun*, April 9, 1899.

96 Whittaker, 20.

97 Deposition 2 – Pedro Pacheco, Oct. 12, 1869, San Francisco, California. Claim of Thos. H. Monstery vs. Mexican Government, Memorial, filed November 1869.

98 Deposition 4 – Ignacio Quiroga, Nov. 25, 1869, resident of Almaden, Santa Clara Co., California, a miner (occupation). Claim of Thos. H. Monstery vs. Mexican Government, Memorial, filed November 1869.

99 *New York Sun*, April 9, 1899.

100 Whittaker, 21.

101 See Chapter XI of *King of the Swordsmen.*

102 See Chapter VIII of *King of the Swordsmen.*

103 *Utica Saturday Globe,* August 10, 1895.

104 *New York Sun*, April 9, 1899.

105 Rafael Reyes, *Nociones de historia del Salvador: precedidas de un resúmen de historia universal* (Barcelona, España: Talleres Gráficos de José Casamelo, 1910), 109.

106*New York Sun*, April 9, 1899.

107Whittaker, 30.

108Ibid., 20.

109*Daily Inter Ocean*, April 18, 1887.

110Aldo Lauria-Santiago, *An Agrarian Republic: Commercial Agriculture and the Politics of Peasant Communities in El Salvador, 1823–1914* (Pittsburgh: University of Pittsburgh Press, 1999), 115.

111Whittaker, 20-21.

112*Daily Inter Ocean*, July 15, 1888.

113Whittaker, 20-21.

114*Daily Inter Ocean*, July 15, 1888.

115Whittaker, 20-21.

116*Daily Inter Ocean*, July 15, 1888.

117Lauria-Santiago, 115-116.

118*Daily Inter Ocean*, July 15, 1888.

119*New York Sun*, April 9, 1899.

120*Daily Inter Ocean*, April 18, 1887.

121Whittaker, 20.

122*New York Sun*, April 9, 1899.

123*Utica Saturday Globe*, August 10, 1895.

124Whittaker, 20.

125*Utica Saturday Globe*, August 10, 1895.

126Mexican and American Commision. T.H. Monstery vs. Mexican Republic. No. 376. Opening Brief for Mexican Republic on Motion to Dismiss. Claim of Thos. H. Monstery vs. Mexican Government, Memorial, filed November 1869.

127Whittaker, 21-22.

128*Utica Saturday Globe*, August 10, 1895.

129*New York Sun*, April 9, 1899.

130Ibid.

131Ibid.

132Ibid.

133*Mexican Herald*, December 20, 1900.

134*Utica Saturday Globe*, August 10, 1895.

135*New York Sun*, April 9, 1899.

136Mexican and American Commision. T.H. Monstery vs. Mexican Republic. No. 376. Claim of Thos. H. Monstery vs. Mexican Government, Memorial, filed November 1869.

137Whittaker, 22.

138Deposition 2 – Pedro Pacheco, Oct. 12, 1869, San Francisco, California. Claim of Thos. H. Monstery vs. Mexican Government, Memorial, filed November 1869.

139Deposition 3 – Antonio Zema, Nov. 15, 1869, Los Angeles, California. Claim of Thos. H. Monstery vs. Mexican Government, Memorial, filed November 1869.

140Deposition 4 – Ignacio Quiroga, Nov. 25, 1869, resident of Almaden, Santa Clara Co., California, a miner (occupation). Claim of Thos. H. Monstery vs. Mexican Government, Memorial, filed November 1869.

141Mexican and American Commision. T.H. Monstery vs. Mexican Republic. No. 376. Opening Brief for Mexican Republic on Motion to Dismiss. Claim of Thos. H. Monstery vs. Mexican Government, Memorial, filed November 1869.

142*Chicago Tribune,* October 10, 1870.

143*The Two Republics*, March 18, 1871.

144*New York Sun*, April 9, 1899.

145Whittaker, 22.

146*Mexican Herald,* December 20, 1900.

147Whittaker, 22.

148*Mexican Herald,* December 20, 1900.

149Whittaker, 22.

150*Daily Alta California,* April 12, 1861.

151*Utica Saturday Globe,* August 10, 1895.

152*Weekly Alta California*, May 11, 1867. Whittaker, 23. From 1861 till at least 1868, children Berguita, Manuela, William, Ole and Consuello were born to Thomas and Carmen.

153*Daily Alta California,* August 13, 1867.

154*Daily Alta California,* September 14, 1867:

155Whittaker, 25.

156New York, Passenger Lists, 1820-1957, Year: 1867; Arrival: New York, New York; Microfilm Serial: M237, 1820-1897; Microfilm Roll: Roll 287; Line: 1; List Number: 1058.

157Whittaker, 23.

158Ibid., 23.

159*El Monitor Republicano*, February 15, 1868.

160*La Sociedad*, February 21, 1865.

161*El Monitor Republicano*, March 17, 1868.

162Angel Escudero, *El Duelo en México* (Mexico City: Imprenta Mundial, 1936), 24, 104, 131-136, 153, 233. Arturo Gomez-Martinez, "L'Escrime au Mexique" in *L'Escrime Francaise,* February 1959.

163Whittaker, 23.

164Ibid., 23-24.

165*Two Republics,* March 7, 1868.

166*El Monitor Republicano*, March 21, 1868.

167*El Monitor Republicano*, March 17, 1868.

168William H. Beezley, *Judas at the Jockey Club and Other Episodes of Porfirian Mexico* (Lincoln: University of Nebraska Press, 2018), 32.

169Whittaker, 24.

170*Utica Saturday Globe,* August 10, 1895.

171Whittaker, 24-25.

172Beezley, 32. *El Monitor Republicano*, March 17, 1868.

173*Daily Alta*, July 12th, 1887.

174*Dallas Morning News*, January 26, 1902.

175*New York Sun*, April 9, 1899.

176*New York Herald*, June 14, 1868.

177*Daily Alta California*, 15 February 1869.

178In 1870, Monstery was teaching at Arbor Hall, 50 West Houston Street, New York City. In 1871 he opened a school at 26 West Fourth Street; then moved it to 55 Bleecker Street, and again to 18 Clinton Place, where he remained until 1874. He then moved his academy to 619 Sixth Avenue. In 1879, he was also teaching "Physical Culture" at the Hellenic Institute on 1481 Broadway. In 1880–81 he was listed at 811 Sixth Avenue. See: Albert Johannsen, *The House of Beadle and Adams and its Dime and Nickel Novels, Vol. 2* (Norman: University of Oklahoma Press, 1962), 202. *New York Clipper*, Sep. 24, 1870. *New York Herald*, Sep. 17, 1871. *New York Tribune*, Mar. 13, 1879, 6.

179*Dallas Morning News*, January 26, 1902.

180*Turf, Field, and Farm,* January 16, 1874.

181Ibid.

182*New York Herald*, Mar. 23, 1879.

183*New York Herald*, Mar. 16, 1880.

184*New York Herald*, Mar. 18, 1880.

185*New York World*, April 11, 1876.

186*New York Daily Graphic*, Mar. 10, 1876.

187*Turf, Field, and Farm*, Mar. 3, 1876. Ben Miller, "A Grand Assault-of-Arms in Old New York, directed by Col. Thomas Monstery" (https://outofthiscentury.wordpress.com/2015/04/09/a-grand-assault-of-arms-in-old-new-york-directed-by-col-thomas-monstery/ last accessed on 7/24/2018).

188Monstery, *Self-Defense for Ladies and Gentlemen*.

189*Mexican Herald*, December 20, 1900. *Chicago Daily News,* March 21, 1883.

190*Chicago Daily Tribune,* February 2, 1896.

191*Chicago Daily News*, February 17, 1883.

192*New York Sun*, April 9, 1899.

193Monstery, *Self-Defense for Ladies and Gentlemen*, 67.

194*New York World*, March 10, 1876. *Turf, Field, and Farm*, March 17, 1876.

195Ole's spurs and pistol holster reside today at the San Jacinto Museum of History; provenance notes by the museum indicate: "Made by donor's father, Ole A. Monsterry, who used it on the Chisholm Trail."

196"Col. T. H. Monstery, the world's expert swordsman...was formerly a prominent figure in Havana, where as a fencing master he held a commission in the Spanish army some twenty-five years ago, previous to his entry into the military service of Mexico. He married here, and upon his departure from Cuba left behind an interesting little family, related to some of the bluest blooded people of Camaguey. Rita, the eldest girl, grew into womanhood among Havana's upper ten...She brought an American bicycle along and was the first Cuban woman to ride a wheel in Havana. The act shocked local society, and after being arrested and fined by the police, she was promptly cut by most of her girlhood acquaintances." *New York Telegraph,* April 29, 1900. It is perhaps worth noting that another of Col. Monstery's daughters, Ana Monstery, married the Spanish general Lino Galan.

197*Dallas Morning News,* January 26, 1902.

198*New York Sun*, April 9, 1899.

199*Chicago Tribune,* December 9, 1900.

200*Mexican Herald,* December 20, 1900.

201*Mexican Herald,* May 19, 1901.

202*Elkhart Daily Review*, August 30, 1901.

203*Chicago Tribune*, Sept. 22, 1901.

204*Mexican Herald,* January 7, 1902.

205*Turf, Field, and Farm*, January 24, 1902.

206*Mexican Herald,* January 7, 1902.

207*Everybody's Magazine,* October, 1902.

208*New York Herald*, April 11, 1908.

209*Jersey Journal*, April 11, 1908.

Maps of Monstery's Journeys

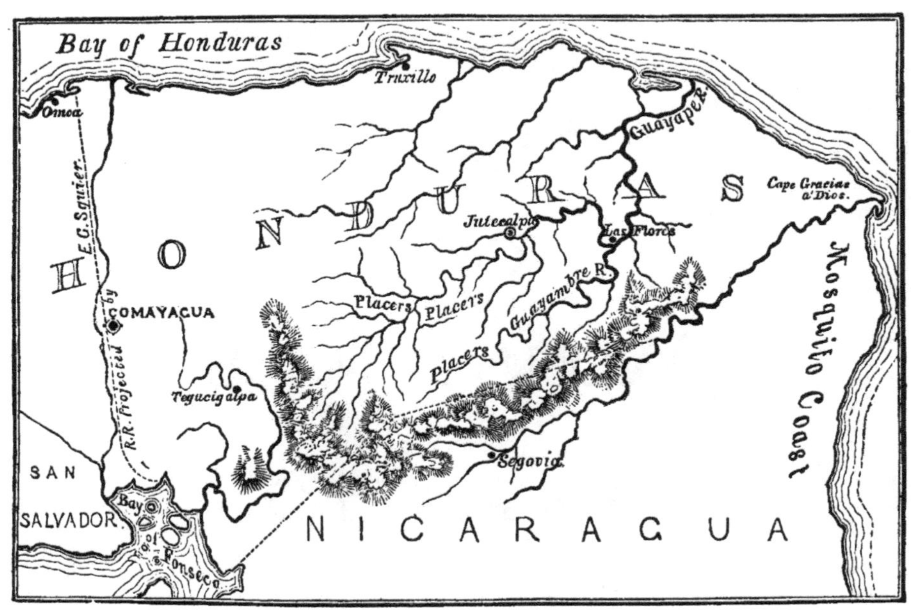

Honduras, 1856.

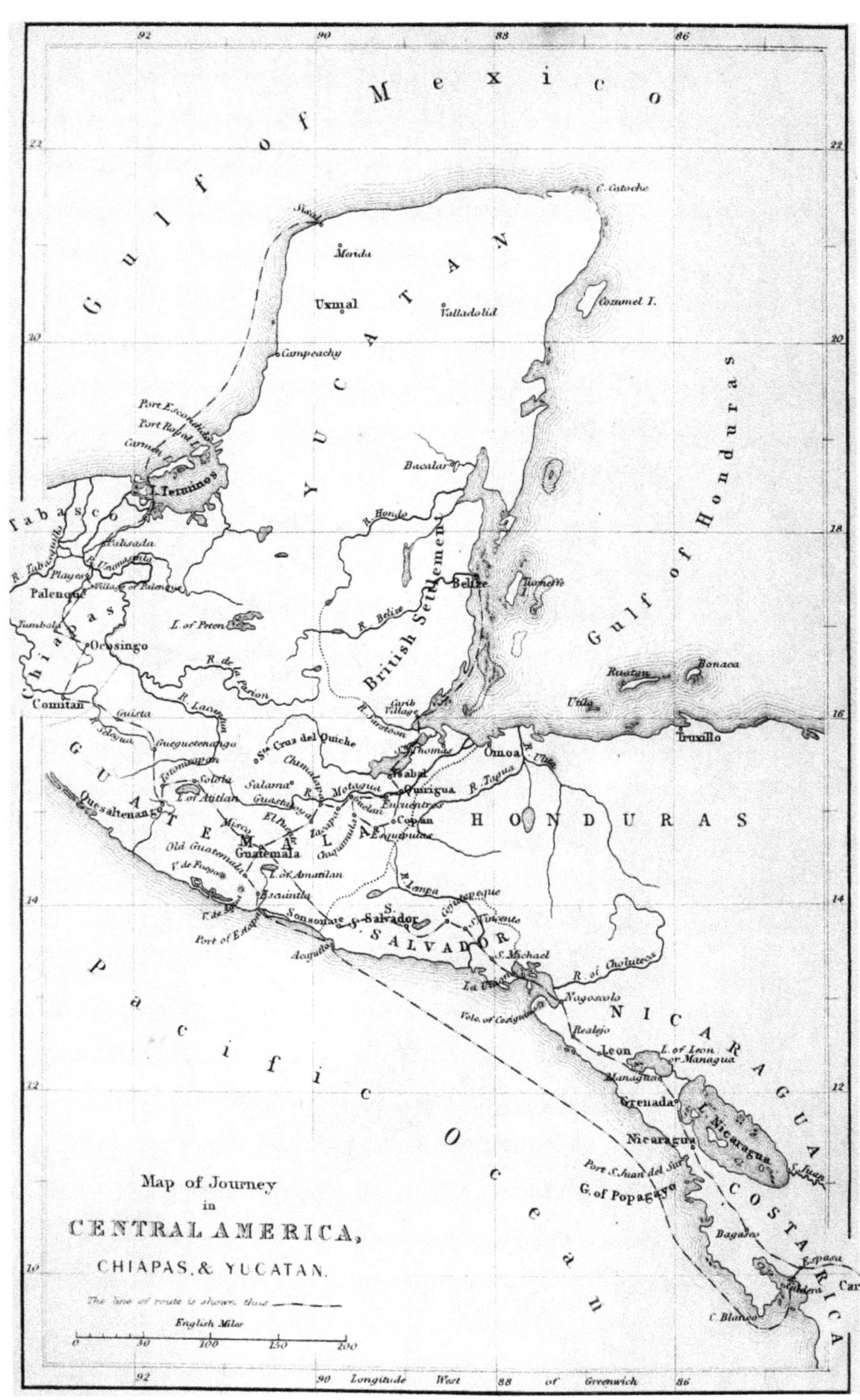

Central America, 1854.

Southeastern Mexico, 1897.

Environs of Mexico City, 1890.

Note to the Reader

The author of this book, which was first published in 1881, has used ethnic and cultural references that may be offensive to some modern readers. However, these do not represent the views of the editor or publisher of the current edition, and instead reflect the language, attitudes, and notions of the nineteenth century.

EL RUBIO BRAVO,

King of the Swordsmen;

OR,

THE TERRIBLE BROTHERS OF TABASCO.

A Story of Tropical Love and Adventure.

BY COL. THOMAS HOYER MONSTERY,

Champion-at-Arms of the Two Americas.

AUTHOR OF "IRON WRIST, THE SWORDMASTER," "THE DEMON DUELIST,"
"THE CZAR'S SPY," ETC., ETC., ETC.

TRUXILLO.
A
D
E
F
G
H

Chapter I.

Three to One.

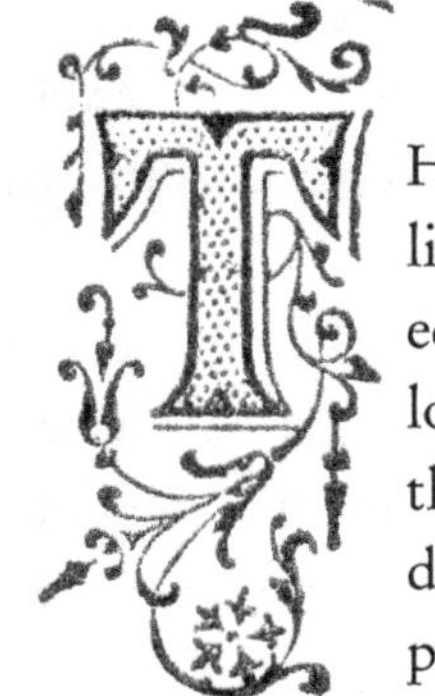

HE independent State of Honduras in Central America, lies between thirteen and sixteen degrees north of the equator, and is traversed by several volcanic chains of lofty mountains, some of them covered with snow all the year round. Consequently, Honduras enjoys a great diversity of climate. Down by the sea level, the atmosphere resembles a vapour bath most of the year, varied by furious hurricanes in the rainy season. On the high table lands of the interior the climate is cool and temperate, with pure bracing air that intoxicates the senses like a draught of wine, and, up in the snow-line, no one lives but the condors, who carry thither the prey they find below.

The town of Truxillo lies on the coast, in the vapour bath region, but is cooled by the trade winds, or no one could live there. As it is, there are only a few hundred people in and around it, and the houses have a dilapidated appearance. But, spite of the fact that there is little in Truxillo to tempt an invader, it has a fort to guard it, and the fort contains a garrison. The fort is a ruinous structure of stone, built in the days when Morgan* and his buccaneers used to raid Spanish America, and the garrison is proportioned to the monetary resources of the government which happens to possess Honduras at the time. The time is usually short; Central America having a cheerful habit of revolutions, which occur about once a quarter.

At the time when our story opens, the President of the Republic of Honduras was a half-bred Indian named Guartiola†, and he had held power for very newly two years, without being killed. To be sure, there was a reason for this unusual good luck, and it was not altogether owing to Guartiola's own abilities. The fact is that the people of Central America are a very different race from those who inhabit the United States, and cannot get along without plenty of fighting. They are the descendants of the old Spanish *Conquistadors*, or Conquerors, who were all soldiers; and they retain the tastes and habits of their ancestors. The people of the United States come from a line of farmers and other hard-working colonists, who never fought except from necessity, and got through with it as soon as possible, with a view to the accumulation of wealth. The Spaniards went in to conquer the empires they found established, with the idea of making the people slaves and living in idleness, and they have kept up the idea to the present day.

Consequently, while the United States has grown in riches, its people passing their time in accumulating, the Central Americans have been equally happy after their fashion in fighting. Failing outside enemies, they fight each other for fun; and the result is that they are fast approaching the condition of the Kilkenny Cats.‡

---

* Sir Henry Morgan (1635–1688), a famous Welsh privateer, feared and renowned for his acts of piracy, fought for the English against the Spanish in the Caribbean.

† General José Santos Guardiola Bustillo (1816–1862) served as President of Honduras from February 17, 1856, to January 11, 1862, when he was assassinated by his personal guard.

‡ *Kilkenny cats:* Tenacious fighters; those who would fight on, heedless of their own destruction. The origin of the expression "to fight like Kilkenny cats," which, according to the legend, fought till only their tails were left, has been the subject of many conjectures.

But if any President can give them an outside enemy to fight, he is a happy man until the war is over, secure from revolutions. It was President Guartiola's luck to give his people an outside enemy in the person of *"Los Yanquis."* All the factions in Honduras were as one in their hatred of *los yanquis* and when the enemy came in the form of the *"Filibustiero"* Walker*, the people were happy in a real war of their own and Guartiola was happiest of all.

But at last came the day when Walker, thanks to the American Government ships and marines, was taken and shot, and then Guartiola began to feel uneasy for himself. War being over, revolutions were next in order.

It was just at this time that a large steamer, full of *yanquis*, came to Truxillo, a week late for Walker's ball, and her people came ashore and took the town. Not much trouble about that, for the garrison of the fort —called the "Castle" by compliments—consisted of Major Don Rafael Balderamos, Captain Don Domingo Senas, Corporal Jose Jesus Diaz, and one soldier, who officiated as sentry and answered to the name of Manuel. But when the visitors heard that the filibuster Walker had been shot, and that all filibusters were to be treated in the same way, with the aid of the English and American squadrons promised to the government, they said no more of taking Truxillo, but allowed Truxillo to take them in the most peaceful fashion. They said they were all quiet travellers, merchants, and what not else, come to see the country, and they submitted to be examined by Don Rafael Balderamos, who allowed most of them to re-embark and go to Belize, leaving a good deal of hard American cash in the major's pocket, but very glad to get off even so as peaceable citizens.

There was only one passenger out of the Yankee steamer whom Balderamos would not pass over with a certificate. He pronounced him a suspicious character, a soldier certainly, a filibuster probably; and,

* William Walker (1824–1860) was an American mercenary who organized several private military expeditions into Latin America, with the intention of establishing colonies under his control, an activity then known as "filibustering". After usurping the presidency of Nicaragua in 1856, Walker ruled briefly, but was defeated by an alliance of Central American armies. After another filibustering expedition in Honduras, he was captured and executed in 1860.

anyhow, he ordered him to be closely confined to the limits of the castle, and killed if he attempted to escape.

The reasons for this severity in the passenger's case were two. First, the stranger had no money to bribe Balderamos; second, his baggage consisted of two huge chests labelled

"ARMS."

So the steamer with the disappointed, would-be filibusters sailed away, and the solitary prisoner watched them off from the summit of a ruined tower in the castle limits, and said to himself, in a mournful sort of way,

"Olaf, my boy, you were a fool to come to this dog-hole of a place, where they kill you with as little glory as a rat in a trap. You will never see your *Carmelita* again."

He was a man about thirty, straight as an arrow, with a slim waist and an appearance of slightness that was very deceptive. Had you seen him stripped, you would have noticed a forty-inch chest, with lean, muscular arms and legs as hard as iron, and a wiry appearance indicative of unusual strength and activity. He stood about five feet ten, and looked taller, while his complexion and hair were remarkable among the dark, sallow men of the tropics, with their black hair and eyes.

This man was a regular white blonde such as the Spaniards call a *"Rubio,"* with fierce blue eyes and hair so light that it looked like spun flax in the sun, for he wore it long and curly. His dress at the time he grumbled to himself about his fate, consisted of a white shirt and trousers, both the worse for the heat, and a battered old straw hat. His feet were bare, and so were his arms to the shoulders.

The garrison of the castle was lounging about, paying no attention to the prisoner. That is to say, the captain and the corporal were smoking together, and the solitary sentry was standing by the broken gate, looking out to sea. The prisoner also looked out seaward and watched the vanishing column of smoke of the steamer till it faded away to the north-west, when he turned away with a sigh, went down to the court and approached the shady corner in which Major Balderamos had caused his baggage to be placed. He unlocked one of the huge chests labeled

"Arms," and showed that it contained a good deal of clothing, in the shape of uniforms and handsome dresses of all kinds.

Captain Don Domingo Senas was sitting so that he could see the open chest, and his eyes glittered with cupidity; but he said nothing as the captive pulled out a box of cigars, put two or three in his pocket, and then began to smoke another. Then he locked the chest, and paced in a gloomy manner up and down the court smoking, and never deigning to notice the captain and the corporal, though the commissioned officer coughed thrice.

"The man is a low *yanqui* without manners," observed the captain spitefully. "He has six boxes of cigars there. I saw them. And he has not offered *me*—the acting commandant—so much as one."

"We can have them all in five minutes, *señor*," suggested the corporal, with a favour-currying smile, "if the prisoner only gets near enough to Manuel." The captain nodded and grinned. Several guns, with bayonets on, were leaning against the corner in which they were sitting.

Meantime the prisoner was walking up and down, muttering to himself in English: "I could lick these three like children, but I can't lick a whole nation, and they'll all be down on me. I was a fool to be led away by those fine stories about Walker. The whole country is not worth stealing."

He paused in his walk, and looked out to sea in a wistful way. He was standing by the open gate, which had only one leaf, and nothing prevented his walking out but the presence of Manuel, who was leaning on his musket, half asleep.

With a sullen puff of his cigar the prisoner resumed his stroll; and as he passed the captain and corporal, cast a scornful angry glance at them, as if they were noxious vermin. When he came back toward the gate he walked a little out, so as to see further, when Captain Senas suddenly yelled "Manuel, the prisoner is escaping! Kill him! Kill the accursed *yanqui*."

Immediately Manuel, who was a squat, surly-looking Indian, uttered a fierce Spanish oath and made a jab at the prisoner with all his force.

The stranger evaded the thrust by an active spring, and immediately grasped the musket shouting fiercely: "What the devil do you mean?"

"Treason," yelled Captain Senas jumping up and grabbing a musket.

"Help! Murder," roared Corporal Diaz, as he followed his chief's example, and then away they rushed for the prisoner.

The fair-haired man looked round and saw them coming, when he uttered an impatient English curse and dealt the struggling Manuel a kick in the diaphragm that doubled up that hero in a moment and made him relinquish his gun.

Then the stranger turned and met Don Domingo, who made a vicious thrust at him with his bayonet.

It was parried by *"El Rubio"* with a slight motion of his own bayonet that sent the other whirling round, and the next moment the whole garrison was fiercely stabbing and cursing at the active stranger, who had to leap from side to side to keep his enemies behind each other, while he parried their thrusts, whirled them round, knocked their muskets flying out of their hands, but never offered to thrust back.

He adopted the easiest of attitudes, with his musket butt on his right hip, where it rested immovable, and always parried with a slight motion of the bayonet, which sent the opposing bayonet far out of the line with apparent ease.*

He sprang from right and left, disarmed all his opponents successively, but inasmuch as he never offered to kill one of them, though he could have done it over and over again; they returned to the attack. And three to one, with the thermometer at a hundred in the shade makes it pretty hard work for the toughest single man. The fair-haired stranger got red in the face, then pale; the sweat was pouring off him, and he muttered desperately, "I must kill them all, or I'll be killed."

He leaped back for the last time, with a shout in Spanish of "Go away, I tell you," when he happened to cast his eyes to the gate, in the hope of running out, and there beheld a tall dark man with a huge moustache, who stood with his arms folded, critically watching the whole

* In his biography, Monstery refers to this method as the "Nachtegall system." A more detailed description of this method can be found on page *xxvi* of the Introduction.

scene. It was Don Rafael Balderamos, the supreme commander of the whole garrison.

The persecuted stranger gave a last parry which sent Don Domingo's musket flying for the fifth time out of his hands, and rushed over to Balderamos, crying:

"Señor Mayor, salva me, por l'amor de Dios!" [Mr. Major, save me for the love of Heaven!]

Balderamos threw up his big hands with a cry of intense surprise, as he saw his captain disarmed, and exclaimed: *"Se pued' un hombr' aprender eso?"* [Can a man learn that?]

The stranger wheeled round and flung his musket full in the face of Corporal Diaz, flooring that worthy before he answered. Then he went up to Balderamos, ran his arm through that of the Spaniard and replied coolly: "Certainly, *señor*, it is my business to teach it. I am a master of the sword."

The garrison had stopped to wipe its face—for only Manuel was left armed—and Balderamos, with an expression of the most reverential admiration, answered: "*Señor*, you are a king of all weapons, and we thought you were a common *yanqui* filibustero. This is amazing. What is your honourable name?"

The stranger smiled.

"If you will come to my arms chest, I will show you."

Balderamos followed him in silence, the discomfited garrison wiping its face and staring, and the prisoner opened the chest, disclosing, besides the handsome dresses, a number of swords, foils, breastplates, and the other apparatus of a fencing-master. From the corner of the box he produced a couple of large parchments, which he opened and spread out.

"Behold, *señor*," he said, "first my patent as colonel, swordmaster-general, to the Emperor of Russia. I held that post till I resigned it. Here is my commission as Colonel Instructor-at-Arms to the army his Majesty of Spain, and here that of Instructor-General in Cuba. I resigned in consequence of yellow fever, and came here because I heard that your people in Honduras are fond of the exercises of arms. I came in search of my fortune, and my name is Olaf Svenson, at your service, and your prisoner."

"Prisoner no more; my guest, my friend, my hero!" cried Balderamos, enthusiastically. "*Señor Don Olavo Svensoné*, I am proud to have the honour of knowing him of whom I have often heard, *El Rubio Bravo*. The President shall hear of you; you shall be invited to Comayagua; you shall be anything you like in Honduras. We adore arms, we adore you!"

And Don Rafael fairly hugged his late prisoner, while Captain Senas and his garrison waved their hats and roared: "*El Rubio Bravo* for ever!"

Such it is to be among people who fight for the love of fighting. El Rubio Bravo was changed from a prisoner to the hero of Truxillo, and a courier was sent off post-haste to Guartiola to tell him, that the king of all swordsmen was in Honduras.

The whole town went mad over him as soon as they heard that he was a famous fighter, and he was at once escorted out of the castle by the whole garrison, with drums beating—Manuel did that—colours flying—Captain Senas carried it—and trumpets sounding—Don Rafael Balderamos did the blowing—till he was safely installed in the private mansion of Balderamos himself.

"The City of Tegucigalpa"

Chapter II.

The Woman in the Case.

A FEW days after the fight in the castle, Balderamos came to his new friend in a great excitement.

"It is all arranged, my hero. President Guartiola bids me offer you the post of Instructor-General of Arms to the forces of the State of Honduras, with the rank of colonel. Your fortune is made."

Olaf did not seem to be very much impressed by the news. In fact, since his release from the castle he had been, if possible, a little more restless and uneasy than before.

"What will the pay be?" he asked, with a yawn.

"The pay, my dear friend? Anything you want; *anything*. We adore you."

Olaf yawned again as he answered:

"I don't want much; only the nine as I got in Cuba. The glory is not much here."

Balderamos coughed as he asked, timidly:

"And how much did you get in Cuba, colonel?"

"Two hundred dollars in gold a month and three rations, with forage," answered Olaf.

The major's eyes opened wide as he ejaculated:

"Eh, *Sante Dios!* Two hundred in gold a month! Why, the whole State of Honduras could not pay such a salary. Be moderate, my friend. The prime minister only receives fifty dollars a month, and President Guartiola twice that sum."

Olaf yawned worse than ever, as he retorted:

"So much the worse for Honduras. I shall not take service here. By the by, have you in your very rich state such a place as Tegucigalpa?"

"Tegucigalpa? Certainly. The President is there, now."

Olaf looked more interested, and he pursued:

"Are there any Spanish merchants there? I mean real Spaniards of the old blood." Balderamos thought a moment ere he replied:

"Only one, and he came very recently from Spain with his daughter."

Olaf looked decidedly interested now.

"A daughter! What is his name, if you remember?"

"His name—let me see—oh yes. Don Carlos—Carlos Ximenes."

Olaf laid his hand on the other's arm.

"You are sure he is in Tegucigalpa, and the daughter, too? What is he doing there?"

"He is a trader in indigo, and makes a good deal of money, they say, by controlling all the crops of the State. President Guartiola treats him with great favour, and they do say that—"

The major hesitated.

"What?" asked Olaf, with a singular glitter of his eyes.

"Well, they do say that the *señorita* plays her cards for her father, and treats Guartiola like a fish on a hook, with smiles and—Why, what is the matter?"

He started back at the sight of the other's face, which was looking with a passion, the intensity of which fairly appalled Balderamos.

The dark men of the South are quick to anger, but their rage is not deep, and their lack of self-control deprives it of dignity; but when the cold, reserved blonde of the North shows his anger in his face, it is apt to be very fierce and dangerous.

Olaf's eyes were glaring at Balderamos, the red veins in the corners standing prominently out, the face as pale as ashes, and the strong jaw muscles, standing out like bunches, showing the firmness with which the teeth were clenched.

"What is the matter, *señor*?" faltered Balderamos.

Olaf's face instantly resumed its usual iron calm.

"It is nothing. I had a twinge of pain from an old wound. Go on, please. You say that President Guartiola makes the *Señorita* Ximenes his favourite in public, shows favour to her father—"

"Yes, yes. He gives all sorts of monopolies to the old man, and the daughter leads all the public balls, and sits in Guartiola's box at all bull fights. Of course this is not all done for nothing, *señor*."

Olaf turned away his head and lighted a cigar with his usual coolness, but Balderamos noticed that he bit off nearly half the cigar with a snap, and that he smoked with a furious energy that betokened a disturbance of some sort in his mind.

And the major, not being deficient in penetration, at once divined that there was a lady in the case somewhere; in other words, that El Rubio Bravo had at some time been acquainted with *Señorita* Ximenes.

He hesitated, stammered, and finally asked:

"Is the lady a friend, *señor*?"

"No!" was the blunt response.

Balderamos coughed.

"Indeed. I thought—"

"Think nothing. I wish I had never come to this accursed country."

Olaf was evidently in a very bad humour.

"But, *señor*, if you choose to accept the President's very liberal offer, your fortune is made."

"I don't want such a beggarly fortune."

The major coughed again.

"It might be prudent to accept it, colonel."

The other started angrily.

"Why, why?"

"Simply because, if you do not go, I have orders to arrest you on the spot, if it takes all the people in Truxillo."

Olaf stared angrily at him for a moment, and then gave a peculiar scornful laugh.

"Balderamos, you are a fool; so is Guartiola. I will go. I was only joking. But some of your fighting men will wish I had not come before I go. I have money with me, but I have in my chests nearly five thousand dollars' worth of arms, clothes, jewels, and so on. Have you a money-lender in town? If so send him to me so I can go to Tegucigalpa as becomes a swordmaster."

Balderamos smiled as affably as ever, as he said:

"Certainly. There is an Italian Jew called Baroni who would accommodate you at once."

"Can I get a decent horse here?" pursued Olaf. "It is true I am a Dane and was bred a sailor, but I can ride a horse too, and I like a good one."

Balderamos rubbed his hands and chuckled.

"You shall have a wonder, for a hundred dollars, a regular angel of a horse, who can trot and amble and waltz and stop at full gallop inside our castle flag."

"Be it so."

And the Dane threw away his cigar and lit another, when he fell into a brown study*, from which Balderamos did not venture to disturb him, so the major went away to find the Jew money-lender.

Left thus alone, Olaf began to mutter to himself.

"What a fool I am to come here in pursuit of a coquette. I might have known—she would not live like a nun for my sake, and there is the father, who hates me, against me too. But if it be true as this infernal

---

* *Brown study:* a mood of deep absorption or thoughtfulness; reverie; gloomy meditation or melancholy.

Greaser hints that Guartiola—Bah! it is a fable. She can play with these fools of the South and wind them round her finger—but if—if—"

He ground his teeth so that they could be heard in the next room and growled out: "Let them all look to themselves. When my race strikes, it slugs hard and is remembered. Carmelita Ximenes, if you play me false, so much the worse for you and yours."

He went out into the town to cool off his excitement and strolled down to the beach. A few naked Caribs were fishing from their canoes outside the breakers. He beckoned in one of them, and went out into deep water, where he amused himself by tossing his last silver coins overboard and watching the little Indians dive after them and catch them before they vanished.

He was roused from his abstraction by the voice of Balderamos, hailing him from the shore.

"*Señor* Colonel, news. Come in."

The fact was that Balderamos feared El Rubio was trying to escape, and wanted to have him safe in.

Olaf came in, and was saluted with cordiality.

"Baroni will lend you all you want and you can be on the road tomorrow morning. But I have more news than that. Pepe Gomez is at Tegucigalpa and has heard of your arrival."

"And who the deuce is Pepe Gomez?"

Balderamos stared as if he hardly believed his ears.

"What! have you never heard of the Gomez brothers, the Terrible Seven of Tabasco?"

Olaf yawned.

"Never, on my honour."

"Oh, *Jesu Maria!* what a thing is fame! Why, they are seven Mexicans, brothers, from the State of Tabasco, and the most famous of all the *espadachíns* in Spanish America."

Olaf looked more interested.

"*Espadachíns*—you mean swordsmen?"

"Of course. They have killed—some say—as many as two hundred people."

"Oh, come, nonsense. Take off half."

"Not a man, *señor*. You see they have very wonderful advantages."

"Indeed? What are they?"

"Well, you see, in the first place, they are all powerful men, strong and supple."

"Granted. So are other men. But two hundred—"

"You forgot there are seven of them."

"Well, what of that?"

"Simply this, that no man can fight seven."

"Of course not all at once; but singly, why not?"

"There it is, *señor*. Any man who touches one of this seven, touches all of them. If he wounds one, he has to fight all the rest."

"And if he kills one?"

"That is impossible. At least I have never heard of its being done."

"Plainly, or they would be no longer seven. But go on. This Pepe, where are his brothers?"

"In Tabasco. Pepe is the oldest, and has come out to coax a few duels out of our people. The others stay home, and if Pepe comes back all right, with plenty of money, well and good. Another goes out."

"Plenty of money? How does he get it?"

Balderamos shrugged his shoulders.

"By betting. We will wager a thousand dollars of our money—that is about two hundred of your *yanqui* dollars—that he will disable the best man in a town. If he wins, well and good."

"I see; he is a prize-fighter."

"Yes, senor, with a sword. But if he gets hurt, and comes back without money and with wounds, then the other six vow the death of the man who has hurt him, and they all go out in a body to kill him."

Olaf looked thoughtful.

"So your brothers are assassins."

"Yes, *señor*."

"Very well, Balderamos. I see a way to beat them. This Pepe must not be allowed to go home. That's all."

"How to prevent it, *señor*?"

"Simply by killing Pepe. It's a hard thing to do, and one I've never done in my life; but self-preservation before all, my friend."

Balderamos smiled.

"Oh, if you can only beat the Terrible Seven you will be a hero, and all the people will worship you."

The Dane smiled slightly.

"They are after all only the heroes of a little province. I have beaten the best men in Europe. Come. Let us go."

They strolled along toward Baroni's; and next day at dawn, Colonel Olaf Svenson, El Rubio Bravo, was riding on his way to Tegucigalpa on a splendid horse, dressed in all the bravery of a Spanish American cavalier.

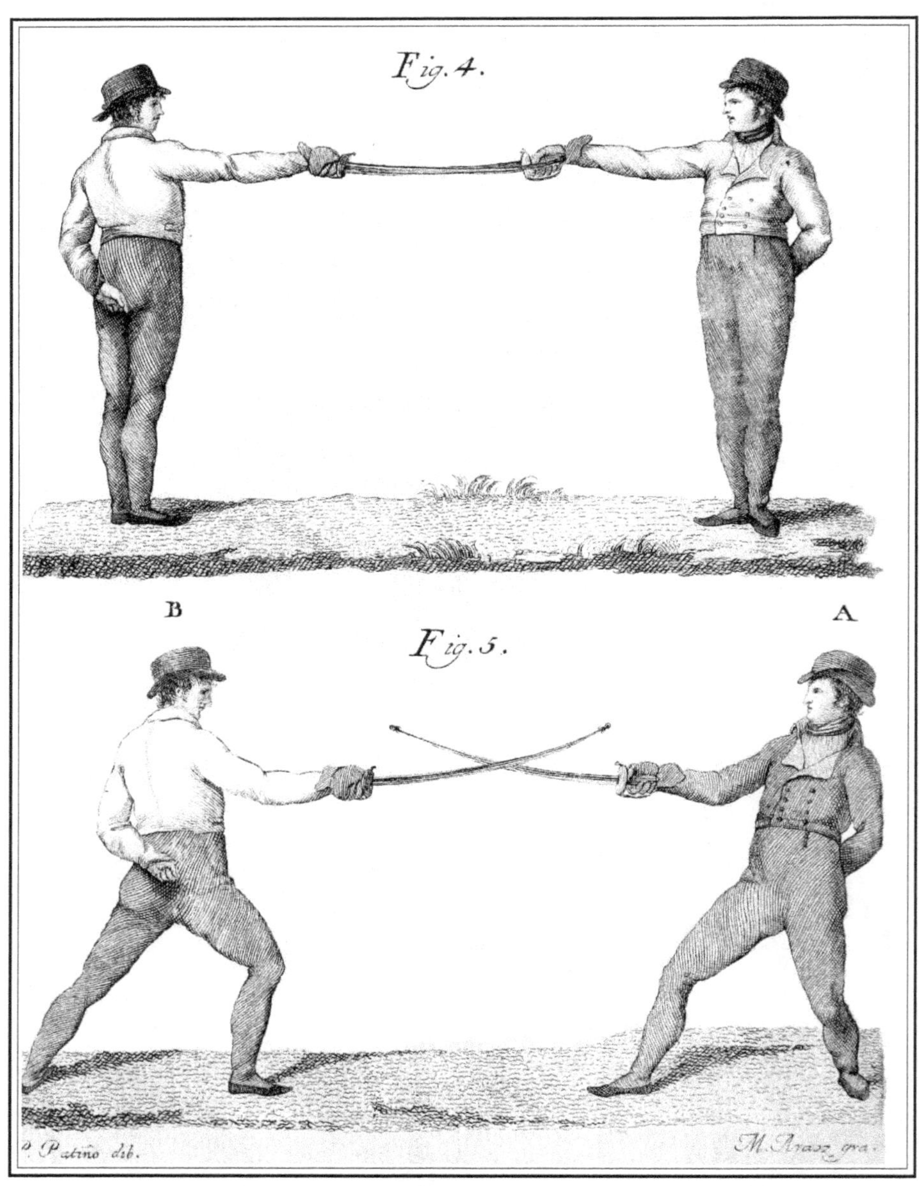

Tratado Elemental de la Destreza del Sable (Mexico: 1809)

CHAPTER III.

THE ESPADACHINS.

THE great square of Tegucigalpa was full of people in the cool of the afternoon, when the shadow of Mount Matador covered the city and everything was pleasant.

In the midst of the crowd an open space had been cleared beside a platform, and on the platform were seated President Guartiola, with all his ministers, and a little group of ladies in the picturesque costumes known as the "*say a y manto*," a short skirt, and a coquettish veil of black lace.

Beside Guartiola sat a particularly beautiful lady of slender, graceful figure; whose large dark eyes, oval face and pure profile showed her to be a different race from the flat-faced Greasers around. This lady had the smallest feet in the neatest satin slippers ever seen, and she flirted her large fan with a languid and haughty grace that was inexpressibly provoking.

Guartiola, a fat, sensual-looking man, with a cruel mouth, seemed to think so, for he was evidently infatuated with the lady and constantly appealed to her decision on all sorts of points.

Below, in the open space, was a group of bronzed, powerfully built men, who all carried huge swords, and were dressed in a glittering costume, much resembling that worn by bull-fighters. In the midst of these was one man whose frame was heavier than that of his fellows, and whose face wore an expression of brutal triumph as he said:

"You've no *espadachíns* in this town. They are all babies. See, here are a thousand good dollars in this bag, and I'll claim no stakes if I don't disable my man."

He jingled a leathern bag of silver as he spoke, and the other *espadachíns* looked at each other as if they would like to take him up, but dared not.

At last one said in a surly way:

"We haven't got that much money but for the honour of Tegucigalpa, I'll go a hundred."

"Agreed!" cried the other eagerly. "Pepe Gomez is well satisfied to make a hundred when thousands are scarce. Out with the money."

The *espadachín*, rather slowly and with a sullen face, took out his little bag of money and laid it at the feet of President Guartiola, who smiled and said:

"Fight hard for the glory of Tegucigalpa, Martino."

As for Martino, the work before him was too serious for smiling, so he only bowed and stripped off his gay jacket, while Pepe Gomez counted out his money before the President, and then cried out:

"Now, *señors* and *señoras*, you shall see Pepe Gomez slash this fellow to pieces in five minutes."

He grasped his long sword and took his place with the confident brutal glee of an old prize-fighter who sees in his opponent a novice, and was just about to begin the duel when a stir and shouting rose in the crowd outside, which presently resolved themselves into:

"El Rubio Bravo! El Rey Espada! Viva! Viva!"

Pepe Gomez listened and Martino with him; and as they did so the lady beside Guartiola, whispered to him something which made him say:

"Certainly, *señorita*, with much pleasure."

Then he called out to the *espadachíns*:

"*Señores*, we will postpone this battle, for here, if I mistake not, comes the king of you all, El Rubio Bravo."

There was an immediate chorus of gabble below, in the midst of which a horseman in velvet and gold lace, with long fair curls flowing down over his shoulders from under a broad hat, rode through the crowd and bowed to the President, calling out:

"I am charmed to behold your excellency at last. I am Colonel Olaf Svenson."

"*El Rey Espada*, the king of swordsmen," cried Guartiola enthusiastically.

"You are but just in time, colonel, to give a boasting Mexican a lesson —or take one."

He added the last words under his breath, and Olaf smiled and bowed as he replied:

"Nothing like commencing business early, your excellency; where is the gentleman with whom I am to fight?"

"Here he stands," cried Gomez, slapping his broad chest and speaking in a deep bass voice. "Head of the Terrible Seven of Tabasco, of whom you have heard, and able to kill any *maldito Gringo* like you for a thousand dollars. Aha!"

Olaf turned to him as he sat on his horse and surveyed him critically.

"You seem to be a pretty good man, and I have but just ridden in from a long journey. Can you let it go till tomorrow at the same hour?"

"Now, now," growled Gomez. "Aha! the *Gringo* is afraid of my sword, I see."

Olaf smiled and looked round up at the platform, where his eyes met those of the beautiful lady, who slowly waved her fan to and fro, but gave no sign of the least recognition.

His face changed on the instant and a frown crossed it as he looked. The frown was there again as he swung off his horse, went up to Gomez and said to him in a stern voice: "You lie!"

With the word, standing close to the other, he let fly his right hand, coming up from the hip with the force of a pile-driver, catching the boasting *espadachín* on the left cheek under the eye, with a crack that echoed over the square, and cutting a deep gash.*

Under that blow, so unexpected from a man of his slender appearance, Gomez tottered a moment and sank down with a stupid smile on his face, while Olaf, in the midst of a deep silence, said:

"When I meet brave gentlemen I use the sword. To ruffians like that I take the weapons of nature alone. They are quite enough for my purpose."

A thrill of amazement and terror went through the crowd; for it is a curious trait of Spanish-Americans that while they will face steel they are mortally afraid of revolvers or the fist of a boxer.

Even Guartiola turned pale, but the lady by his side smiled as one well pleased, and said in a clear voice:

"Well done, Rubio. I told your excellency he was no child to be cowed by Gomez."

But Pepe Gomez, though completely stunned for a few moments by the well delivered "brain blow" of Olaf, was too tough a subject to be settled for good. He rose up with a growl and reached for his sword, which had escaped from his hands as he fell.

"We will see," he hissed, "if you are as good with the sword as your hands. Cover my money or back out."

Olaf took out a little bag of gold.

"Here are five hundred of your dollars, one hundred of ours. It's all I have. Who will back me for the rest?"

The beautiful lady spoke out:

"I will. Lend me the money, Guartiola."

---

* Monstery instructs precisely how to deliver this strike, in chapter two of his martial arts treatise. See Monstery, *Self-Defense for Gentlemen and Ladies*, pages 77-78.

Guartiola was all willingness, and El Rubio allowed a smile to cross his face as he said:

"*La señorita* is very good. I will win the money for her."

A moment later he had thrown aside his gaudy velvet jacket, and had drawn from where it hung at his saddle-bow a long slender Toledo blade with a basket hilt.

"Clear the road," he cried. "Now let us see what the Terrible Seven are made of."

The circle was cleared like magic and the antagonists stood facing each other, about twelve feet apart, when Gomez executed a spring like a tiger and delivered a furious cut at Olaf's head.

It never fell, however, for as soon as the Dane's sword rose, as it did like a flash to parry the blow, the *espadachín* drew off before the blades touched, and made another grand leap past Olaf to the left, when he thrust at him savagely.

With the slightest movement of the sword-arm, Olaf wheeled on his heel, and stood with his sword pointed straight at Gomez's eyes, and again the *espadachín* was foiled.

In this singular fashion three good minutes passed, Gomez leaping from side to side, constantly threatening, but never allowing the sharp blades to cross, while the Danish master kept wheeling on his right heel, constantly facing his foe, his sword always pointed at the other's face.

This sort of work soon tired out even the powerful and active Gomez, who stopped, panting for breath.

The moment he stopped Olaf advanced, one step at a time, but straight and rapid as a dart, and though Gomez fell back he could not keep the swords from clashing in parrying a straight lunge.

"I have you now!" cried the Dane with a fierce laugh that blended with the clash.

With the sword he plied the other with thrusts he could no longer evade, drove him all round the ring, and at last sent a straight lunge into his body below the right shoulder, under which the boastful *espadachín* uttered a howl of pain and dropped his sword as he fell.

Olaf calmly wiped his own sword and said:

"If the other six are no better than you, I pity their chances, my friend. Good-night."

He turned away, resumed his jacket, and bowed low to Guartiola.

"Your excellency is satisfied, I hope, and I have won the stakes fairly."

Guartiola raised his hands in wonder.

"You are the king of the sword in truth. Such fencing never was seen. Now you will come to my palace, and you shall be treated in royal style."

He kept his word, for that very evening the palace—a two story house of *adobe* with clay floors below—was lighted up from top to bottom; and El Rubio Bravo was treated to a truly royal Honduras banquet, in which Guartiola exhibited his taste for imported luxury, by bringing out some English plum pudding in tin cans, together with three dozen bottles of Bass's pale ale.

But if the banquet was ludicrous in its bad taste, the ball was a success, on the green grass under a grove of palm trees, hung with coloured lanterns; and here at last the famous swordsman received, as a distinguished honour from Guartiola, an introduction to *Señorita* Carmelita Ximenes, who amazed and astounded her presidential admirer to the verge of an apoplectic stroke by saying calmly:

"Colonel Svenson and I need no introduction, *señor*. We have known each other for three years."

Then she took his arm and strolled off under the palms, while Guartiola grew green with jealousy, muttering:

"Old acquaintances! And so she has fooled me after all. Well, we shall see."

As the Dane strolled away with his beautiful partner he remained quite silent, with a strange expression of anger and reserve on his face, till she burst out laughing.

"Why, Don Olavo, one would think you had seen a ghost instead of me. Why don't you ask where is my father?"

"Because, *señorita*," he said, gravely, "I would rather see you with *him*, though he hates me, than alone in the court of this vulgar Guartiola. *Señor* Ximenes is a gentleman."

She smiled at him coquettishly, as she said:

"You men of the North have no feeling. One would think you would enjoy your good luck to be alone with me after we have been parted a year. My father went to Comayagua last week, and we expect him back to-morrow. Then farewell to moonlight music, love, and all that is sweet. To-night let us enjoy ourselves."

"And Guartiola," he said hesitatingly, for he could not resist those eyes and tones.

"Guartiola is an ox, and I lead him by a ring in his nose," she answered saucily. "I would not give my Rubio Bravo for a hundred such things."

Chapter IV.

The Cock-Fight.

THE town of Tegucigalpa, was all excitement next evening, for there was to be a famous cock-fight in the Plaza de Armas. Spanish-Americans are devoted to cock-fights, bull-fights, man-fights and every other kind of contest, while they are equally fond of betting on their favourite; and in this instance all the population were enlisted on one side or the other.

The *Gran Matador* of Comayagua, who had vanquished all opponents for nearly three years, was going to fight a Mexican bird from the province of Tabasco, who went by the name of *El Imperador*—the Emperor.

Of course public opinion in Tegucigalpa was on the side of the Honduras bird, on account, not so much of his prowess, as of his being a specimen of home talent.

The other bird was backed by a few Mexican merchants in town.

The President and all his cabinet were of course at the cock-fight, and there was no lack of ladies, who were as ready to bet as the men, though a little risky as to the payment of losses.

Conspicuous among the President's suite could be seen El Rubio Bravo, in a sort of uniform invented by himself which set off his handsome figure well. Since his arrival, the *Señorita* Ximenes had not been seen near the President, and rumour at Tegucigalpa said that she and El Rubio Bravo were old lovers, who had been parted by a cruel father, and that now it was all right again between them, at least till *Señor* Ximenes came back from his trip to the Indigo planters.

He did come back on the evening of the great cock-fight, and was seen to greet El Rubio Bravo with a cold civility that confirmed the story, after which he and Guartiola sat side by side, muttering under their breath to each other, while Carmelita and Olaf made love in the most open way right under the President's nose.

But now the birds were brought out and placed in the ring singly, for the people to admire, when the betting began. *El Matador*—the killer—was a very handsome black and red cock, who crowed loudly as soon as he got his feet, while *El Imperador* was still in his handler's arms. The people cheered him and voices shouted all sorts of bets on his victory.

President Guartiola turned round with a sort of veiled sneer to Olaf.

"You don't know much about this in your country, colonel."

Olaf bowed as he answered:

"No, *señor*. Our people prohibit it by law and I used to think it a stupid, brutal sport, till I went to Havana and learned the points. It is a contest of skill and strength, and I call myself a judge now."

Guartiola sneered again.

"Ah, indeed? Perhaps you'll bet against *El Matador* then?"

"Not yet, your excellency."

"Why not?"

"I have not seen the other bird yet."

Guartiola nodded and whispered to Carmelita's father, a stout, white-headed gentleman:

"He is cautious, but we'll clean him out yet."

Ximenes whispered back:

"You shall have all the money you need; if you will get rid of him. He has bewitched the girl with his ways, and she scorns reason."

Just then *El Matador*'s handler took him up, and a squat Mexican in velvet and gold threw El Imperador down into the ring, shouting out:

"Make your bets, *señores*. Here stands *El Imperador* to back them."

A roar of disdainful laughter was heard from the throats of the people, and a babel of voices broke out with bets against the bird. El Imperador was a simple black cock apparently without a strain of game blood in him, who stood in the pit and began picking at the dirt without so much as a crow.

But he was stoutly built and several pounds heavier than *El Matador*.

"Well Don Olavo, do you see any chance to make money?" sneered Guartiola.

"I do," replied the Dane quietly.

The creole was up in a moment.

"What is it? Name your bet."

"I await your excellency's."

"Very well then, a thousand on *El Matador*."

"I'll take it, *señor*, and make it eight if you like," replied the Dane. "El Imperador is going to win this fight."

Guartiola put up a bag of silver.

"There's my money. *Señor* Ximenes shall hold it. Where is yours?"

He knew that the Dane had only his winnings of the previous night.

What was his surprise when Olaf showed him a leathern bag of gold eagles of the United States.

"Here are a thousand dollars of our money, or eight of yours. The *señor* can hold them."

The old Spaniard gravely took the bags. He had no idea where Olaf had got the money, but he had a suspicion that his daughter knew something about it.

Then the birds were put into the pit, which was only a carpet spread on the ground, and the next moment they were standing by the scratch, their feathers bristling, as they crept to and fro, watching for a chance to spring.

The clamour of bets was great and the confusion deafening, but all became still as death a moment later, when both birds sprang aloft and met with a clash.

To the amazement and horror of the men of Tegucigalpa, *El Imperador* sent *El Matador* over on his back with a single kick, pounced on him as he lay, caught him with his beak by the back of the head and began to trample the life out of him with a power to which the other with all his pluck and activity, could interpose no effectual resistance.

It was simply overmastering strength that did not bungle or show cowardice, against pluck that had no power to back it. The three pounds extra weight settled the fight. In fact it was no fight, but a massacre, for El Imperador held on like a bull-dog till he killed his bird, and then uttered a regular dung-hill crow, deep and hoarse, in the midst of which the abashed creoles of Tegucigalpa began to hand over their money to the little party of Mexicans, and *Señor* Ximenes, with the sourest of faces, said to Olaf:

"The President's wager is yours, *señor*. I wish you luck of it all."

The Dane took the bags of money and called to his Indian servant, whom he bid take the bag of huge "copper dollars"*, wagered by Guartiola, to his quarters, while he put the gold back into his pockets and whispered to Carmelita:

Our little firm progresses fast. We shall have enough to marry before we leave this country."

And Carmelita only swung her fan and said:

"*Quien, sabe*, who knows?"

Then the assembly broke up with glum faces, and *Señor* Ximenes called roughly to his daughter:

"Carmelita, come hither. I wish to see you."

---

* *Copper dollars:* When economic conditions deteriorated in Honduras, President Guardiola issued copper coins. According to Monstery: "These dollars were worth twelve and one-half cents a piece. When they dropped to eight cents they were bought up by an English syndicate which rehabilitated the currency with guarantees, disposed of them at par and quit the country." *Everybody Magazine,* October, 1902.

The girl cast a regretful look at her lover, but obeyed quietly, and as Ximenes went away he began in a low, angry tone:

"How often am I to tell you you must not encourage that beggar? You may be the first lady in the State if you play your cards well, and make me a millionaire, and here you are compromising yourself with an adventurer who has nothing but his sword. I will not permit it any more. Do you hear?"

"Yes, *papa mio*," she answered, with the most touching humility. "Just as you shall be best pleased. Only I have told you that I cannot marry that Guartiola. He is a miserable *mestizo*[*] and you know we are proud of our *sangre azul*.[†] You would not have me sully our name."

The handsome selfish face of the old man flushed slightly, as he answered in a tone of impatience:

"What do you know about it? You are a child, who would throw herself away if she had no one to take care of her. I wish you to marry him, and drive off this reckless *espadachín*. Why, we do not even know who he is or where he comes from."

"I know," she answered quietly.

He shook her arm.

"Hold your tongue, I tell you. I am your father, and it is your place to obey me."

"Yes, papa."

And she did not say another word till she was alone in her room in the large, old-fashioned house which had come down from the days of the old Spanish occupation, and cost about ten dollars a year to rent.

Then she went softly to the window and put a candle in it for a moment; then withdrew it and repeated the operation thrice, after which she blew it out and watched.

The house faced on the plaza and was just opposite to the large mansion devoted to the suite of the Instructor General at Arms of the

---

* *Mestizo:* Traditionally, a term used in Spain and Spanish America originally denoting a person of mixed European and Native American ancestry.

† *Sangre azul:* Literally, "blue blood"—a person of pure Spanish Castilian descent, claiming to never to have intermarried with Moors, Jews, or other ethnicities; a person "from Spain, of high rank and birth, of the *sangre azul*, the blue blood."

State of Honduras, otherwise known as El Rubio Bravo, who, on a salary of thirty dollars a month, (and pickings) already supported three horses and five or six servants.

No sooner had Carmelita's light disappeared than a tall figure wrapped in a cloak left the door of the swordmaster's house and strolled across the plaza in the dusk; for it was already evening, and tropical twilight is short at the best.

He came under the lady's window and a little white note came fluttering down at his feet, with which he stalked away past Guartiola's palace and so into the town, where he was suddenly jostled by an individual who said in English and Spanish mixed:

"Excuse me—I mean—what the deuce is it in this blooming lingo—oh yes—*mil perdonas, señor—muy—muy*—oh, I wish I knew the confounded stuff—very sorry, I mean."

Olaf looked at him closer and saw the unmistakable face of an Englishman—fat, rosy, and fair-haired, and he exclaimed:

"Is it possible? I thought there were none but Greasers in this place. Why, how are you, my friend, and who are you?"

The Englishman, as far as he could be seen in the dark, was a burly, heavy-built man, and he at once answered:

"Well, by Jove, this is an unexpected pleasure, you know. 'Tisn't often a fellow can see a countryman abroad, and when it comes to these beastly Greasers, ye know, why they're enough to turn your stomach, when you've seen as much of them as I have. My name? Oh, yes. I am Dr. Brown, licensed last year, ye know, St. Bartholomew's Hospital and all that sort of thing, and, by Jove, I came out here to seek my fortune. And whom have I the pleasure of addressing?"

Olaf and he shook hands as the sword-master said, gaily:

"I am not an Englishman, but I am of the race that gives England all her strength. I am a Norseman, sir, and we are all one. I am Olaf Svenson, a Danish Yankee, by the great roost of St. James. Now we must find a *posada*,[*] for you and I cannot part without cracking a bottle together."

When two men of the so-called Anglo-Saxon race meet in a strange place, their first of thoughts is to take a drink, and our friends were no exception to the rule.

As for Olaf, in his excitement he actually forgot all about the note he had in his bosom from his adored Carmelita, till he and Dr. Brown were sitting by a table with a bottle of Spanish wine beside them, in a humble *posada* or inn, when the Dane suddenly started and said:

"Excuse me a moment, while I read a letter. It is from a lady you know."

The English doctor—he was quite a young fellow, now he was in the full light of a lamp—smiled.

"Aha! An adventure, I see. All right, old boy. Count on me if you need any help."

"I certainly will," answered Olaf, cordially. Then he opened his note and read in Spanish the following effusion:

> "MY SOUL:—My father is determined I shall marry the infamous Guartiola, and I can only depend on your courage and address to save us both. They are hatching a plot to get rid of you. Be on your guard, and always believe in the undying love of
>
> Your own
>
> CARMELITA."

Doctor Brown kept his head discreetly turned away white his comrade was reading, but when Olaf had finished the Dane struck his fist on the table with a force that made the glasses ring.

"It is my Danish luck. Always a fight and always a whitehead for a comrade. My friend, can you shoot and box?"

The big Englishman stared and laughed.

---

* *Posada*: During the period, an inn or lodge in a Spanish-speaking country; literally, a place for stopping.

"As for boxing, I can take good care of myself as well as the next man. As for shooting, I can hit a silver dollar every time at twenty yards. Do you expect to do any shooting here?"

"One never knows what may happen, doctor."

CHAPTER V.

OLAF'S STORY.

DR. BROWN—better known among the creoles as *Dr. Carlos*, his Christian name being Charles—was little more than twenty years old, and his passion for roving had sent him, as a medical student, to the climes of Central America, where he at once dropped into a lucrative practice. He worked when he pleased, had the whole State of Honduras to himself, got ten dollars a visit, and had the honour—if honour it was—of being court physician to the amiable Guartiola.

And still he was not happy, for he had no one to whom he could talk his native tongue, and he made but a poor fist of Spanish.[†] Being full of animal spirits and strength, he was very fond of drinking and boxing, while he was surrounded by temperate Spanish Americans, who never

† *Make a poor fist of:* To do a very poor job of something. An idiom primarily used in the United Kingdom and Australia.

drank anything strong, and who had a horror of what they called "*La Boxia*."[*]

He had heard of El Rubio Bravo, but had never imagined him as anything but a Spaniard, and had not been present when the Dane fought his duel with Gomez, though he had afterward been called on to treat the fallen *espadachín* for a sword thrust through the right lung.

His meeting with Olaf, therefore, was like a godsend to him, and he could not tear himself away from the Dane.

"And how gets on my friend Pepe Gomez?" asked the sword-master, after they had exchanged confidences over the third bottle. "Is he going to be able to travel to Tabasco in a hurry?"

"Not under six months if he does well, you know," answered the *medico* a little thickly; "but then, you know, the beggar's got a devil of a temper and keeps tossing and cursing, so he's in a hot fever half the time. He wants to send a message to a lot of his relations out in Tabasco, but as the brute can't read and I can't write Spanish, it's pretty hard lines[‡], you know."

Olaf told him what he had heard about the Terrible Seven of Tabasco and the doctor pursued:

"Oh, I say. I didn't know that. The black muzzled thief! So he wants to set the whole gang on you, does he? Not if the court know herself, which she thinks she do. He can carry his own message when he gets well, and I've a very good mind not to treat him any more."

"Oh, no. Treat him and cure him for my sake, my dear friend."

"Well, I will, but I don't like this. And how do you like this country, my dear colonel?"

"The country is grand," cried Olaf; "but the people are—well, you know."

"I should think I did. A lot of rascally Greasers, with only one aim in life, to cut each others' throats! Even the women go to see cock-fights and bull fights and holler as loud as the men."

---

* In 1878, Monstery recounted, "I have found, in my travels among the desperadoes of Mexico and Central America, that the worst ruffians were more afraid of my fist than of sword or knife." Monstery, *Self-Defense for Gentlemen and Ladies,* Chapter II.

‡ *Hard lines:* bad misfortune.

"What! Do they have bull-fights here?"

"Yes. What *they* call bull-fights, but bless your soul, nothing like the real thing, you know. Tame bulls, and they saw their horns off. It's a beastly sell."

"Still, every one goes, I suppose."

"Oh, yes. Every Sunday. To-morrow's Sunday, by the by. Are you going?"

"Of course, my friend. We'll meet there. Now it is time to say good-night."

But the doctor insisted on seeing the Dane home, and would not leave him till they had sworn eternal friendship, while he was round at the other's quarters in the morning long before breakfast, and did not leave him for the rest of the day.

Yet Olaf noticed, with all the young doctor's hard drinking and reckless ways, that he was a perfect gentleman.

He had never asked the Dane a single private or personal question, though he would not have been human had he not felt some curiosity as to Olaf's love affair. He simply waited till the other was ready to tell him, which occurred just after the people were coming out from mass, and while the *torreadors* were fixing up the bull ring in true creole style.

"My friend," said the Dane, "I want your help, and to make you understand things, I must tell you a story."

"All right, old fellow, I'm agreeable," was the truly British reply, as the doctor lighted a cigar and composed himself to listen.

"You must know," began Olaf, "that there is a lady in the case."

"Of course. There always is. Pretty?"

"As an angel!"

The doctor gave a heavy puff but said nothing.

"You have seen her," pursued Olaf.

"Who! I?"

"Yes. You know Don Carlos Ximenes?"

"Old Indigo. I should say so. Came here only six months ago, and is worth more than any man in Honduras to-day."

"Very well. His daughter is the lady."

Brown whistled.

"By Jove, I say, you've dashed good taste, and all that sort of thing, but then—"

"Then what?"

"Why, you know, Old Wickedness is sweet there, and you've no chance."

"Who's Old Wickedness?"

Brown lowered his voice.

"By Jove, it's risky to talk too loud about him. I mean Guartiola."

"Why do they call him Old Wickedness?"

"Don't you know?"

The ruddy face of the young doctor was a trifle pale, and his voice sank to a whisper.

"There is not a bigger blackguard this side of the hot place downstairs. Why he's—never mind. Picture murder—his own brother, one of the poor fellows—robbery—he called it confiscation--poisonings and all sorts of crimes against men, with a record on the woman side too horrible to talk of. That's old Wickedness. There's nothing bad he hasn't done, I believe."

"How do you know all this?"

"I hear it everywhere. People confide in a doctor or a priest, you know. If he's set eyes on that girl, he'll have her."

Olaf frowned slightly.

"By the great roost of St. James, he'll not."

"Ah you don't know him, colonel."

"On the contrary, he does not know me. A man who has beaten Czar Nicholas on his throne, is not likely to be beaten by a Greaser like Guartiola."

Brown looked obstinate.

"He'll have you assassinated."

"If he can catch me in the dark unarmed. But I don't go about in that fashion."

"All right, colonel. I'll stand by you, revolver and all."

The doctor threw back the loose coat he wore, and showed a pair of navy revolvers in a belt at his back.

Olaf smiled approvingly.

"Our race stand by each other. Now I'll tell you all about this."

"I am listening."

"Three years ago I met Ximenes and his daughter in Spain. I was a colonel at court, and had plenty of money; he a rich Cuban on a visit to Madrid. I went to Havana in the same ship with him as Instructor to the Cuban forces. On the voyage they had a great hurricane, and the *señorita*, who insisted on being on deck, was washed overboard by a wave. I took a life-buoy and jumped after her in all the tempest. Well, we were saved, and thenceforward she loved me a little. At Havana I beat all the fencers, and and fought nine duels for her. At the ninth she loved me entirely. Then I took yellow fever, and one of my rivals, a fencing-master of Havana, bribed a barber to bleed me in such a way as to disable me, while I was delirious. When I recovered, the tendon of my right arm was cut nearly through, and it healed up short, so that I had to give up my situation. Then, when I was penniless, Ximenes, who had fawned on me in my prosperity, turned against me, forbid me his house, and finally carried off his daughter to Honduras, and leaving me, as all thought, a cripple for life. I was far too disabled and unwell to attempt to take any steps to detain them."

"Hard lines," observed Brown, sagaciously.

"Yes, indeed. But my race are hard to beat. My arm was shrunk up, but I set to work to get it straight."

"How is that?" asked the doctor incredulously.

"By hard work at it. Oh, how it hurt at first. When I struck out I had to grind my teeth to keep from yelling out. But I kept on at it, and about a month ago got the tendon stretched and the arm straight at last. Then, when my savings were nearly gone, I came here to search for my Carmelita, and I found her making eyes at Guartiola."

The doctor coughed.

"Are you quite sure that..."

"That what? Speak out!"

"It may offend you."

"I shall not be offended."

"Well, then, are you quite sure your Carmelita is a good woman to tie to?"

The Dane hesitated, gnawed his lip, and then broke out: "No, I'm not."

"Then why do you follow her?"

"Because—because I am infatuated with her. She is a coquette, and I am jealous, but she is only coquettish, and she is so beautiful."

"That is true. But beauty is only skin deep."

"Oh, a truce to proverbs! I want you to help me."

"All right. As I said, I am ready."

"I am going to try and see Carmelita. Her father keeps her in the house except when she goes out in public in Guartiola's company, and I have no chance except at a ball, but I know a way. I will climb up from the garden to her window, if you will watch below."

The doctor laughed heartily.

"With pleasure. And I have a scheme of my own. While you meet the *señorita* upstairs, I will have my little affair downstairs."

"With whom?—Excuse me, I did not mean to ask—never mind."

And Olaf laughed at his slip of manners.

Doctor Brown smiled.

"It is no secret. Don Ramon Garcia, the Prime Minister, has a daughter too, and she is teaching me Spanish. I can't learn from a master, so I'm trying a mistress. I'll take a Spanish lesson in the garden, and if any one comes, he can look out for squalls."

"All right, doctor," and so it was arranged.

Then the plaza began to fill with people and the two new-made friends strolled over to see the bull-fight, which turned out to be, as the doctor had said, a "complete sell," as far as regarded excitement and danger—compared with the real thing as carried on at Madrid or even Havana—these bulls being tame and stupid, with little capacity to fight.

Indeed Olaf was so scornful of the whole business, that he cried out in Guartiola's hearing "Bah! call those men *torreadores!* I believe I could kill such bulls as they have here myself."

Instantly the President turned his evil face toward him and sneered: "*You* kill bulls? Bah! I will bet you twenty thousand dollars you dare not stay in the ring when the bull makes for you in earnest."

"I'll take the bet," cried Olaf recklessly, and Guartiola eagerly snapped out: "Done! I'll have the bull ready next Sunday, and then take care of yourself, my bold Rubio."

The swordmaster bowed and said in a low tone to Brown: "They don't back our race down, do they?"

To which the young Briton answered: "The beastly Greaser will try to put up a job on you, colonel. See if he doesn't."

Guartiola glanced suspiciously at them, for he did not understand English, but he made no remark, and the crowd soon after broke up when Olaf and Brown repaired to the former's quarters, and the Dane said gravely: "Now, my friend, I shall really need your help. I was never in a bull-ring in my life, and I have only a week in which to study bull anatomy, and the science of the *torreador*. Tomorrow morning we must take a ride to old Garcia's *estancia* and get our first lesson."

"Agreed," said Brown, cordially. "But how about our little interviews in the garden to-night? Do they go on?"

Olaf shook his head dryly:

"One thing at a time. The love-making can wait; the bulls won't wait."

Chapter VI.

A Lesson in Killing Cows.

JUST as the early streaks of dawn hung grey over the summit of Monte Balboa in the east, two men on handsome little horses drew rein before a long stone building some miles from Tegucigalpa, and the biggest of the two shouted in his broken Spanish:

"Holloa! Pedrillo! *Venga, venga*—what the deuce do you call it—come out here! *venaca! venaca!* We want a cow, a bull, an ox. *Vaca! Vaca!*"

A little shrivelled Indian came out with a grin on his face, saying:

"Como lo pasa, señor, como lo pasa? Su criado de usted. Quequiere vuesa merced?" [How are you, sir, how are you? Your worship's servant. What does your worship want?]

It was Olaf who answered:

"We want to learn how to kill a bull, my friend. How much will you charge to let us try?"

The old Indian looked astonished.

"To kill a bull? But your worship is not a butcher or a bull-fighter."

"Never mind. How do you sell your cattle?"

"Two dollars apiece; *señor*. Do you wish it tied or loose?"

Pedrillo realized that he had before him an original.

"Tied for to-day and I need your help," was the answer. "I'll buy three beasts at once, no matter what kind."

The two men dismounted and tied their horses, while the old Indian jumped on a pony close by, went down to the open fields round the *estancia*, and presently came back dragging a vicious looking red cow at the end of a lasso, full tilt.

The two Anglo-Saxons had to scamper out of the way as the beast came up, for it made a vicious dash at them as it passed, and Pedrillo cried out:

"Here is your animal, *señores*. Kill it and welcome."

"The grinning old scoundrel is trying to fool us," growled Brown. "Tell him to take the brute to the killing wheel."

Olaf obeyed the injunction and Pedrillo galloped away dragging the cow after him, till he came to a huge wheel with a small barrel, round which was coiled a stout rope with a noose at the end.

"Throw the noose over, *señores*," he shouted.

Olaf ran forward, picked up the noose as the Indian dragged the cow near the wheel, and cast it over the horns of the struggling animal, just in time to escape the dig of her sharp horns.

With a malicious grin at the clumsiness of the "*gringos*," Pedrillo let go the other lasso from the horn of his saddle and away went the cow jumping and shaking her head to the end of the second lasso, the wheel whizzing round til she reached the end of the lasso, then stopping with a shock that tested the heavy framework severely. Then the animal went ramping around at the end of the lasso, while Pedrillo sat on his horse laughing, and the two *gringos* stood looking doubtfully on.

"I say," observed Brown, "that crazy brute isn't so easy to kill, is she? If that's the way the cows go on, old man, what will you do with the bulls?"

Olaf compressed his lips.

"I have a job before me," he said. "It is like learning a new weapon. But I'll master it in a week. See if I don't."

He called to Pedrillo angrily.

"Stop your grinning and come here. Now tell us what we are to do."

"Why, kill the cow, of course, *señores.*" Pedrillo was civil but sly. Olaf drew out a revolver.

"That's easily done, my friend, but I don't want to use this. Show me how you would go to work yourself to kill her."

"Me, *señor!* Oh, if I wanted to kill that cow I would wind her up first and then give her the *matador* stab."

Olaf drew out a couple of dollars.

"Go to work and do it."

Instantly Pedrillo was off like a shot. He jumped from his horse, ran in, nimbly evading a side rush of the cow and in another moment was turning the huge wheel as hard as he could turn it.

The cow, seeing an enemy, came plunging in with a slack rope, and thus was wound up short without any trouble, till she came to the wheel, when she was checked in trying to get round it at the Indian, and both stuck fast.

"Tease her out, *señores*, or I can't get her wound up," cried Pedrillo, impatiently. "Don't you understand?"

Olaf ran in and yelled at the angry cow, which instantly turned on him and cleared herself of the wheel.

No sooner was the lasso stretched again than the old Indian commenced winding it up again; and in a few seconds, thanks to the tremendous power of the wheel, the poor cow was wound up with her head against the barrel of the machine, kicking and bellowing, but powerless.

Pedrillo quietly put the check rope on one of the spokes of the wheel and said to Olaf:

"There is your cow, *señor,* kill her."

"Show me how to do it first," said the Dane.

Pedrillo grinned again and walked over to the barrel of the wheel.

"You see the cow's neck?" he said. "Just here, where the shoulders begin in one place, and here at the root of the horns is another. Shall I kill her or will you?"

"I will try," said Olaf, and he drew his sword. "Which is the place to strike in a bull-fight?"

"Here," replied Pedrillo. "With full force and let the sword pierce the heart."

The swordmaster plunged the blade into the animal, and Pedrillo nodded.

"Good! I could not have done better myself. You see, she is dead."

And it was true, for the cow had dropped as if struck by lightning, and when they let down the rope not a quiver could be seen in the carcass.

"We will try another cow, Pedrillo," said the swordmaster quietly. "Bring her up and I'll try her without the wheel."

Pedrillo did not grin any more as he set out.

"Your worship learns quickly," he said.

Presently he brought up a young steer wilder than the cow, and dragged it to Olaf, plunging and kicking, when the Dane, with an exertion of all his agility and watchfulness, rushed in and tried to inflict the fatal stab.

But he found that a lively steer even at the end of a rope, is not so easy to kill, and it was only at a third attempt, and after having twice wounded the poor creature, that he was able to plant the stab of the *matador*.

"That is enough for to-day, doctor," he observed. "The sun is getting up, and we want to be back in Tegucigalpa before they find out where we have been."

"That's the ticket," responded Brown, in his most sententious manner. "Don't let the Greasers know how you know, or what you know. Keep dark, till the bull-fight."

They paid Pedrillo for his cattle, with strict injunctions to keep secret the fact of their being there, and rode back to the city.

As they rode into the *piazza*, they saw Don Ramon Garcia, owner of the *estancia* to which they had just been, coming out of the President's palace, and saluted him cordially.

"Beautiful morning for a ride, Don Ramon."

"Beautiful, *señores*. But I prefer my bed."

Chapter VII.

Tropical Evenings.

THE night before the bull-fight in which El Rubio Bravo was to kill his bull on a bet with the president was full moonlight. The city was full of excitement at the prospect of a novelty, and it was whispered about that the President had sent to one of his own private *haciendas,* far up in the mountains, for a fierce bull, who was said to be a *sequidor.*

A *sequidor,* or "follower," is the most ferocious and dangerous of his kind, and much feared by the boldest bull-fighters.

The ordinary bull, when he is teased by the *picadors* and *banderilleros* —prickers and flagmen—exhausts himself in a series of straight rushes, and shuts his eyes at the moment he thinks he can hit his enemy.

This is the salvation of the *torreador*—or bull-man, a name including all kinds engaged in the sport. He has only to spring to one side to be safe, and long practice gives him wonderful skill and daring, in waiting for the last moment. But there are bulls now and then which do not shut their eyes, and which turn on a single *torreador,* following him up, and not permitting the others to divert their attention from a victim.

These *sequidors* are justly dreaded, and it was rumoured that Guartiola had secured such a beast to fight the boasting American.

"Serve him right," growled one of the regular staff of the bull-ring. "He must needs come round here, bragging about what he has seen, and calling our bulls fools. We'll see if he can kill one, or whether the bull will kill him. He'll find it is not as easy as it looks."

Master Pepe Gomez, sitting up in bed and coughing horribly in a spasm of pain, heard the news and ground his teeth with great satisfaction.

"Maybe the bull will avenge me before I can get news to my brothers. Why is it I cannot find a man to go to them?"

The wounded *espadachín* was worn to a shadow of his former confident, hectoring self, under the drain of his lung wound, and had but little money left.

As he lay looking from the window, he saw the erect, lithe figure of the Dane cross the plaza in the cool of the evening, arm in arm with the burly English doctor, and he cursed him heartily as he shook his fist in impotent rage.

"What is it *señor*? Why do you curse so?" asked a gentle oleagineous* sort of voice at that moment.

Pepe Gomez looked round and saw the smooth face of Don Ramon Garcia.

"I am tied here hand and foot," he groaned, "and I cannot get word to my brothers of where I am."

"That is very sad," said Ramon soothingly. "I am told that you have seven brothers."

"Six, and my cousin, Isidoro Bragamonte," was the eager answer, for Pepe began to suspect that the Prime Minister of Honduras had not entered his hovel for nothing.

---

* *Oleagineous*: rich in oil or grease; exaggeratedly and distastefully complimentary; obsequious.

It was only a hovel, where Gomez was waited on by a single Indian servant, and yet here was Don Ramon Garcia, stealing in as softly as a cat, to sit by the bedside of a dying *espadachín*.

"Six and Bragamonte?" he repeated musingly. "They are all good men with the sword?"

"As good as I, *señor*. Bragamonte is, however, better than any of us."

Don Ramon looked cautiously round to see that no one was listening, and then said:

"You were wounded by the American and you want revenge. Is it not so?"

"Yes. But how am I to get it?"

"How *could* you get it?"

"If I could get word to my brothers."

"Write a letter then, and I will send it."

Pepe looked confused.

"*Señor*, I cannot—I cannot write."

"I can. Tell me what you want to say?"

The Don took out a pocket inkstand, a pen and some paper, as if he had come fully prepared, and sat down.

"How shall I begin? To whom shall I write?"

Pepe's eyes glistened.

"To General Isidoro Bragamonte, at San Miguel."

Garcia wrote.

"What next?"

"Write this: 'My dear cousin.'"

"My dear cousin," repeated Garcia.

"I have been hurt by an American who fences like a devil. His name is Olavo Svensone, and they call him El Rubio Bravo. He is here now. He is a good man on whom to try your private wrist trick. Tell the brothers, and come quickly."

"Is that all?" asked Garcia, after a good deal of scratching away.

"That is all. He will know."

"But you must sign this."

Pepe took the pen, and made a cross at the bottom of the paper.

"That will do as soon as my cousin sees it. He will not escape from Bragamonte's sword. How will you send it?"

"By a special messenger."

Pepe grinned, but presently said:

"How is it that you are willing to do this, when this man is in the service of your own government, and a friend of the President?"

Don Ramon smiled slightly.

"Who knows? Perhaps the President is tired of him; perhaps he fears him; perhaps he is jealous of him. Anyhow, he is dangerous, and we must get rid of him."

Pepe nodded.

"He shall be got rid of. Bragamonte will tell the rest, and he cannot escape all."

"Your brothers will waylay him?" said the minister inquiringly.

Pepe shook his head, frowning.

"No, no, they are not assassins but honest *espadachíns*. They will challenge him when they meet him, one after another, and then let the Rubio look out for himself. Every one has a different style."

"How do you mean?"

"I mean a different style of fighting. There is Pedrillo whose *forte* is the creep and spring; Jose Jesus and Jose Maria who do it by main strength; Gil, whose best point is with the knife, and in throwing it; Domingo who excels in the rally; Martino, who has lamed all his opponents; and Bragamonte, whose wrist trick is effective against the best fencers particularly. Between then, they can kill any man alive."

Don Ramon nodded, as one very well satisfied, and rose to depart, just as the full moon looked in at the window.

"Keep up your spirits, Pepe, and you shall be avenged," he said, and then went away.

Being after sunset, the twilight being over, it was already dark in the shadows of the moon, but the minister was surprised to see in the moonlight a man stealing away from behind Pepe's cabin, in whom he thought he recognized the figure of his own *vaquero*[*], Pedrillo.

How the man came there he could not imagine, as his duties led him to the city only on a holiday; but he could not be sure it was Pedrillo, for when he called to the stealthy figure, it ran on and was soon lost to sight in the shadows of a side street.

Don Ramon returned to his own house buried in thought, muttering:

"If that man was Pedrillo, he heard our talk. But what of that? He is my peon, and if he is too open-mouthed I may have to shut it and him up together."

Already the town was sunk in repose, for the people were early sleepers, except when there was a ball on foot.

The only beings awake were the lovers, who were tinkling mandolins in the gardens, and singing confidentially to each other.

Don Ramon returned to his own house full of virtuous respectability, found everything as quiet as could be, and went over to smoke a *cigarito* with his neighbour, Don Carlos Ximenes, when the two old gentlemen discussed the nuisance of having the *Americanos* in the State; and the Honduras Don confided to the Cuban Don the fact that another gringo, that English *medico,* seemed to be more than a little agreeable to little Pepita, "my child, *señor,* and one whom I destined for my friend, Don Isidoro Bragamonte, chief of cavalry in the service of San Salvador; but since that big Rubio has come here, she thinks of nothing else but learning the English tongue, and teaching him Spanish."

"Then you should forbid him the house," said the Cuban decidedly. "That is what I did when my daughter showed too much favour to Rubio."

"But this fellow is a court physician, and a great favourite of Guartiola's. There is no way to get rid of him except—except—"

"Except what, my friend?"

Don Ramon lowered his voice.

"Except a *pronunciamento* and another revolution."

---

* *Vaquero:* In Spanish America and the Iberian Peninsula, a cowboy or herdsman. From the Vulgar Latin *vaccārius* ("cowherder").

Don Carlos threw up his hands in horror.

"By no means. I have put all my money into indigo, and have not a bag shipped yet. Postpone it, my friend, till next month at the very least. Give me time to realize."

"But in the meantime my daughter may run away with this *maldito Gringo.*"

"Not she. Leave it to me. I will devise a scheme by which we will keep this big lubberly Rubio from coming near your house for months to come."

"But in a revolution, my friend, we could kill him and get rid of him for good. You see half the army would follow me, and all are tired of Guartiola. It is only necessary to kill him first, for many fear him."

"And who would be the new President?" asked the Cuban curiously.

"Hard to tell. You see I should issue a general proclamation, calling on the people to revise the constitution and proclaiming an election. Then the troops rise and we kill Guartiola. Then the people vote, and generally choose the man who has killed the last ruler."

"Then *you* would be President," said Ximenes.

"Possibly. In the meantime try another of my *puros.* They smoke well."

Thus they tranquilly discussed revolution for the sake of breaking off a love affair, and after quite a long conversation went to their hammocks in tranquility.

Don Ramon went to his own house by a back way through the garden door, and was surprised to find it wide open.

Instantly suspecting an intrigue, he went back for Don Carlos, called him; and the two old gentlemen, one carrying a long knife, the other a sword-cane, began to prowl about in the shrubbery of Don Ramon's house, but all in vain.

They could see no one and hear nothing.

"Wait a moment," quoth the Prime Minister, and he ran up to his daughter's room, which he found empty, and then came down stairs with pale rage, hissing:

"She has gone to meet this Gringo. Where are they?"

"How should I know?" quoth Don Carlos in a testy way. "I don't keep watch over *your* daughter, it is enough to look after *my own.*"

"They are great friends," whispered Don Ramon. "They may be in your garden now. Let us search."

The supposition was too much for the Cuban.

"In *my* garden? Then that infernal Rubio Bravo is at the bottom of it. Come, let us go!"

They hurried round to the next wall, and as they had begun to expect, found the door of the garden unlocked.

Softly they stole in, and presently Don Ramon pulled the sleeve of Ximenes.

They could hear the murmur of voices among the leaves of the orange trees.

Presently the sounds became plain and this was what the two old gentlemen heard. First there was a deep powerful male voice talking in execrable Spanish, then came a sweet girlish treble giving out broken English; and they seemed to be rehearsing a lesson.

The male voice spoke first.

"*Yo ti amo*—is that the way to say it?"

"*Si, si,*" with a little giggle. "*Yo ti amo, yo ti amo*. You say eem ver' vell. Dat mean 'I loaf you' in *Ingles*."

"Say it again, Pepita. You didn't pronounce that right. Say 'I love you.'"

"I loave you," said the girl's voice, and then they heard a slight osculation.

"Now let's get on to the rest of the lesson," said the male voice. "What do you call this in Spanish?"

"*Mis manos,*" said the girl. "Vat you say *en Ingles,* Carlos, *mi vida?*"

"Those? Those are my hands, Pepita, my hands."

"*Mai andes*—ah! dat is not eet—*Ma handos*—no—'ow you say 'eem?"

"My hands, Pepita; no, I mean your hand, that is to say it's yours now, but it will be mine very soon; so I may as well kiss it for luck."

"Ah! Carlos!"

Then there was another little giggle and Don Ramon ground his teeth.

They stole forward and beheld in the moonlight among the orange trees Dr. Brown, his hat off and his flaxen curly head gleaming in the light, while one arm was passed around the waist of a very pretty Spanish girl, whose black hair was lying all over his white jacket; for Charley Brown dressed in the coolest of tropical garments, loose and easy.

"I wonder," remarked Dr. Charley presently, "whether Ole and Carmen are enjoying themselves as much as you and I, Pepita. They're quiet enough over it, if they are."

The girl evidently did not understand all his English, for she answered:

"Vat you mean, Carlos? Say eem in *Español.*"

Charley scratched his head.

"*Quiero decir*—I mean to say that Ole and Carmen are very quiet—*muy—muy*—what do you call quiet?"

The answer was not destined to be given that night, for Don Ramon could no longer contain his fury, and he rushed forward with a string of Spanish imprecations to grasp his daughter's arm, while she jumped up with a shriek, and Charley caught her to his breast and whipped out a revolver as quick as a flash, crying:

"Halt, you blooming Greaser assassin! Who are you trying your tricks on?"

"*Oh, Carlos, es mi padre!*" faltered the girl, turning deadly pale, and Don Ramon, who had recoiled before the muzzle of the revolver, hissed out:

"Yes, sir, her father—you hear? her father—Give me my daughter—*Carajo!*"

Charley Brown put up his weapon.

"Of course, I don't want to hurt you, sir. I expect to have you for a father-in-law some day, but in the meantime I can't let you hurt this young lady. It's not our way."

The creole did not understand him fully, but he repeated more quietly:

"Give me my daughter."

And Pepita—not half so much afraid as she might have looked, came over to him and was about to be carried off, when Don Carlos Ximenes uttered a cry of rage, and dashed into a neighbouring thicket, where he found Carmelita and the Danish sword-master, sitting with their arms around each other, looking on quietly through the screen of leaves.

The old Cuban rushed at his daughter and shook her soundly, when Charley Brown dashed after him and tore him away, saying:

"Come, old fellow, *you're* not going to be my father-in-law, so I can handle you. Leave that lady alone. Ole, do me the same favour, you understand?"

The quick-witted Dane jumped up and ran after Don Ramon whom he brought back to Charley with Pepita on his arm.

"Take care of your own girl, Charley," he said. "I'll take care of the old man."

"And I'll take care of yours," was the reply. "You're not supposed to punch your own father-in-law you know; but you can punch mine all you like and vice versa."

Then was beheld a curious spectacle. Doctor Charley had Don Carlos Ximenes by the collar with one hand, while he wrenched away from him with the other the sword-cane which the old man was too nervous to use.

On the other side, El Rubio Bravo had Don Ramon Garcia by the hair of the head with one hand while he threatened him with the knife he had just taken from him.

And thus it came to pass that on one side Pepita Garcia was on her knees to Olaf imploring him to spare her father's life, while Carmelita Ximenes, on the other, was saying:

"Ah, *Señor* Don Carlos, do not hurt him! He is my father."

But both men were inexorably stern and deaf to the voice of the charmer, perhaps because they did not dare to do otherwise for fear of exciting jealousies.

As for the two old men, the situation was full of hardship to them, for each was in the power of a man who could strangle him and over whom he had no control. And the only way of escape for either was to call on his daughter's lover for help which each hated to do.

Thus matters stood for about half a minute when Charley Brown cried out in English:

"I'm going to thrash your father-in-law, Ole."

And the Dane retorted:

"Then I shall pummel yours, Charley."

And they both began to shake their victims till Don Carlos screamed out:

"Help, Don Olavo, this English brute will kill me. Quick! Quick!"

Olaf only shook Don Ramon harder, till the old creole cried to Charley for help.

Then both men dropped their prisoners and sprang to the assistance of the old gentlemen, and in a moment all was peace.

Ten minutes later the garden was empty and two men were entering the quarters of El Rubio Bravo, followed by a third, who was telling them something.

The third man was Pedrillo, the *vaquero*.

A Honduran bull-fight.

Chapter VIII.

El Sequidor.

SUNDAY had come; mass was over; the people of Tegucigalpa had dined, and the bull ring, with its rows upon rows of seats, one above the other, was packed with bright colours from the palisades to the top boxes.

Rancheros and indigo planters, with their wives and daughters, in picturesque costumes, with velvet and gold jackets for the men, silk shirts and black lace *mantillas* for the girls, crowded the bull-ring.

Conspicuous above all was President Guartiola's box, full of brilliant uniforms and bright dresses of ladies. Doctor Charley was there in uniform as surgeon-general to the armies of Honduras, for titles were cheap at Guartiola's court.

But around and below all were the real masters of Honduras in the people, who felt that they could always change their government when they pleased, by the simple process of revolution.

Guartiola, with all his capacity, cruelty and murders, with all the forms of outward respect that surrounded him, yet realized that he was but a servant to the mob that surrounded him and began to feel more and more uneasy every day.

And now it was nearly four in the afternoon, and the shadow of Monte del Matador fell on the plaza, and the people round the bulls-ring began to stamp and shout:

"El toro, el toro!" [The bull, the bull!]

They were impatient to begin.

After a little more delay there was a sound of drums and trumpets the gates to the ring flew open, and in rode the four *picadors* on lean, worn-out old horses, only fit to die.

The men were dressed in gay silk jackets and ribboned hats, their legs and thighs to the waist protected by heavy leathern guards, and they carried long spears in their hands. They rode round twice and were followed by the *banderilleros*, a score of clean-built, active young fellows, in gay silk jackets, short breeches and stockings, with the lightest of slippers, who bounded into the ring, with little red flags, and bundles of small darts carrying long streamers of ribbon.

Then the procession passed out, and the cry of *"El toro!"* was renewed, louder than ever.

Presently the trumpets sounded again, the gates were flung open and into the ring, followed by a spitting shower of crackers, dashed a handsome red bull, with a lean wiry look about him that portended a good fight, and made the people roar with delight at the sight. Not for long did they remain pleased, however. The bull ramped up and down, smelt at the barriers all round as if to find a way to escape, and finally uttered a low bellow of dissatisfaction.

Then the people howled out:

"Los picadores! Los picadores!"

The *picadores* or pikemen took the hint and rode in, when the bull, being a good fighter charged them at once.

There were four *picadores*, and each tried to divert the bull from his comrades by pricking him in the rear whenever he charged one of the number. They could not divert this bull, however. He gored one horse the first rush, and then knelt on the carcass to jab his horn into the struggling rider.

When the other *picadores* stabbed him in the rear, he only went more fiercely at the fallen man, and they had to call in all the *banderilleros* together to attract his attention elsewhere, and save the life of the victim of his fury.

Then he dashed away at the other *picadores* and gored a second horse, and a third in less than two minutes. The last *picador* was glad to get off his horse and climb over the barrier to escape.

Then the *banderilleros* began to play about the bull, throwing darts into his skin and trying how close they could come to his horns without being gored.

But the fact of this bull being a *sequidor* or "follower" was soon plainly visible, for he chased individual *banderillos* so fiercely, that one by one he drove them out of the ring and people began to roar again:

"El Matador! El Matador!"

Doctor Charley Brown, who had looked on at the bull-fight so far with much indifference, now began to manifest a great deal of uneasiness.

He made his way down to the edge of the bull-ring, where he suddenly produced a pair of navy revolvers, from which all the neighborhood shrank back, and laid them on the railing beside him, where he sat with his legs dangling over, ready to jump down into the ring.

The cries of *"El Matador!"* (The Killer) went on, and presently the trumpets sounded again, and into the ring walked El Rubio Bravo himself, in his usual dress, carrying a drawn sword and a broad square flag of bright scarlet.

The *banderillos* made a grand rush at the bull as soon as Olaf entered, yelling at the beast, flinging showers of darts, most of which had lighted squibs at the hinder end, and generally using all their endeavours to excite the utmost possible burst of rage.

In this they were completely successful, for the bull was not by any means exhausted, and it was only by working on perfect concert in his rear, that they succeeded in saving one of their number from death.

Then came a second blast of trumpets and all scattered and leaped over the barriers, leaving the bull and the *matador* face to face.

Olaf was just bowing to the President's box where were seated Carmelita and Pepita side by side, when the bull caught sight of him, uttered a low bellow and came for him on a rush.

The Dane did not alter one iota of the profundity of his salute till it was completed and the bull was within ten feet of him, when he turned and flapped his red banner into the animal's face with a step to one side that brought down the house, so coolly was it done.

The foiled bull rushed on only a few feet when it turned again and made a second savage rush.

Flap came the scarlet banner in his face and again he was foiled.

But this time he turned inward on Olaf and the next moment was following the Dane closely round the ring, step for step, the man springing from side to side behind the red flag; the bull shaking his head, lunging desperately and coming closer all the time.

The people howled and shouted with glee, for they saw the bull was getting the better of the man, and their sympathies were against the boastful foreigner whose brag had been magnified by hundreds of envious tongues.

"Bravo, toro, bravo!" they reared, and Olaf who had all he could do to keep out of the way of the furious bull, heard the cry, and felt for the first time, a sensation very like despair.

He found that bull-fighting, even in Honduras, was not such an easy affair after all, and that the position of a *matador*, though only requiring him to deliver a single blow, was yet one requiring more skill and nerve than all the rest.

He could see the spot where he knew the sword must be plunged plain enough, but the trouble was to get the bull to hold still long enough to enable him to plant the thrust.

And in the meantime he had to keep out of the way of the bull's horns, which were shaking and stabbing within a few inches of his body, while the people were hooting and jeering and he knew that Guartiola was smiling to think how his plan had succeeded.

Doctor Charley Brown saw the danger and he picked up and cocked both his pistols, shouting defiantly:

"Give him fair play! I'll shoot the first man that interferes!"

Then came a roar from the people as the matador's foot slipped and he nearly fell. In most cases such an accident would have provoked a rush of *torreros* to the rescue, but the sympathy was against Olaf, and the populace only jeered.

Olaf heard the jeer and it stung him to the core, for he was an intensely vain man.

He ran several feet to one side making for the bull's tail, thereby securing nearly a second of time and held the banner before him with the left, while he poised the sword with his right.

Inside the second the bull was on him and there was no chance to escape.

The flag was in its face, but the horns were touching the Dane's body when he fell forward on the bull's neck, burying the sword up to the very hilt.

The bull dropped as if struck by lightning. The impetus it had acquired pitched it on its knees and head, but that was all. It was stone dead before it reached the ground.

The Dane's sword had made a master's stroke, dividing the spinal marrow and splitting the heart in twain.

Half-incredulous himself of his own good luck, he was yet quick-witted enough to embrace it and turn it to advantage, so he turned to the box where Guartiola sat and saluted it with a low bow and a wave of the sword toward the dead bull, executed with distinguished grace.

For a moment the people were silent, and then they burst into a perfect whirlwind of applause.

"El Rubio Bravo! *El Rey Espado!*"

The Dane had conquered them, and no one but himself knew how nearly he had fallen in the effort.

As it was, they attributed his previous conduct before the bull, not to awkwardness or fear but simply to a deliberate provocation to increase the excitement and suspense.

They swarmed over the barriers, invaded the ring, seized the triumphant *matador* and carried him on their shoulders to the President's box, where he was received by Guartiola with distinguished civility in presence of so many people, though the half-breed's heart was inwardly raging over the renewed triumph of one he began to hate as his rival in love.

Moreover, he had just lost twenty thousand dollars, for Olaf had killed the bull as he had said he would and as Guartiola had bet he would not. And that made thirty six thousand dollars which the Scandinavian swordsman had beaten out of Guartiola from first to last.

True, they were only Honduras dollars, so debased as to be worth only twelve-and-a-half cents apiece; but even so, there were forty-five hundred good solid gold dollars involved in the swordmaster's winnings, and the loss was more than Guartiola could afford.

He paid over the money with a sour face, but from that moment Olaf saw that his doom was sealed if he remained in the city of Tegucigalpa, and he began to cast about him for means of escape.

Fig. 1.
B.
Hat innere Qu
gestossen.
ner Second
Fig. 2.
A.
ch mit Second,
chzeitig vor
esarmiren.
B.
Stösst Quart i

Chapter IX.

Bragamonte.

THREE weeks after the bull-fight in which Olaf had so astonished the natives, he was lying in bed in the early dawn of the morning, half asleep, when his door was burst violently open, and in rushed a tall, dark man, with a ferocious moustache on his face and a drawn sword in his hand. The swordmaster's room was on the ground floor—in fact, most Central American houses are of one story on account of earthquakes—and the door opened on the plaza.

"Come out, and fight me," roared the man with the huge moustache, and as he spoke he drew back his sword as if to make a thrust at the recumbent Dane.

But Olaf was not used to carry his life in his hand for nothing, and the door had hardly opened before the revolver under his pillow was cocked and leveled, while he growled:

"Stay where you are or—!"

The sight and sound of the clicking lock, overawed the other who recoiled to the door and the Dane went on:

"Who are you? What do you want?"

"I am General Isidoro Bragamonte, chief of cavalry to the State of Guatemala, and I challenge you to follow me to the plaza and give me a chance to avenge my honour and that of my family."

The dark man roared this in a tone that would have overawed most men, but he did not advance on the pistol.

Olaf smiled composedly.

"You do not want me to go out in my shirt, I suppose, Bragamonte?"

"No matter how. You must come or I will proclaim you a coward who has wounded my cousin Gomez by foul play," bellowed Bragamonte, flourishing his sword furiously.

"Get out of that!" suddenly hissed Dame and he started, up in bed and looked so dangerous behind his pistol that the dark man went through the door like a shot.

Olaf ran to the doorway and fired a bullet through his hat, when he took to his heels, and the Dane rapidly pulled on his trousers and boots and went out. He saw Bragamonte in the middle of the plaza and heard him yelling:

"The sword! the sword! You dare not face my sword, coward of a *Rubio!*"

El Rubio Bravo saw a crowd of men gathering to watch the antics of this seeming madman, and noticed his friend Charley Brown hurrying toward him with his inevitable revolver in each hand.

He stalked back into his quarters, picked up his sword and came out again.

"See fair play, Charley," was all he said to the young Briton. "This is Bragamonte, that Pedrillo told us of."

Charley nodded and waved his pistols in such a way that scattered the creole crowd in a moment, when Olaf stalked up to Bragamonte with the curt salute:

"I'm ready. Come on!"

He had heard of Bragamonte from Don Ramon's *vaquero*, Pedrillo, who had listened to the interview between his master and Gomez, and knew that although a furious braggart, he was also counted the most dangerous man in Honduras.

No sooner did Bragamonte see him than he rushed at him, and began to cut in the same blind, furious way which marked the practice of the ordinary *espadachín*, but without as much leaping as had marked the play of his cousin Gomez.

Olaf watched him closely in the same way he had watched Pepe, keeping his point to the other's face, and presently Bragamonte tried to confuse him by a high feint at his head ending in a furious cut down at his very toes.

The Dane felt himself cut and the sting made him savage. He made a furious blow at the other's head which was parried in *carte*, then beat over in *tierce*. The moment he did so Bragamonte drove his own blade high in air and made a clutch at the Dane's sword-wrist with his left hand.

"Aha!"

Olaf uttered a savage shout and the next moment had drawn his sword out of danger, grasped the other's sword wrist like a flash, and driven his blade through the centre of the bully's body a foot beyond his back.

Bragamonte uttered a choking roar of rage, pain and despair and fell back on the plaza, Olaf leaping back holding his bloody sword and crying out:

"Take care all. Don't come near us yet."

But if he had thought the duel not over he was mistaken, for there lay the once boastful Bragamonte in a pool of blood, his face pale, his eyes glassy, and the Dane remarked grimly:

"One more of the Terrible Seven, and he is not so terrible after all."

Then he turned and went back to his quarters, while the people came and picked up Bragamonte, and carried him to the same hut in which Pepe Gomez was lying partially convalescent. As for El Rubio Bravo, he looked gloomy and depressed as he went back with his friend Brown, and he remarked as soon as they were out of hearing: "Doctor, this is only the beginning. I never yet killed a man in a duel but I shall have to kill seven before these fellows will let me alone. I am going to leave Tegucigalpa."

"With all my heart," returned the doctor in a tone that showed he meant it. "I've turned my money into gold and diamonds. How's yours?"

"The same. I am an old campaigner and always ready to travel. How many horses have you?"

"One and three mules."

"Let us be off, then. I have four horses and that will carry all we need, including—"

"Including what?"

"Including our wives," was, the composed answer of the Dane.

Doctor Charley shrugged his shoulders.

"And what shall we do with them? They can't stand hardship."

"They will come with us if they love us," said the swordmaster obstinately.

Doctor Charley shook his head.

"I shall not ask Pepita to ride off with me on any such wild goose chase. Where do you propose to go to go?"

"To Guatemala."

"And suppose Guartiola sends after us?"

"He will not. We shall have enough men to stop pursuit."

"And where will you get them?"

Olaf smiled.

"My dear friend, you do not know that I have had plenty of pupils since I have been here."

"Yes. I do. Heaven knows you've made noise enough teaching them. I've heard you shouting for hours at a time."

"Very well. All these men adore me and among them are twenty Indians, whom I have taught how to use a lance as they never did before. They have already promised to follow me to the death."

"And you expect—"

"To take them with me and strike through the forest into the State of Guatemala, where I have received offers of a place worth three times as much as this. Is it not worth the experiment?"

They were interrupted by the sound of fire-arms in the plaza.

Doctor Charley jumped up and ran to the window where he watched a moment, then shouted excitedly:

"By Jove, another revolution."

CHAPTER X.

THE REVOLUTION.

THE two friends hurried to call their servants, arm all hands and saddle up; for in Central American revolutions the rule is, every one for himself, the only point of union being that of opposition to the government.

The whole of Guartiola's army had turned out, to the number of about a hundred men; and a general free fusillade was going on at the opposite side of the plaza.

In a very short time the whole town was aroused and had taken sides, and a man on horseback came tearing across to the quarters of El Rubio Bravo, imploring him to come to the rescue of the President, and "cut down the insolent rebels."

Olaf by that time was all ready, and he mounted his horse and called to the doctor.

As they rode out into the plaza, there arose a general shout for "El Rubio Bravo," and the bullets began to patter round him—not very thickly because fire-arms were not plentiful, but enough to show that he was marked by one party or the other. A moment later came a clattering and shouting, as a whole troop of cavalry, armed in all sorts of ways, came galloping into the plaza yelling:

"Viva Don Ramon! Abajo Guartiola! Muerta! Muerta a Guartiola!"

[Long live Ramon! Down with Guartiola! Death! Death to Guartiola!]

The cry was caught up till it swelled into a mighty chorus, and Doctor Charley observed to Olaf in his sagacious way:

"The jig's up! Guartiola's chances are not worth a rap. We must run for it. Old Ramon's at the head of the move, and we'll be killed if we stay."

Just as he spoke they heard a great shouting and rumbling, and into the plaza rattled two brass guns at full gallop.

"That's Ortega's battery," observed Olaf. "He'll scatter the rebels."

"Wait a bit and see!" quoth Charley.

And lo and behold!

Instead of firing at the rebels, Ortega jumped off his horse, unlimbered one gun with his own hands, and sent a round of grape crashing into the ranks of Guartiola's supporters, who incontinently broke and fled, while the whole mob swarmed into the palace and the firing was drowned in the exultant shouts of the victors.

"Now, Colonel," quoth the Briton, "take my advice. The quicker we're out of this the better. They have a pleasant little habit of massacring prisoners here, and we belong to the losing party."

The Dane looked sullenly at the other side of the plaza and ground his teeth.

"I wish my twenty Indians were here instead of on Ramon's *hacienda*," he growled. "I'd like to try one charge on that scum."

"But they not being here, I'm going," quoth the doctor, and he rode off as he spoke.

Olaf hesitated a moment, and then followed his example, for he was all alone save for his three Indian servants, who had already loaded up his baggage and were waiting to depart.

They trotted slowly out of Tegucigalpa on the westward side, and Brown remarked:

"Only six months in this wretched country and one practice broken up already. I wonder how long they'll let us stay in the next place, colonel?"

"I don't know, and I don't care," said Olaf in a savage way. "All I regret is that I didn't cut my way through them and carry off Carmelita."

Brown laughed.

"And where should we be now, with a woman in our party? Give the devil his due; these creoles never hurt women. I believe they inherit that much chivalry from the old Conquistadores. Your girl and mine are both safe, and by this time old Guartiola's dead, so he can't marry Carmelita. As for my girl, you've just laid out her intended, Bragamonte; for which, by-the-by, I'm very much obliged, old fellow."

They rode quietly on, no man offering to pursue them, and began to ascend the side of the mountains.

The higher they went the cooler it became, till, by the time it was hot, sweltering noon in Tegucigalpa, below them, the air about them was cool and bracing, while over their heads they could see the edge of the snow line, and the condors were wheeling about on a level with their horses' feet.

The view around them was one full of the most picturesque sublimity; for they had come to a ridge whence they could see on one side the waters of the Caribbean sea, and on the other the dim distant line of the broad Pacific ocean, while a wilderness of mountain and forest, lake and savanna, spread on either side from sea to sea.

And, saving the town of Tegucigalpa, in all that expanse they could see no sign of human habitation, save that they were on a sort of track marked by mule's feet, and to be traced ahead by the white "blaze" of the trees.

"This is the road to old Guatemala," said the doctor. "It passes to the south of Comayagua and runs into the Lost People Road, further."

Olaf looked surprised.

"The Lost People Road! What's that?"

"Well, it's pretty hard to say. You know the Indians around here are queer people and the whites don't know the language of half of them. It's called Maya."

"So I've heard. Here's Maso, my horse-boy, is a Maya, by-the-by. But what of it?"

"Well, you see, I believe they are a superstitious lot of fellows, you know."

"I know that too."

"And they have a tradition among them that, somewhere in these mountains, there exists a lost city, inhabited by a lot of ancient Mexicans, who ran away when Cortez took the country, found a place where no one can get at them, and are living to-day in just the same style as that in which their ancestors did in the days of Montezuma."

The Dane looked very much interested.

"I never heard of that before; but it sounds as if it were reasonable. Let us go and find this place."

Brown shook his head.

"No use; no one ever got there and came back alive."

"Perhaps no one ever tried very hard."

"Perhaps not. These Greasers are lazy brutes, not worth licking, and the Indians, if they have ever been there and come back, won't tell a soul. But I've heard of at least two white men who went in search of the Lost City and never were heard of again."

Olaf pulled his long moustache in a meditative manner.

"And where is this Lost City supposed to be?"

"Somewhere beyond old Guatemala, on the road to Chiapas and Tabasco."

"My friend," said Olaf enthusiastically, "let us go there. These Greasers are not Norsemen. *Our* race goes anywhere and everywhere. We will find the Lost City or die in the attempt."

Brown shrugged his shoulders.

"It may be all a sell, you know?"

"How a sell?"

"Well, the whole country is full of these ruined cities, that some people think are many thousands of years old, while others are just as sure that they are remnants of the same cities that Cortez found, full of Mexicans."

"Well, what of that?"

"Well, this may only be another of them, colonel."

"Another what?"

"Another ruin. You see, no white man has ever been there, and it's surrounded by dense forests, but so are Uxmal and Palenque and the other ruins. I'm told old Padre Gil Perez has seen something he thinks is the town, on a clear morning from the mountains, but after all it may only be another ruin."

"Ruin or town," returned Olaf obstinately, "I'm going to try and get there."

The doctor made no reply and they rode on along the trail till the blitzed line crossed a ridge, and plunged downward into a dense sea of dark green foliage.

They rode on, the atmosphere becoming by slow degrees warmer as they descended, till sunset surprised them in the midst of great groves of India-rubber trees with their broad leathery leaves, their trunks half-strangled by leaves and vines, while troops of howling monkeys began to make night hideous, and the occasional roar of a jaguar showed them that the South American animals had spread into their vicinity.

It was but a cheerless place to camp, for everything was damp around them and they had no food with them, but they were soon cheered as they rode along by the gleam of a light in the dark forest ahead, and coming up to it, discovered the hut of a native india-rubber gatherer who was clipping away at some new troughs for his next day's work.

He was an Indian of the Maya family like most of the labourers in that region; but he understood Spanish and talked it in a broken fashion that was not unpleasing.

His name was Lupo, he said, and he made his living by carrying india-rubber to the coast traders when he wanted money.

"I don't want much, *señores*. It is only for tobacco and cocoa, and one trip a year gives me enough of that."

"And have you any neighbours?" asked Olaf.

The Indian smiled.

"Listen, *señor*, and you will hear them."

It was not necessary to listen, for the loud chorus of monkeys, frogs, alligators and other animals from the neighbouring swamps, forced itself on the ear all night long.

By day the silence had been oppressive, but the night seemed to be given over to revelry among the animals which swarmed in the forest, and the sharp buzz of millions of mosquitoes, which drove them to the lee of a smoky fire, where they had to sit up all night.

"This is the way, *señores*. To do my work here we must follow nature and do our sleeping in the day time, for the night is the same all the year round. If we don't have a visit from the jaguars before morning, I shall be much surprised."

And Lupo was right, for the scent of the horses and mules proved so attractive, that the whole party was compelled to turn out before dawn and open fire on a pair of prowling jaguars, one of which was killed and the other sent limping away.

In the dawn they saddled up and proceeded on their journey toward the State of Guatemala.

Mexican *Guerrilleros*, 1848.

Chapter XI.

Don Jose.

OUT in the upper valleys of the Coradilleras*, between the States of Guatemala and Chiapas, one of the provinces of Mexico, a stout and handsome man in the uniform of a Mexican general was riding at the head of a party of some fifty lancers, when he suddenly gave the order for his men to halt, as he espied a figure on the ridge that divided him from the low countries.

The party was in the midst of a grove of palms, whose spiky foliage concealed them from view, and the figure above was clearly outlined against the blue sky, so that they could see it to be an armed horseman.

---

* *Coradilleras:* an extensive chain of mountains or mountain ranges, a continuous sequence of which form the western "backbone" of the Americas.

The officer held his horse reined in and watched. Presently another figure came in sight, and then another till they had counted six, all mounted and coming down into the valley in which they were.

The officer called up one of his followers.

"Captain Robaldo, you have a glass. Can you see who those people are?"

The captain—a swarthy, handsome fellow—nodded as he offered the glass to his commander.

"I have seen them already, general. They are *Yanquis* or English and all well armed. I see rifles and revolvers, but only one wears a sword. He is a *rubio* like yourself, general."

Indeed the general, though evidently of pure Spanish blood, had fair hair and blue eyes. The senior officer reflected a moment and then said: "Let the men dismount. These people may be friends after all. In our State anyone who is not an enemy is welcome."

The men obeyed orders and tied their horses to the palm trees, while the two officers rode out to meet the coming party which had been, when first seen, about two miles off.

They kept among the trees so as not to be seen, and finally came out into a pretty little meadow surrounded by forest, where they could see the other party advancing. Captain Robaldo here ventured to say:

"Is it quite prudent to go any further? These people may attempt—"

The general waved his hand.

"They are Americans and I fear nothing. If they were our own countrymen, now, you might talk, Robaldo."

"But we do not know them, and they might shoot at us for fun."

"Not they, captain. They see that we are not handling our weapons."

They rode on accordingly and as they came nearer the other party, saw that it was headed by two men, whose light hair and general appearance showed them to be probably Americans.

One of them was slim and military-looking, the other large and burly; but both had pistols in their hands and looked suspicious.

Presently they came within hailing distance, when the slim man, who had a long pointed moustache, called out:

"Who are you, gentlemen? Halt, please."

He pointed his pistol, and the two Mexicans halted, but neither offered to throw his hand forward while the senior said:

"I am Don Jose Ramirez, late general of cavalry in Chiapas, now a free lance on my way to hunt up recruits for Ortega.[†] This is my aide, Captain Robaldo. To whom I have the honour of speaking?"

"I am Colonel Olaf Svenson, late Instructor at Arms of Honduras, now a free rover and looking for a service. This is my friend, Don Carlos Brown, in the same predicament," was the answer of our friend the swordmaster.

The Mexican general burst out laughing.

"I could have sworn you were, like myself, a soldier of fortune, down on his luck. Come, *señor*, my party is down today, but this is a land of fluctuations. Join forces with me and who knows what we three *rubios* may accomplish? I can promise you under my chief as good a place as that you have lost. The pay it is true is only enough for cigars, but then *por Dios, tenemos onglas libres*[*] [we have nails free by heaven] and you do not need to be told what that means."

Olaf smiled.

"Nails free! It is a picturesque phrase, and means, I suppose, that you have plenty of pickings. Who knows, Don Jose, I may accept your offer."

"Hands upon it then," cried the other frankly. "We are cavaliers and we have our arms and horses. Who shall refuse us a forced loan?"

---

† Jesús González Ortega (1822-1881) was a military man and Mexican politician who participated in the fight against the French intervention in Mexico, and in the War of Reform. Monstery, who fought against Ortega in the last conflict, recounted: "There was a man named Ortega who had been the Chiapas Governor of Customs and whose peculations had run into the millions. He had been dismissed from office by the central Liberal Government and in revenge joined [Miguel] Miramon. He was a soldier and a valiant captain, as well as a thief, and one of the most murderous leaders in the history of that land of murder." See page liv of the Introduction.

* *Onglas libres:* Strangely, Monstery uses the Provençal (rather than Spanish) term for "nails." The correct translation of this phrase in Spanish is *uñas libres.*

"Who indeed? A forced loan, I suppose, is—"

"The tribute commerce pays to arms. We come to a town full of merchants and they pay for our protection. You understand, the country is full of *guerrillas* and we are the friends of order. It is proper society should pay for us, my friend."

"I see."

Olaf could not help smiling at the careless recklessness of the handsome Mexican.

"But come, my friend, my party is in camp over yonder in the valley and it is time to eat. Share my hospitality."

"With pleasure, Don Jose."

They rode along to where the lancers were now bivouacked and dismounted, when a bountiful repast was spread before Olaf and his fellow-traveller, causing the Briton to exclaim:

"I say, colonel, you know, if this is the sort of way the 'out' party fares, the 'ins' must live in clover[‡] all the time."

Ramirez asked for a translation of the remark, and laughed heartily.

"This is the country for a soldier of fortune," he said. "Nature and the Indians do the work, and we live on the fat of the land. But it is well understood that we must be ready to fight for our lives all the time. That is the drawback."

Dinner over, they saddled up, and Olaf asked:

"Whither now, Don Jose? This is not the way to Chiapas, but to Guatemala."

"Faith, I hardly know," responded Ramirez. "I have a week in which to roam before we meet my chief, and hardly know what to do. Can you suggest any scheme to fill our purses in the meantime, for our party needs money?"

Olaf nodded.

"I have a scheme on which I was bent, but had not enough men to render it safe."

---

‡ *Live in clover:* To live in a condition of prosperity, luxury, or abundance.

"And what is that?"

"To find the Lost City of the Aztecs."

Ramirez started.

"The Lost City? How did you hear of it? I thought that was a secret among our people."

"I have heard of it."

"Do you know where it is?"

"I know where it is said to be."

The Mexican looked thoughtful for time.

"Do you know, Don Olaf," he said "that I have had a dream of that city haunting me for many years and have never had any opportunity till now of realizing it?"

"Indeed!"

"Yes. What do you know? What have you ever heard about this Lost City?"

"Simply that up in these mountains, and as near as I can find, not far from here, the Indians say there is a hidden city still held by the ancient Aztecs."

"Yes, that is it. But that is not all."

"How not all? What else?"

"Have you not heard of the ransom of the great Montezuma?"

"No. What is it?"

"It is quite a story. It is said that when the great Cortez took Montezuma prisoner and before the Mexicans rose for the *Noche Triste** when they drove the Spaniards from the city, the king offered to pay Cortez a great ransom of gold and sent word to all his chiefs to collect it. But the *Noche Triste* came, the treasure never got to Mexico, but was carried away into these mountains. Then came the conquest and the

---

* *La Noche Triste,* or "The Sad Night", took place on June 30, 1520 during the Spanish conquest of Mexico, when Hernán Cortés and his invading army were defeated and driven out of the Mexican capital following the death of the Aztec king Moctezuma II, who had been held hostage by the Spaniards.

Aztecs were driven out of their old towns while our race took possession of all."

"I have heard all that."

"True, but not of Guatemoezin's sister, Tlahoma."[†]

"No. Who was she?"

"They say she was a princess six feet high and as strong as two common men. Anyway she was the only Aztec who took to the mountains, defied Spain and maintained her freedom."

† *Guatemoezin*: Cuauhtémoc, or Guatimozín, was the last Aztec emperor, and is venerated in Mexico today as a national hero for his desperate defense of besieged Tenochtitlan in 1521. When Aztec forces became overwhelmed, he and his court attempted to flee the city by boat, but were captured and taken prisoner. In 1525, Hernan Cortés took Cuauhtémoc along with him on his expedition to Honduras, as he feared that Cuauhtémoc could have led an insurrection in his absence. While the expedition was stopped in the Maya capital of Itzamkanac, Cortés had Cuauhtémoc executed for allegedly conspiring to kill him and other Spaniards. Bernal Díaz del Castillo, who served under Cortés, described these executions as unjust based on insubstantial evidence, and admits to having liked Cuauhtémoc personally.

"But what has she to do—"

"With the Lost City?"

"Yes."

"Simple enough. She founded it."

"Founded it! Then it is a modern place."

"Not exactly."

"What do you mean?"

"The tradition goes that it was a sacred place, only inhabited by priests and sacred to the God of War, Quetzalcoatl."

"Quetzal—what a name?"

"Yes; we'll call him the War God, it's much easier. Well, the city was built in the midst of mountains like a fortress with only one narrow entrance so that the temple could be defended by twenty men. It was a fitting temple for a War God."

"But Tlahoma—what of her?"

"I'm coming to that. The time came at last when Tlahoma—her band reduced to less than a thousand faithful warriors, was hunted into the mountains and took refuge in the War God's temple. She found the land around it so fair that she made it into a city, and from it planned numerous expeditions into Mexico, all of which succeeded. Therefore, in the Lost City, which was once nothing but a temple, are collected all the treasures of Montezuma's ransom and all the fruits of Tlahoma's raids."

"But what became of her?"

"She married the chief priest of the War God, it is said, and her descendants rule there to this day. But since her death they have never come down out of the mountains. That's all."

"But how did you learn all this?"

"Merely by legend. You know our Indians are very fond of telling legends. It may all be false, but if it be true—"

He paused doubtfully.

"Well, if it be true?"

"Why, then, there must be enough gold and silver in the Lost City to make us all as rich as Cortez."

Olaf nodded.

"Then, why not go and try for it?"

"Why not? Well, you see there are only a hundred and six of us."

"And how many men had Cortez, when he made war on an empire?"

Ramirez shrugged his shoulders.

"You are right. He had only five hundred and fifty, and seventy muskets, with sixteen horses."

"Yet with those he gave Spain an empire. We only seek to find a city and we have a hundred horses, with rifles and revolvers. Your men have their fire-arms; is it not so?"

"They have carbines, swords and lances, no pistols. We depend on the lance most."

"The lance ? I do not think much of that for a weapon, general."

Ramirez flushed up in a moment. It was clear that Olaf had touched him on a sore spot.

"Not trust the lance! Good Heavens, man, it is the queen of *armas blancas* (steel weapons), and our national arm. My men could do nothing without the lance. Why, I could beat any swordsman living with my lance."

Olaf smiled provokingly.

"Any swordsman living is quite a challenge. You may not know I am a master of the sword."

"Master or no master, I can run you through," cried the Mexican, hotly, and as he spoke he caught up his lance, ran to his horse, and vaulted on without the aid of the stirrups. Then he wheeled and galloped off a hundred yards, waved his lance and cried:

"Come on, Don Olafo, or else own the lance is the queen of all weapons."

His tone was gay and courteous as might have become a knight of old, challenging for a tournament.

Olaf smiled and said to himself:

"That is a man after my own heart. He is a born cavalier, but he does not know me."

He mounted his own fiery little horse with a deliberation in strong contrast to the fiery haste of the Mexican, drew his sword, and galloped to meet Ramirez.

The Mexican general rushed in with headlong haste, his lance couched and quivering, while the Dane kept his own horse in a hand-gallop. A moment later they came together, and the Mexican's horse was seen to sway wide of Olaf's body, while the swordmaster turned in toward Ramirez, closed with him, and in a moment later emerged from the fray with Ramirez's hat and lance in his hand.

For a moment the Mexican seemed inclined to be furious, but as he looked at the other, calm and smiling, he exclaimed:

"It is fair; you have beaten me, but by the saints, you are the only man in the world who can do it."

Olaf rode up to him and handed him his hat and lance.

"You play the lance well, but I know a trick in that weapon worth more than yours. We will practice it. In the meantime I will admit that the lance is a good weapon in good hands, and I intend to use one before I leave this country. And now which way shall we go, Don Jose?"

"Yonder. That is the way to the Lost City."

He pointed to the ridge over which Olaf had come when he entered the valley.

CHAPTER XII.

PADRE MIGUEL.

PADRE MIGUEL was the sole remains of the once powerful and flourishing Mission of San Miguel de Guatemala, in the Cordilleras. He had been reared there from the time he was a baby, and had never known who was his mother. He had known the Mission in the old times of the Spanish occupation, when it received tithes from a large space of country below, and had a good two hundred monks when he was an acolyte, and he had seen it dwindle to a hundred when he was a deacon, and sink to fifty after he had become a full priest.

After the numerous revolutions that shook the land round them, varied by earthquakes and hurricanes, Padre Miguel found his head growing white, with only two old monks to keep him company, and finally they dropped off.

Then Padre Miguel was left all alone in the huge, ruinous building, cracked by the innumerable earthquakes but still fairly habitable, surrounded by a garden full of every variety of fruits, with two Indian servants for his sole flock.

Nevertheless, he was too old to change, and he had lived there ever since, with plenty to eat and drink, and performing mass as regularly in the Mission chapel, as if he had been in a city full of people.

Padre Miguel in his black cassock and huge hat, sat at the door of the Mission and looked over as fair a picture as ever gladdened the eye of man.

Before him, about three miles off across a broad and lovely valley, rose the foot-hills, of a sea of mountains, and from where he was he could see the blue line of the Pacific over the top of another sea of woods. Thirty or forty miles off among the mountains rose a trio of lofty peaks crowned with snow, and it was at these that the old monk was gazing wistfully when he heard the clatter of hoofs, and saw a cavalcade of lancers coming towards the Mission.

Padre Miguel was all in a flutter. Such a sight had not been seen in San Miguel for fifty years. He remembered once in the old Spanish times having been visited by a party of "patriots," but the Mission was too lonely ever since to attract anyone.

He saw at the head of them all, three men with fair hair and blue eyes.

One was dressed in the showy uniform of a Mexican general, with a gold-laced cocked hat; the second was likewise in uniform, but of a plainer cut; the third wore white clothes and a pugaree* hat, such as the *padre* had never seen before.

Behind them rode at least a hundred men in velveteen jackets and bell-bottomed trousers, with broad, shiny hats on their heads, brass-sheathed sabres at their sides, carbines strapped to their saddles, and long lances in their hands.

Padre Miguel got up, trembling.

"Good-day gentlemen. What are you pleased to want to-day? We have no money left."

---

* *Pugaree:* a wide-brimmed slouch hat, so-named for its distinctive band. Often pinned or cocked on one side, it was popular with many Western military units.

The Mexican general laughed.

"We want none father. Nothing but your blessing and permission to halt and pick a little of your fruit for my men."

"Certainly, certainly, my son. The blessing of the church is the right of her sons."

The Mexican dismounted and knelt down in the most respectful manner before the priest, who extended his tremulous bands over his head with a fervent benediction.

Then the whole party got off their horses and spread about the Mission, while the officers asked the good *padre* if he would not honour them by taking dinner with them, as they had killed enough game in the forest to supply all, and it would only spoil if kept.

The *padre* was not loth, and the fires were soon lighted, before which sundry legs of peccary, ant-eater, monkey and other savoury, but peculiar game, were soon roasting, while the chiefs entered into conversation with the of numerous questions.

"You seem pretty lonely here, *padre*?"

"Pretty lonely. Yes, my son. But few people come by here, except those that are running from one State to another, in these terrible times of revolution. Ah, how different to the peace and quiet when Our Mother Spain ruled us!"

"Aha! *Padre*, you remember the Spanish colonial times, then?"

"Yes, my son, yes. Don't tell any one, but I wish they were back. The church had her rights and respect, then. Now—you see how her Missions are decayed."

"Any travellers passed lately?"

"Last week, my son; a small party with two ladies in it. Heaven help them."

"Ladies! Here!"

It was Olaf who spoke.

"You may well wonder, my son. Yes; it was true, indeed. They were ladies."

"Where from, father?"

"They both come from Tegucigalpa, on it account of the revolution there. They belonged to the party that was beaten. One of them belonged to a Cuban merchant called Ximenes—"

"Ximenes! *Dios!*"

"What is the matter, my son?"

"Nothing, father. Go on."

"The other was called Garcia. They were with their fathers and had five mules loaded with gold, all their fortunes, going to Mexico."

Olaf turned to Charlie Brown.

"You hear that?" he said in English.

"Of course I do. I'm not such a stupid idiot; I can understand Spanish if I can't speak it. I told you our girls were safe."

"But how came they here?"

"Blest if I knew. S'pose Old Wickedness got the best of them after all, and they had to pull up stakes and run."

"Then we shall find them in Mexico."

"Perhaps," said Charlie doubtfully.

"Why not?"

"Because Mexico's as full of *guerrillas* and other robbers as an egg's full of meat. Five mules loaded with gold! That's enough to tempt a saint. And no escort I suppose."

"Ask the old man."

"Padre," said Olaf, turning to the old priest, "did these travellers have any soldiers with them when they passed?"

"Not one, my son. There were two old men and three Indian peons."

"Then they're gone up sure," muttered the young doctor.

"Which road were they to take, father?"

The old man reflected.

"I think, my son, if I remember right, they were to go by the Lost City road to Chiapas, because no one passes that way, on account of the legends of ghosts at night. I recommended it to them as safest for them. If there are ghosts on the roads, at least there are no robbers, and five mule loads of gold is a great temptation."

Olaf nodded to Brown, well pleased.

"We are in luck. We shall overtake them."

Here Ramirez, to whom their questions were enigmatical, broke in:

"Do you know this party, gentlemen?"

Olaf made him a sign to restrain his questions for the present and answered:

"Yes, they are friends of ours. We may save them from danger before they reach Mexico."

Then Don Jose called them to dinner, and over the savoury fumes of roast monkey—than which is no better eating, it is said—they entered into further conversation with the old priest, who had lived all his life in that spot.

"You have seen a good deal of the Indians, *padre*, is it not so?"

"I was brought up among them my son, and I talk all their dialects."

"How many are there, father?"

"There are enumerated one hundred and thirty-seven varieties more or less distinct, of the Maya stock," began the old man, who was evidently riding a hobby. "I devoted much time and attention to the subject, because I had nothing else to do, and I am satisfied that the Maya is the original language of the Aztec nation, that was conquered by the great Cortez."

"And have you ever heard from them of the Lost City, father?"

The *padre*'s voice sank to a low impressive key as he said solemnly:

"My sons, I have seen the Lost City."

Olaf started up full of excitement.

"You! Why, I thought no white man had ever been there and come back alive!"

"I did not go there, my son. Heaven forbid. I should not be alive now had I done so. But I have seen it with these two eyes when they were many years younger and better than they are now, and I shall never forget the sight."

His hearers much interested, began to ask questions again.

"When was it? How was it? What did you see? Is it a ruin? Does it have any people in it?"

"I saw it when I was a young novice, before I took even deacon's orders. I went on a long tramp among the mountains in my novitiate to meditate on holy things, with no one to make my thoughts wander. I wandered on till I lost my way in the forest and among the passes."

"Could you find the way again?" asked Don Jose eagerly.

"I could, my son. I took precautions, as you shall hear, to mark the trail as I came back, and I have dreamed ever since of some day going back there. But it is all over now. I am an old man and I shall never see with my living eyes that wondrous city again."

He fell into a fit of musing again from which he was wakened by Brown asking:

"Was it a ruin, father?"

The English doctor blushed all over at his first attempt at connected Spanish, and the *padre* answered absently:

"No, no, it is no ruin. It is a real city, with real people; but such a city, such a people I never saw. Ah, *señores*, some have said that the *conquistadores* were cruel, that they murdered innocent Aztecs. I tell you if they were all like these people, Cortez was a scourge sent from God to punish them for their sins."

Now perfectly burning with curiosity, Olaf cried out:

"For Heaven's sake, *padre*, tell us the story. How did you come on them, and what did you see?"

The old monk looked at him doubtfully.

"You know, I am not certain if I saw them, *señor*," he said quietly.

"Not certain? What do you mean?"

"I mean that it is all so strange, so very strange, that I have often wondered since if it were not all a dream."

"Well, dream or reality, tell us. You say you lost your way in the mountains. How was it?"

"I lost my way in the forest, not in the mountains. It was in the mountains I found it again, *señores*. But I may as well begin at the beginning, and tell you all about it."

The padre took a pinch of snuff—his only vice—and began his story.

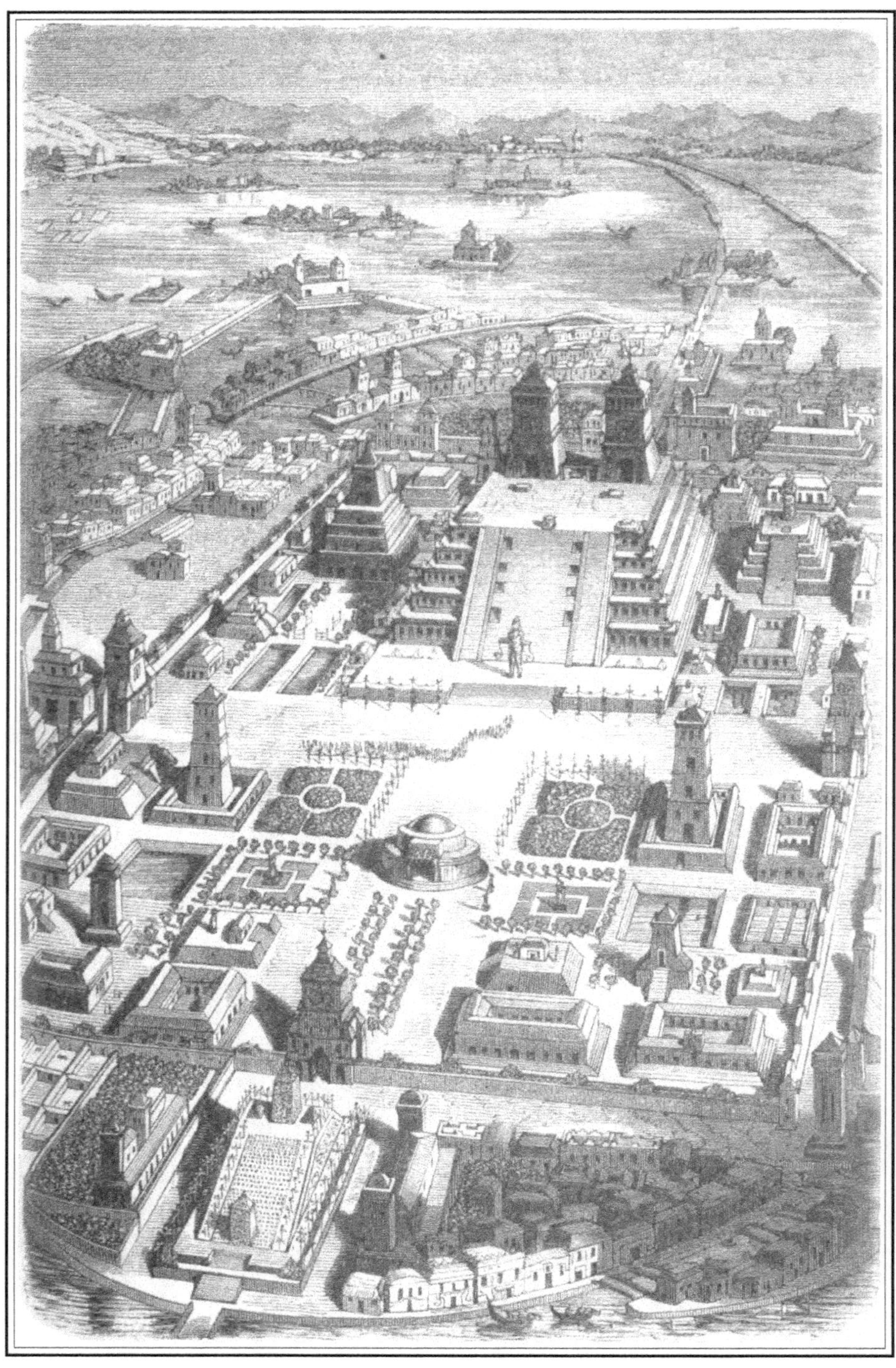

CHAPTER XIII.

THE PADRE'S STORY.

"YOU know, *señores*, even if you are not Catholics, that we Catholics frequently make what we call retreats."

Don Jose nodded.

"This would be a nice place to make one."

"Very true, *señor*. Whenever you wish to come, you shall be welcome."

Olaf interrupted him.

"But *I* do not know what is a retreat."

"It is a season of retirement from the world, to fast and pray, *señor*, and good Catholics make it once a year. Well, it was my turn to make a retreat in my novitiate, and I asked the Father Superior's permission to make mine, in the mountains towards the Lost City, because it was said that there were terrible spirits in that direction, and wished to do battle with them for the church. Alas, I saw none, unless you call human beings such. Well, I went there with the father's advice, and I was so much wrapped up in any thoughts that I went three days and nights without food, and on the fourth day found myself in a strange place, where I had never been before."

"What was it like?"

"It was an open forest, without under-wood, with tall *cascarilla* trees at the foot of a rock which I could see towering up, so straight that it looked like a wall. Down the middle of it came a little stream of water, as cold as ice, and this had worn a passage into the rock, up which I climbed."

"Were you strong enough to climb, after three days' fast?"

"Three days is nothing, my son. I have fasted ten at a time, and have seen visions."

"Well, go on."

"I will admit that I was very hungry, my son; but there was nothing to eat, so I had to go on, after drinking of that beautiful water. It seemed to give me immediate strength, and I went up the bed of the stream, which led me on finally into a sort of tunnel or cave, clown which the stream cut its way, and finally brought me out on a table-land of rock, in the midst of which the stream had made a pool, coming from the side of a vast snow-crowned mountain, out of which shot the spur of rock on which I stood. On that side there was nothing but the huge mountain and the sky above, but on the other side I saw—"

"What? The Lost City?" cried Olaf eagerly.

"No, my son," said Padre Miguel, smiling. "Not the Lost City, but this Mission."

"Then if you saw the Mission from there, we can see the rock from here," said Brown, with British logic and common sense.

"Certainly, my son, yonder it is. I cannot see it, but your eyes are young. I know the direction."

He pointed off to the east across the sea of dark forest under his feet—for the Mission was built on a lofty table-land—to where a chain of snow-capped mountains rose up, about forty miles off.

"Can you see a white spur of rock over the forest at the foot of the mountains, *señores*, with a stream of water that sparkles, if the sun is in the right quarter?"

"I see it," quoth Ramirez.

"So do I," said Brown.

Olaf deliberately levelled a strong field-glass at it, before he would declare:

"I too. Yes, there is the stream and the pool of which you spoke. Yes, and there is a cavern beyond, out of which the stream runs."

"That is the place, and there I found myself. Well, you may be sure by that time I began to wish I had not made my retreat so *very* far, and to think about something to eat, if only some berries."

"Very natural, *padre*."

"Yes, *señores*, the flesh is weak with the best of intentions; and though I had been so busy in my thoughts I had forgotten all about my hunger, the moment I remembered my hunger I had forgot my prayers. I actually wished I had a gun to shoot something but I had not so much as a knife, nothing but my nails."

"Well what did you do, *padre*?"

"I wandered along the foot of the mountain on that table rock, looking for some wild bananas or pine-apples or something; but of course found none, and the consequence was that I went on round the shoulder of the mountain and came into a side valley, where I discovered, to my great joy, a little pool of water, full of tortoises and frogs."

"And did you eat them?"

"Indeed I did, *señores*."

"But how did you kill and cook them?"

"There were plenty of sharp flints lying round, and you know, *señores*, we people are half Indians round here. We know how to make and use flint knives. As for fire, I know how to make that too, for there was plenty of dry moss on the rocks, and flints to strike fire with. In short I cooked and ate a good-sized tortoise, and then felt so much ashamed of myself that I prayed to be forgiven, and resolved to do penance for my sins by fasting for a week longer, and wandering out of sight of any place where I could get help. I tell you I felt strong to resist the devil and all his imps, at that time of my life."

Olaf interrupted him here.

"Are we getting near the Lost City yet?"

"All in good time, my son; I did not see it for three days after that."

Olaf groaned with impatience.

Brown shrugged his shoulders and smiled.

Ramirez lighted a cigarette.

The *padre* placidly proceeded:

"I skirted that mountain and got to the next, then went on to a pass between two others, and finally found myself surrounded with hills of all sorts, and once more completely lost.

"Only there was this difference.

"In the forest I did not know how I got there, but in the mountains I was able to go back the way I came; retracing my course by the landmarks."

"How long before you found you were lost?" asked Olaf abruptly.

"Three days, *señor*."

"Thank Heaven!"

"Why, *señor*?"

"Because we are so much nearer to the Lost City, father."

The old priest smiled.

"Don't be impatient, my son. It was noon on the third that I again began to feel hunger, and determined not to give way to it. I went recklessly on till I came to the other side of the mountains, where I saw below me a green valley of surpassing and wonderful richness, evidently the property of men; for I could see gardens and herds of sheep, cattle and horses, grazing on a level savanna in the midst of palm-groves. I was so much disgusted at the sight—for I thought I had come into the State of

Honduras by mistake—that I turned round, re-entered the pass I had left, and sank down to rest under a rock, where I speedily fell asleep."

"Well, *padre*," said Olaf, resignedly, I suppose you have about as little curiosity as any man. I should not have gone to sleep in *your* place."

"But I did. It is true, my son. I slept till the middle of the night, and dreamed a very strange dream. I thought that I had gone on into the valley and found in its midst the Lost City of the Aztecs, crowned with a huge *teocalli*[*] to the War God, to whom they were offering human victims. I was so much impressed by the dream that I woke in a profuse sweat, and, as I did so, heard in good earnest the very drums and cymbals I had heard in my dream from the priests of the War God. They were all round me, and seemed to echo from every rock, but I could see nothing. I thought it was the work of the evil one, so I fell on my knees and prayed most heartily to be spared. It was then quite dark.

"Just then a bright light shone up the pass, and I saw, coming toward me, a crowd of men in gorgeous feather dresses carrying long spears, and bearing in their midst a white man, stripped and crowned with flowers, whom they were leading along with ropes covered, as if in grim mockery, with garlands of flowers.

"I was frightened to death, and shrank back into my dark hole in the rock and so the great rabble passed me, singing in the Maya tongue a hymn to the god Quetzalcoatl.

"I saw too well what it was. In one single moment it flashed on me. These were the men of the Lost City, in the same state as Cortez had found them, centuries ago, and they had by some means captured a white man and were leading him as a victim to the altar.

"He was a young man, fair and handsome, a *rubio* like you, and I heard him praying to himself in some foreign language as he walked along, the Aztecs yelling and singing round him.

"They never saw me, but passed on to the valley I had seen, when I followed them, as if compelled by a horrible fascination. They went on,

---

* *Teocalli*: In Nahuatl, "God-house." A Mesoamerican pyramid surmounted by a temple.

and I watched them in the dark night, like a trail of fire, for they all carried torches, going along the side of the mountain.

"Below me the valley seemed to be all ablaze with lights, and as I went on, I saw that a tall white *teocalli* was erected at the end of the valley, with a huge bonfire blazing on its summit, around which the priests of the War God were dancing and singing, while processions with torches were winding to and fro beneath.

"I could see the whole city, and a grand one it was, with white palaces and houses, all surrounded by trees and gardens, a lake in the valley covered with boats, and a stream running out to the lower end.

"I went as far as I dared, and found that the valley was surrounded by perpendicular walls, except in one place, where there was a narrow road down which the procession was passing.

"Then I hid in some bushes and watched.

"I was not eight hundred feet from the summit of the great *teocalli* and could see it plainly, for my eyes were very good in those days.

"I saw the procession with the white victim go down into the valley and up the side of the *teocalli*; I saw them lay the victim on the great black stone of sacrifice, just as we read about in the days of Cortez; and I saw them finally cut out his heart with two fearful gashes, and hold it up to the War God.

"Then, I own, *señores*, that my senses seemed to give way. I felt as if I were going mad, and I leaped up and fled like a deer.

"I don't even know how long I fled or where I was; but when I came to my senses I found myself by the little pool with the turtles, cutting one of them apart and devouring it raw like a wild beast."

The old man shuddered and hid his face.

"Don't be so shocked;" observed Don Jose, soothingly. "You were excusable. I should have done the same in your place."

"I suppose so, *señor*, but you are not a priest sworn to mortify the flesh. I was shocked and terrified beyond measure, added to which I was assailed by the most horrible pains."

"No wonder, eating raw flesh after a five or six day's fast."

"I do not know how long it was, *señor*, but I know I fell sick by that pool and very nearly died; and when I finally got back to the convent they had given me up as being killed by jaguars."

He stopped as if he had finished, and Olaf asked, with some disappointment "Is that all, *padre*?"

"That is all, my son. I have never seen the Lost City since."

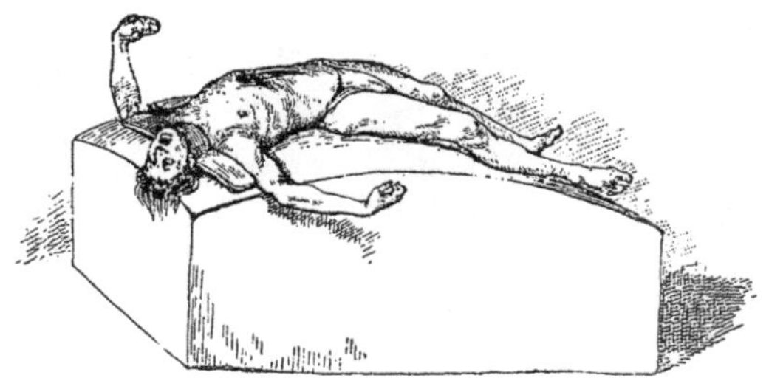

Chapter XIV.

Setting out.

"BUT surely you have spoken of it to others," said Don Jose, earnestly. "Why, they have even a road which they call the Lost City road somewhere here."

"It is true, my son; they have such a road, but it is nowhere near the Lost City, though I am inclined to think that the people of the Lost City sometimes go out in raids on that road."

"What makes you think so?"

"From the fact of their having a white man for their captive when I saw them. Of course I told my superior of my adventure, and he cautioned me never to speak of it, for he attributed it to a dream brought on by extreme hunger, and doubted my sanity at the time. In fact, I hardly know to-day if I did not dream it all."

"Did you over hear of any traveller being missed about that time?" asked Brown, thoughtfully.

The *padre* sighed deeply.

"Yes, my son; and that is one of my reasons for believing I did not dream."

"How? Why?"

"There was a party of engineers making a survey at the time, and they were all found dead on the Lost City road. And a strange and terrible peculiarity of their death was that every one seemed to have had his heart cut out of his body."

"That settles it," observed Olaf, rising; "and it settles another thing. These wretches are the same that Cortez found, and it is our place to drive them from the face of the earth. It is too late in the world's history for human sacrifices, *padre*."

Padre Miguel shook his head gravely.

"My son, beware of passion. It is true that these men are wicked devils, but it is not for us to punish them. I have thought over that."

"But you say they infest the Lost City road, and make travelling unsafe there. Why even now there are two ladies there. Suppose these fiends should attack *them*?"

The possibility so excited the Dane that he paced up and down the room with his hands in his hair.

Padre Miguel spoke as calmly as ever.

"I think there is no danger, my son."

"Why not?"

"Because in all the seventy years of my life I have never heard of but two parties being killed on the Lost City road."

"And what were those?"

"One was the surveying party of which I have spoken, the other a French naturalist, who went up into the mountains on that road."

"And what do you infer from that?"

"Simply this: that the people of the Lost City keep a watch over that road from some unseen post, but that they are only bent on preserving the secret of their own existence."

"I don't understand you."

"It is enough, my son. If they kept the road in turmoil all the time it would attract attention to it."

"I see that of course."

"But if they find any person making a long stay on the road and trying to penetrate into the country where they are hidden, they fear an attempt on their liberty, and in that case they always kill every soul of the party coming."

"Are you sure of that?"

"Yes. Those that are not found dead with their hearts cut out disappear. No one ever escaped from them only wounded."

"Yet the legend has spread."

"True; but that is all on account of the Indians, some of who have visited the town, and all of whom are friendly to it."

"How comes that, father?"

"Simple enough, my son. These Indians know they come of a conquered race, and cherish dreams of some day recovering their independence. And more than that: they hope to regain it by means of the people of this very Lost City, whom they respect and admire. Therefore you may lay it down as an axiom that none of our Indians will ever betray the secret of the Lost City, and that its people will always have scores of spies on our side ready to tell them of any effort to discover its whereabouts."

"Do any of them know that you have seen the city, *padre*?"

"No, my son. I did not dare to speak of it for many years, and it was not till the death of the Father Superior released me from my promise, that I mentioned it by chance to the French naturalist of whom I spoke. Poor fellow! It was probably the cause of his death. If the Indians about here knew that I had seen with my own eyes the Lost City, I think they would kill me, and I am sorry I told you. It was only the joy of seeing you after so long a period of loneliness, I suppose, that opened my heart to you, but I shall never cease to regret it if it be the cause of your death."

Olaf and Don Jose smiled with some contempt.

"The Indian does not live that can kill a Goth of the ancient blood," said Ramirez with all the pride of a Spaniard. "Here are we three *rubios*, all of the same stock, the old Goths that destroyed the Roman Empire. One branch settled in Scandinavia and called it Gothland, another in Spain, another in Angle land, and here we are all three, the conquering races of the earth."

Padre Miguel stared. He had never heard this branch of ethnography discussed before.

"Whatever you may be *señores*," he observed, "I would not advise you to try to go to the Lost City. I was there in the night by an an accident not likely to happen again, but I saw enough to convince me that none but a powerful army could penetrate there."

"Why? How?"

"The people are numerous and well-armed, and we know from all past and present history that they are as brave as lions in battle. See what trouble they gave Cortez."

"But he beat them with his guns. They have no artillery or gunpowder."

"How do you know that, *señores*?"

The *padre* looked very wise as he said this.

Don Jose laughed.

"Oh, come, *padre*, you don't think they have."

"Why not, *señores*? Our Indians can shoot and do shoot, and some of them make guns and *trabucos*.* Why not these men? They are not slow to learn, I can tell you."

"But you saw no firearms among them did you?"

"No, *señor*, nothing but spears. But I saw they had horses, cattle and sheep, all of which they must have taken from the whites in former times. It is reasonable to suppose that they must know about our weapons, and equally reasonable to suppose that they have copied them

---

* *Trabuco:* a blunderbuss.

to some extent, knowing the terrible advantage they gave Cortez in his struggle with their ancestors."

Olaf thought a moment, and then burst out:

"Don Jose, if you'll go, I'll follow. I am resolved to see this Lost City before I die, if I die in getting there."

They got up from the table and took their leave of the old monk, after receiving from him full instructions about the Lost City road, which went on the other side of the mountains from that on which the *padre* himself had ascended on his famous "retreat."

The Dane himself was sorely tempted to try the regular track, taking his chance of stumbling on the outlying post of the mysterious people, but Brown, with his stolid British sagacity, observed:

"And if you do, that's just what the beggars want, colonel. They don't believe it possible for anyone to get up on this side, or else Padre Miguel would have run on some of them in his little trip."

Don Jose backed Brown in this opinion, but Olaf persisted, and finally gave his reasons.

"If we ride fast we are likely to over-take the party that has gone on ahead with five mules loaded with treasure and with two ladies who are the affianced, respectively, of the doctor and myself. We may save their lives, for if these fiends come down on them they will kill the whole party and very possibly carry off the girls to offer as a sacrifice to some god who likes young virgins cut up before him."

"In that case," said Don Jose, "we shall be better able to rescue them if they be taken by coming on the captors by surprise. I am still in favour of trying the *padre*'s route."

And after some discussion it was so agreed.

Padre Miguel told them that the spot where the English surveying party, and the French naturalist had been killed, was at least a hundred and fifty miles off by a long circuit, while the Lost City could not be more than seventy in a straight line from the Mission.

"And you will be able to get there long before the slow-travelling mules of that party get to the dangerous place, *señores*. Therefore, God speed you and fare you well."

The old man stood waving his hat as they rode away and watched them down into the forests of the lowlands.

When he hobbled back to his arm-chair he said to himself mournfully:

"I shall never see them again. And they are so young and brave-looking too! It is a pity!"

Meantime the party of lancers, in all their glory of glittering steel and brass, with their spirited and well-shaped little horses, rode down the slope from the mission, and found themselves on broad lonely savannas that had not known a scythe for fifty years, and yet stood out green and waving with luxuriant crops of wild wheat and barley, remnants of what had once been the farm of the Mission.

They travelled on till the sun was low in the sky, when they went into camp at the edge of a dense forest, whose tangled vines and undergrowth proclaimed the near vicinity of a swamp.

"To-morrow, if we keep our course right, we shall reach the *padre*'s rock," said Don Jose. "After that, our real work begins."

The Fugitives

CHAPTER XV.

THE FUGITIVES.

OUT on a lonely bridle-path, that wound to and fro among gigantic trees, faintly indicated by a series of white "blazes" on the tall trunks, full of mud holes and pools of water, a small caravan of loaded mules was stringing wearily forward on the road to Chiapas, under the shadows of the grand Cordilleras.

Down in the forest one could not see far in any direction, but whenever it opened into a glade, there overhead towered the silent, solemn mountains crowned with snow.

There were about twenty mules in the party, of which only six were ridden, the rest plodding sullenly along after an old white mare with a bell round her neck trotting at the head of the caravan and known as the *madrina*—little mother.

Of the ridden mules, two were mounted by old men dressed as rich Spanish merchants or *rancheros*; two carried armed servants, and two bore ladies.

Three Indian muleteers trudged along in the mud beside the mules, and the whole party looked weary and haggard.

"If we only get to Chiapas safe, I shall not mind the privations, Don Ramon," said old Ximenes, with a sigh, "but I fear very much we shall not get there without meeting some *guerrilleros*. Padre Miguel said that they—"

"For the love of Heaven, Don Carlos, don't let us anticipate trouble," interrupted Don Ramon irritably. "It's had enough to know we have failed, and, to see Ortega plucking the fruit we ripened, without imagining all sorts of evil before it comes."

Don Carlos Ximenes groaned.

"I have all the savings of my life on those mules, and you tell me not to be anxious."

"Anxiety won't help us. We are in the hands of Providence, my friend," retorted Don Ramon. "Do you suppose I feel very jolly in my turn? But Padre Miguel says that we are in no danger on this road. The only men ever seen on it are the Gomez brothers, and they have not been out this year."

"All the more reason for them to be out now," answered Ximenes, obstinately. "I tell you, Don Ramon; I shall not be easy till I am safe inside the gates of the city."

"And that is the very place where we may be in most danger, Don Carlos."

"Why, my friend?"

"Because I hear that they have a change of government there also."

"What! Another revolution? *Dios!* Why did I not stay in Cuba? There was not so much money there, but it was safe, at least."

"That is your affair."

"I know it. But who is in Chiapas now?"

"A namesake of the man who cheated me out of the presidency of Honduras, General Ortega. I hear he is levying forced loans to make an effort against the central power in Mexico. He has a dashing scamp for a lieutenant called Ramirez who is said to be out even now scouring the country."

"Heaven grant we do not meet him," groaned Ximenes, in great tribulation. "Oh! My mules! To think I should have—"

"Hush! No need of telling our secrets, Don Carlos. It is enough we know the amount of our savings, without telling the servants."

Don Ramon looked round cautiously, and then went on in a low voice:

"I don't know but we might do well if we met Ramirez."

"Why, my friend?"

"Because he is said to be a good fellow, who will listen to reason."

"To reason? How?"

"I mean that it will be better to give him half our savings if he will convey us to Vera Cruz; than to lose all to some band of *guerrilleros*, who would cut our throats and carry off our daughters into the bargain."

Don Carlos turned pale, and trembled.

"Is that possible, Don Ramon?"

"It is what the Gomez brothers did to a friend of mine only three years ago."

Don Carlos made no answer, but rode on, looking nervously to right and left.

Presently the ground began to rise, and they came to a very pretty savanna where the mules, tired and hungry, refused to proceed further, and began to lie down. When a loaded mule lies down it is a sign that he is determined to have rest, and the muleteers suggested that this was a good place to go into camp till the evening, and let the beasts feed.

The two old men, though loth to halt, were persuaded, and in a few minutes the animals were unsaddled and the little party began to eat what dinner they had, with the foot of the mountain a few hundred yards off.

Pedrillo, the *vaquero*, who was one of the armed attendants, sat smoking his pipe after dinner, and looking up at the grim face of the mountain so long that Don Ramon asked him:

"What do you see, Pedrillo?"

The old Indian started as if ashamed.

"Nothing, master, nothing."

He moved away to another spot, but his master observed him pretty soon after in the same reflective pose, looking up.

He said nothing, but watched him till he found that the vaquero's gaze was fixed on a ridge of rocks about a thousand feet above, looking like a natural fort or at least a breastwork.

Don Ramon's eyes were not very good, so he went to his saddle-bags and brought out a double glass, with which he examined the breastwork.

He thought he detected a movement above it, and presently was convinced that he did so, by seeing several plumed heads, moving about and evidently watching them as they lay below.

Don Ramon, usually cool and impassive, uttered a slight cry of alarm, and as he took the glass from his eye, became conscious that Pedrillo had seen him.

The *vaquero*'s face wore a decided look of alarm, and he rose up and came to the side of his master, to whom he whispered:

"Show no signs, master, or we are lost. I wish the mules were saddled."

"Who are those people above, Pedrillo?" asked the Don gravely. "Do you know?"

Pedrillo turned away his eyes.

"You have been a good master. Don't make me lie. Let us saddle and pack and be off."

Convinced that some danger existed which Pedrillo would not divulge, the Don, his nerves in a sad tremor, gave the order to catch the mules and leave the place at once, an order quickly obeyed, so far as catching the mules was concerned.

But when it came to saddling up, the case was different, for the mules did not like the idea of leaving so fine a pasture, and they began to roll and kick and behave as only mules can.

Don Ramon, from under the shelter of a tree, furtively watched the rocks above, and saw a man come out openly and signal to some one who seemed to be down in the forest behind them.

Now seriously alarmed, he hurried on the packing operation, and had almost succeeded—thanks to liberal beating—when the whole party was appalled by a tremendous yell that seemed to come from the forest all round them, and the next moment, more than a hundred men poured into the savanna, some on horseback, some afoot.

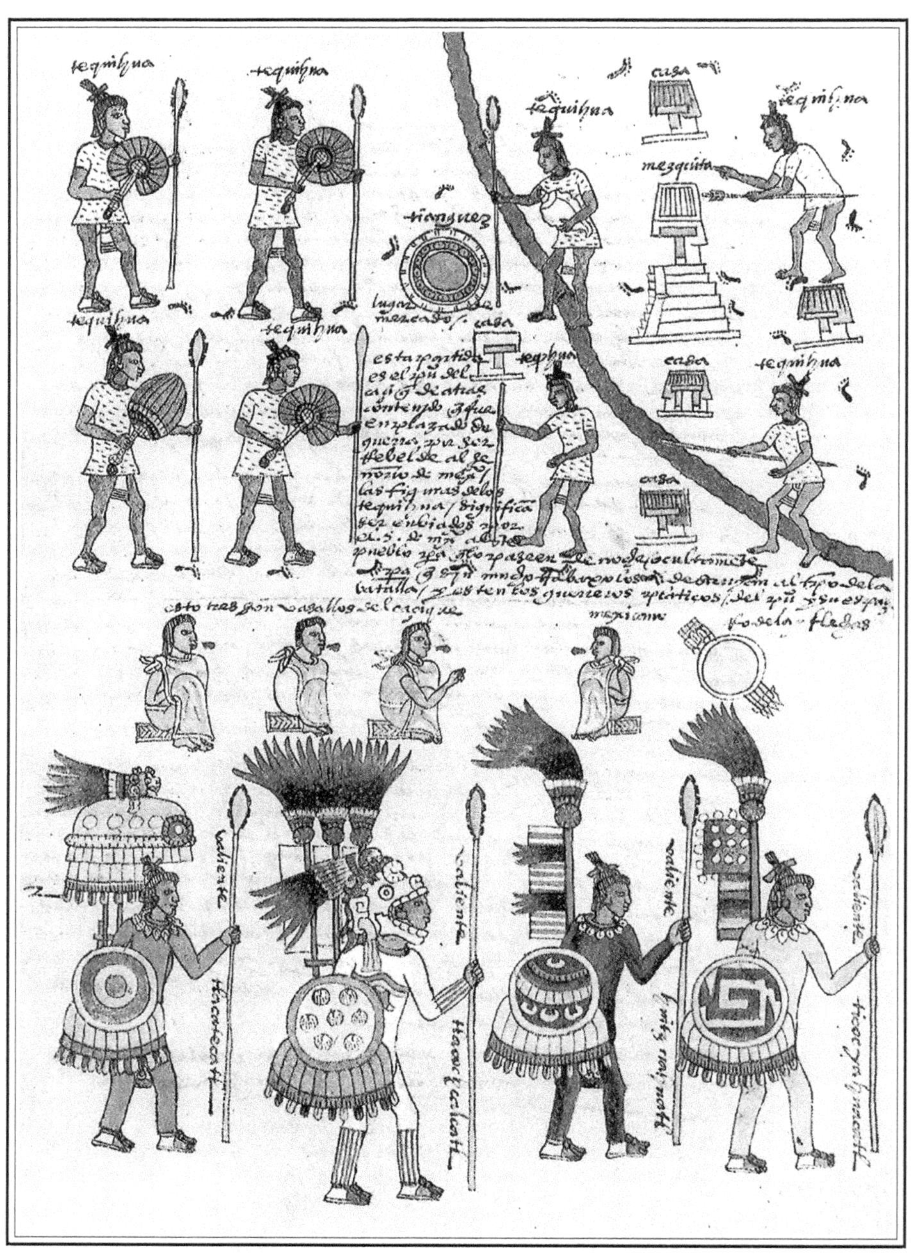

Aztec warriors. From the *Codex Mendoza*.

CHAPTER XVI.

THE CAPTURE.

THE effect produced by the appearance of these men was immediate and terrifying. The five Indians of the party instantly let fall their weapons and occupations and stood with their arms folded and heads bowed, as if awaiting death.

The two girls, who had been sleeping in the shade of a tree, sprang up, screaming, and ran to their fathers, while the men, with hands that trembled violently, shielded them in their arms and awaited their fate.

Of the oncoming men none of the party—at least the whites—had ever seen their like.

That they were Indians their dark faces told, but they were by no means the naked, squalid Indians brutalized by three centuries of slavery.

These men were all dressed in the most gorgeous raiment of featherwork and wore cotton-padded armour, while their heads were covered with wooden helmets of strange device, in imitation of the heads of jaguars, wolves or bears.

They carried copper-tipped spears. and long, wooden swords set with sharp flints, such as had not been seen since the days of the conquest of Mexico.

They came running in with frightful cries, and began to question the Indian servants in the Maya tongue, of which Don Ramon understood a little, Don Carlos, nothing.

"Who are these men, and why are they here?" asked a horseman, who rode bare-backed on a black horse, and seemed be the chief.

"They are travellers, mighty chief, going to the city of Chiapas," replied Pedrillo.

"Why are they spying on us? Do they know who we are?" pursued the chief, fiercely.

"No, mighty chief."

"What have they on those mules?"

"Nothing but merchandise, not worth taking."

"You lie, slave of the white man."

"Yes, mighty chief. As you please."

"They have gold stolen from our land. I see it in those little bags. The men of Iximaya are not blind. The gold is ours."

"Yes, mighty chief."

"You are one of our race. Why do you serve the white devils?"

"Because my father did before me."

"That is no reason. I am Quahotl, the son of a man who was a slave, but he slew his master and fled to lximaya."

Pedrillo made no answer, and the chief called out to his men:

"Drive the beasts off up the mountain. They have gold in their loads. Kill the old men where they stand, and take the girls up to the city to be offered to the Mother of the Gods. Stop!"

He turned Pedrillo.

"Are they married, these women?"

"No. They are virgins."

"Take them away then."

The strange warriors were already raising their spears to kill the two old men, when Pedrillo ventured to speak.

"Mighty chief, spare the old men and make them slaves. It is better than to kill them, and we will go with you then."

Quahotl smiled as one well pleased. He was a handsome young chief and sat on his black horse like a centaur.

"Be it so," he said. "Take them all away. Who knows. The priests may like them, even if they are too tough to be eaten."

In a moment the two old men were torn from their children, and fastened on mules, while the girls, too frightened now even to scream, were bolted away and taken to a couple of stalwart warriors who put them before them on their horses, and then set off at a rapid pace up the mountain side.

They did not seem to mind tiring out their animals, perhaps because these last were so fresh, but tore away at full speed till they gained the rocky breastwork where they rested for awhile.

Then Don Ramon saw that the place was indeed a natural fortification, but much improved internally by art.

A shelf of rock jutted out from the mountain-side, in such a way as to form a sort of parapet enclosing a space of twenty or thirty acres, and then came a sheer wall of rock full of deep cracks and crevices blackened with smoke below.

Behind that parapet from below a thousand men might have lain hidden, and the smoke of their camp-fires be all swallowed up in the bowels of the mountain.

By night any glare of fire would be equally hidden, for every blaze was evidently built deep in a cavern.

And from the parapet what a view was commanded, for a space of a good hundred miles or more to the north and west, the white towers of the Cathedral at Chiapas in plain sight, and miles of dark forest up to the blue waters of the Gulf of Mexico!

Even Don Carlos Ximenes in his miserable plight could not restrain a cry of wonder and admiration at the view, and Quahotl said to Pedrillo:

"Tell the old white thief that my ancestors once owned that country till his fathers came and robbed them of it, but that the men of the city of Iximaya will yet take it back again."

Pedrillo gave the message in Spanish and Don Carlos said, piteously:

"Please tell the gentleman, Pedrillo, that I am not a Mexican, but from Cuba. Surely he has no quarrel with me. What have I done?"

Pedrillo grinned a little sarcastically.

"You'll find that no defence with the men of the Lost City of Iximaya. They believe that the blood of white men is the sweetest of all to the gods of Iximaya. But be easy. I have saved your life for the present and who knows what may happen?"

"You don't care," groaned Ximenes. "Why don't they threaten to kill you?"

"Because I am one of them, though I am fool enough to save a Spaniard's life who gives me no thanks for it," growled the *vaquero*.

Then Don Carlos began to be afraid and to implore the peon.

"Dear Pedrillo, sweet Pedrillo, don't be angry. Get us out of this scrape and I'll make you a rich man for life."

"You'll have naught to do with it with if you get out alive," quoth Pedrillo dryly. "No white man ever escaped from Iximaya."

Then they heard the sharp tones of Quahotl calling out:

"Silence the white thief. Cut his tongue out if he says another word."

You may be sure that after that, for Pedrillo took a malicious pleasure in putting the command into Spanish, Don Carlos Ximenes kept very still.

The whole of the little plateau was strewed with huts of straw and palm leaves in regular streets, and there were signs that the place had been occupied for many years as a garrison.

Pepita Garcia, who having been brought up like most Central Americans by an Indian wet nurse, understood the Maya tongue pretty thor-

oughly, took occasion to try and ingratiate her guards by remarking on the appearance of the fortress.

"The white girl is right," said one. "It is a castle that was first found out by a woman, the great Princess Tlahoma, and we have never left it empty since. From it we can pounce on the town of Chiapas when our time comes, like a condor on a carcass."

"But why should you hurt us, who never harmed you?" asked Pepita insinuatingly.

The Indian's eyes glowed.

"Had our fathers hurt yours that they came across the sea with thunder and fire to kill them? You are their child. All is fair in war."

"But if you could help my father and me to escape," whispered Pepita, "you might be very happy, for we should love you."

In her fears of what was coming she was willing to do anything to save herself from being carried into the midst of the Indians.

Her guardian shrugged his shoulders.

"I shall be happy as it is," he said. "If I ask the chief to give me you for a wife he will do it, but you cannot go from our people. You are pretty, and if you behave well I will ask for you. It is better than to be killed for the Mother of the Gods."

Pepita shuddered. She did not fancy either horn of the dilemma, and had got all she wanted in the way of information.

Quahotl soon afterward ordered out a party of men to take the prisoners and the treasure mules away to the city, still leaving a strong guard behind.

They filed away to the end of the plateau, to where a vast cave mouth opened, the whole mountain seeming to be honey-combed with these excavations, and very soon all disappeared in the bowels of the hills, while the sentries of the Lost City resumed their lonely watch for fresh victims of the race they had learned to hate so bitterly.

Chapter XVII.

Ominous Sounds.

THE sun had sunk to the bosom of the blue, distant Pacific when the last lancer of the party of Ramirez and El Rubio Bravo led his horse out of the narrow passage in the rocks, down which fell the stream that rendered the ascent possible.

"There!" quoth the Don, as he stood on the table land and looked over toward the Mission, "the *padre* did not dream this, at least. So much is certain."

They were on a broad plateau, with a cavern-pierced wall of rock at one side, and a grand view on the other, very like the fortress of Iximaya on the other side the mountain, had they only known it.

Twenty men could have defended the passage against an army, and it would have taken a heavy bombardment of shells to have cleared the plateau of its defences, in any event.

"Now let us find the *padre*'s pool, with the tortoises," observed Ramirez. "For my part, I am no faster, and I love the taste of a stewed terrapin. Even frogs are not bad in their way, well cooked."

They led their horses on, as the old priest had directed, and found the plateau of rock, strewn with boulders fallen from the mountain above, and very rough for near two miles along.

When at last they turned the spur of the mountain he had mentioned, they came into a valley so deliciously green and beautiful that it charmed them all, and there in the midst was a most lovely little pond, about a hundred feet across, into which they saw hundreds of turtles of all sizes, scuttering from the banks in great alarm at the noise of the horsemen.

"There are the turtles, sure enough."

"Good place for a camp."

"Hurrah for roast terrapin."

The gastronomic enthusiasm of the party was evidently at fever heat, and it was not long before the horses were picketed and feeding on the succulent green grass, while the men were wading into the pond which was, as they could see, less than waist deep, hauling up the turtles by main force to shore, where they were soon cut up and roasting over the fire.

"I don't wonder Padre Miguel felt as if he had committed a sin when he'd eaten a whole turtle," said Charley Brown, reflectively, as he threw some bones into the fire. "You see, when a man sets out to mortify his appetites, it's easy enough if he sticks to cold potatoes, porridge, and all that sort of thing. But roast turtle has a way of inducing a man to overeat himself, and I feel as if I couldn't get up and fight just now if the whole army of those Lost City brutes came ramping in here."

The others laughed, but Olaf said:

"It is by no means impossible they may come, and if they do, it is as well to be prepared for their reception."

"You are my chief of staff, Robaldo is my aide, Brown my surgeon-general," returned Don Jose, smiling. "Post your pickets as you please, *señor*, for I feel so much like the doctor here that I am going to sleep."

But the swordmaster, who was of a very temperate habit, and whose caution was developed to a great extent in his character, was not content till he had examined every portion of the little valley and ascertained that it could only be entered from the front as they had come, when he arranged his camp for the defence.

He placed the men outside, next to the entrance, with their saddles in a line, close to each other, lance and carbine resting on the saddles, ready to pour a volley into any intruder.

He had already, during his short service with Ramirez, taught the men how to use the lance on foot as a pike with fearful effect, and felt that they were safe from every front attack.

Then he posted a mounted sentry on the plateau, with orders to fire and ride in, if any enemy appeared, arranged for a relief of this man at each hour of the night, and finally sought his own couch to rest, after looking well to his pistols and rifle, both of the then new Colt's revolving pattern.

How long he had slept he new not, but he was awakened, by what sounded to him, like the booming of a bass drum and distant strains of military music.

Disbelieving his senses, he sat up, rubbed his eyes and listened.

The men were snoring away in chorus, and all was deathly still in the valley, but the regular "*bom! bom! bom! bom!*" of a military band still sounded in his ears.

He looked at Ramirez.

The Spanish *rubio* was fast asleep, his handsome face as peaceful as a church.

Charley Brown was snoring away the remnants of the turtle, and no one but himself seemed to have heard anything.

Softly he rose up and listened.

The sound seemed to him to come from high overhead, and he began to feel superstitious.

Presently he heard some whispering near by, and saw the corporal of the guard with three men crouching over the embers of a fire, talking to each other.

He went up to them.

"Do you hear anything, boys?"

The corporal looked up with a pale face, and his comrades seemed equally afraid.

"*Si señor, son spiritos.*" [Yes, sir, it is spirits.]

Their superstition was evidently aroused.

Olaf smiled contemptuously.

"Spirits! Nonsense, corporal!"

"Then what is it, *señor*?" asked the man eagerly, evidently hungry for something which would relieve his terrors.

"It is a drum from the Lost City," said Olaf decidedly, "and what is more it cannot be very far off."

"But it comes from above, *señor*."

Olaf pointed to a cloud that had settled on the mountains overhead, and spread out far and wide.

"That reflects it down to us, corporal. Moreover, it will rain before morning."

"That is certain, *señor*, about the rain. But do you think that drum is really beaten by mortal hands?"

"Yes; and on the other side of this mountain not ten miles off in a straight line, though it may be a long way over or round the rocks to get there."

Corporal Martinez, pacified for the time, went to call the relief and soothe the outlying vedette's* nerves, while Olaf returned to his couch

---

* *Vedette:* A mounted sentry positioned beyond an army's outposts to observe the movements of the enemy.

and fell asleep, listening to the monotonous "*bom! bom!*" of the distant drum till it soothed him into slumber.

The rays of daylight woke up all hands, and they saddled up and rode away, after having nearly cleared the tiny pond of all but its smallest turtles, follow the level path round the spur of the range, which the young priest had trodden, in his rapt and prayerful meditation, fifty years before.

The contrast between what must have been the bearing of Padre Miguel, and their own trampling pride, struck Olaf so strongly that he said to Ramirez:

"Rather a different man at the gates of the Lost City today than fifty years ago, eh, general?"

Ramirez looked grave.

"I fear so, my friend. And we may not get off so cheaply either. He was unarmed, fasting and on foot, we mounted, armed and well-fed, but he had the good God with him to save him, while we are only soldiers of fortune, who trust to our own arms."

Olaf shrugged his shoulders.

"Heaven helps those who help themselves. Padre Miguel had to run without seeing anything except the *teocalli*. I intend to see the whole city, aye, and walk in it, if I have to storm the *teocalli* to do it. Cortez stormed a *teocalli* in Mexico. We may do it again in the Lost City. I heard the drums beat there last night."

And he told Ramirez how he had been woke up by the weird sound.

Don Jose was a well read man in the history of his own country, and at once remarked:

"Either that was for a sacrifice or for war. From what you say it must have been a very large drum, probably the great war-drum of Quetzalcoatl, covered with snake-skin, and that is never beaten save on great occasions. Of course this is only supposing there *is* a Lost City, inhabited by the same Aztecs that were found by Cortez."

"Whatever it was, it was not very far off, for I heard it distinctly," said Olaf, "I should say it was not ten, perhaps not five miles off."

"It might be that, and still three days' journey round the mountain," answered the general. "We shall see more when we turn into the next valley."

Ominous Sounds

"Seeking the Mysterious City."

Chapter XVIII.

On the Brink.

BUT the adventurers were not destined to behold anything fresh when the came to the next valley, nor the next to that, for a long time.

They passed on between steep mountains and those that sloped graduallay, under sheer precipices and above them, along a track that might be followed by wild *guanacos*[*] but was assuredly not a regular road of any sort.

They noticed, as they went along, scores of places where a dozen men could bar a passage, and where it would be wholly impossible to bring artillery to bear in any manner on the defenders.

"If the other side is as easily defended as this," observed Ramirez, "no wonder Tlahoma held her own. It is absolutely impregnable on this side,

---

* *Guanaco:* A camelid native to South America, closely related to the llama. From the Quechua word *huanaco.*

and I hope no one will offer to prevent our returning, or we shall be in a pretty bad predicament."

Olaf, too, began to feel not a little uneasy as he rode along, and now and now and then looked back at the long file of lancers winding round some sheer precipice on a road ten feet wide, with a second precipice on the other side, a thousand feet deep.

It was absolutely certain that if the men of the Lost City kept any scouts out on that side of the mountain, the whole party of the whites was lost, no matter what the difference in arms between them and their adversaries.

But for all they could see, the mountain-side was utterly deserted, save for a few condors wheeling round it, and the *guanacos* on the rocks above.

No sign of human habitation was anywhere visible.

So the day passed, afternoon came on and deepened into twilight, when they at last rode into a broad pass between the mountains, which Olaf recognized from the description as probably the place in which Padre Miguel, fifty years before, had seen the horrible procession bearing the human victim to sacrifice.

Here Olaf halted and spoke to Ramirez:

"General, the *padre*'s story so far seems to be confirmed; but you will remember that he was surprised by a number of people coming *in his rear*, from this very pass. If so, there must be some rear passage here, and we need it, to cover our retreat."

"Very true, my friend. What do you suggest?" was the immediate reply of Ramirez.

"A reconnaissance from this point, while we can still retreat."

"Aha! my Norse friend, you have more caution than I, after all, if you are a master of the sword."

"It is because I am master of the sword that I am cautious, general. Let the men stop here, while you and I go forward."

"With all my heart."

The two friends rode slowly up the path. They were armed to the teeth; for Olaf, to oblige Ramirez, had taken to himself a lance, the present of his friend, and carried it, besides his rifle and revolvers.

The pass was several miles long, and in places expanded into broad valleys, while in others it sank to the dimensions of a canyon with perpendicular walls. No passages opened on either side, so they rode on, secure from having their retreat cut off.

At last Olaf stopped.

"What is the matter?" asked Ramirez.

"Listen," was the reply.

They listened in silence. The Dane's horse flung up its head, and the rider checked him sharply, saying:

"Be still, fool."

"What do you hear?" asked Ramirez.

"I hear the sound of horses. At least I did, a moment since," was the reply.

"Do you hear it now?"

"No, it has ceased."

"Was it not imagination?"

"No. It was the neigh of a horse, deep and hollow, as if in a stable. My own horse heard it, and pricked his ears."

"But he did not answer it."

"No, because I checked him."

Ramirez looked a little dubious.

"Let us go on, colonel. I heard nothing, and I have sharp ears."

Where they were, the pass was quite broad and heavily clothed with trees; but a little beyond, it narrowed again into a canyon.

The Dane laid his hand on his companion's arm, and said earnestly:

"Will you grant me a favour? Let us ride slowly toward that canyon, keeping in the shade of the trees."

"Certainly, my friend."

They rode in under some trees, and Don Jose proceeded:

"Some thing seems to be on your mind. Tell me what it is. You, usually so reckless, seem to be growing timid."

"I am."

"And why?"

"Listen. Either Padre Miguel saw the Lost City or he dreamed it."

"Certainly."

"But, so far, he seems to have dreamed of nothing that did not actually occur. It is fifty years since he was here, yet we are able to recognize all the localities through which he passed from his description."

"Granted."

"And if he dreamed nothing else, he did not dream of the end at all. Secondly, we have an independent proof that the Lost City is not far off. We heard the war-drum last night reflected from the clouds which clung to the mountain-side."

"I see all that."

"And in that case we are in grave peril from an overpowering multitude of the most cruel and implacable savages, who have us in a position from which escape will be difficult."

"I don't see that, Don Olavo. We can go back the way we came; for we know there is no one behind us."

"Exactly. But if we enter that canyon, we shall not know it."

"Why?"

"Plain enough. It is clear that there, or beyond it, is a passage leading to the other side of the mountain. We dare not pass that passage without exploring it."

Ramirez looked thoughtful.

"You are right. To neglect that would be a military blunder. We will do it."

They rode forward now very cautiously, keeping the shadows of the trees upon them, and presently came to where the walls of the canyon began.

"Now we can see and be seen. Forward at a fast walk, and keep your lance ready," said Ramirez, briskly.

So they entered the canyon.

It turned off sharply to the left after some fifty yards, and ran on straight as a dart, widening every moment, till it ended in what seemed a colossal picture frame.

In the centre of this frame they saw a bare gray mountain, with mists curling around its tops and sides, evidently at the other flank of a deep valley which they could not see, for the floor of the canyon ended abruptly, cutting across the view like a knife.

But what they *could* see was a single tall palm tree, that must have grown on an eminence in the valley, nearly as high as the pass on which they stood. Only the upper half of this tree was visible.

Involuntarily both hatted and listened.

"There!" cried the Dane suddenly. "*Now* do you believe?"

Ramirez bowed his head.

He also had heard the faint, distant, but unmistakable crow of a cock.

"We are near the Lost City," he said gravely; "but where is the other passage?"

Olaf pointed down the pass, not a hundred feet from them, where a slight projection of the wall could be seen.

"It must be behind that shoulder, general."

The general moved his horse forward.

"Let us explore it," he said.

They came up and rode round the little projection, when, to their wonder and alarm, they beheld, not only a branch canyon at right angles to their own, ending in a lofty natural tunnel, but saw in the midst of it a crowd of people coming toward them.

They instantly drew back; but the question remained: had they been seen?

They could not be certain; but of one thing they were convinced, that it was not safe to remain where they were.

Back they rode to the angle of the canyon, hid themselves behind it, and then Olaf dismounted, stuck his lance into the sand, hurriedly tied his horse to it, and said with compressed lips:

"I will defend the pass till you bring back the men, general. My rifle and pistols are sufficient."

Ramirez frowned.

"For what do you take me? I am no run-away. If you are in danger, it is my place to share it. But I prefer the lance, after all."

The Dane shrugged his shoulders.

"Two men cannot hold this place. We must have help. One *must* go back."

"Neither need do it," returned Ramirez, a little sullenly. "To tell the truth, I ordered Robaldo to follow us at the interval of a mile. As soon as he hears shots, he will hurry up."

The Dane looked immensely relieved.

"You are a better soldier than I. Be it so. But at least get off your horse and try a little shooting with me."

"I have no objection to that," was the reply.

Just as the Mexican general joined Olaf, they saw several horsemen ride into the pass, with their backs to them.

Chapter XIX.

The Rout.

"THEY have not seen us," whispered Don Jose to his companion. Olaf nodded and they watched, crouching behind pillars of the black basalt of which the canyon was composed.

The new comers were mounted on small, beautifully shaped horses, and sat in high peaked saddles of the old Spanish style, with heavy stirrups of metal.

"The same saddles Cortez used," muttered Ramirez. "They have copied everything like children. And their dress. See, it is the very same Bernal Diaz describes.* The wooden casques, the armour of cotton and featherwork. What would not some of our antiquaries give to see them!"

---

* *Bernal Díaz del Castillo* (1496–1584): a Spanish soldier and conquistador who took part in the conquest of Mexico under Hernán Cortés. He later wrote an account of these events in his classic 1576 memoir, *Historia verdadera de la conquista de la Nueva España.*

The horsemen they saw carried long lances of cane, with bright copper points, and rode along at an easy amble toward the distant palm-tree.

Olaf found himself trembling with excitement. He was at last on the threshold of the Lost City, and its inhabitants were actually under his very eyes.

Presently out came more horsemen, then a few warriors on foot, and finally came a regular body of spearmen, in uniform dresses of padded white cotton, marching in unison, as if they had been well drilled.

"They have learned that too," whispered Don Jose. "Those fellows are no fools."

As he spoke he heard the clank of weapons in the valley behind him, with the distant neigh of horses.

"Go back," he whispered to Olaf. "It is Robaldo. He will ruin all."

The Dane, full of anxiety, ran back to the edge of the valley and waved his hands frantically to Robaldo to halt.

The Mexican obeyed, and Olaf came hack, satisfied that his support was within few hundred yards.

When he rejoined Ramirez the last of the spearmen were still coming out, and they heard the sound of singing, with the deep "*bom! bom!*" of a drum, from the valley of the palm tree.

The leading horsemen were already going down into it.

The spearmen were in a solid body, marching away down the pass, and they began to think the procession was over, when another group of horsemen came out, closely followed by a string of laden mules, conducted by Indians on foot.

Ramirez uttered a low ejaculation.

"Prisoners! I'm sure of it. Probably white people are coming. It is good for us to be here! *Santa Maria!* We may be able to make a rescue. Call up Robaldo."

Olaf stole away, mounted his horse, and rode off to summon Robaldo, who came up at a walk, his men nervous and excited.

It was indeed a strange position to be in.

They found Ramirez mounted and sitting on his horse in plain view, had any one in the Indian column turned round to look.

He had his lance ready for instant use, and his handsome face was very stern.

The Dane came up beside him and saw a sight he never forgot.

Two old white men, stripped, and bound wrist to wrist, but bedecked with long garlands of flowers, were led in the midst of a procession of Indians, who had the ends of other garlands in their hands, and were dancing and singing as they went.

The Dane understood nothing of the words of the song, but he guessed the truth.

The bound men were victims going to the altar; the song a hymn to the gods.

But the procession was not over yet.

Presently came another little gap; then a mule's head came out, and then, Olaf uttered a deep Danish malediction in his excitement at what he saw.

Carmelita Ximenes and Pepita Garcia, scantily clad in short tunics of feather-work, crowned with flowers and bedecked with garlands, were being led along on foot by two old Indians in long black robes, riding on mules.

Their black hair was floating down behind them, their heads were bowed with shame as they walked, but he knew them in a moment.

So did Charley Brown, who was close behind them, and in a moment the hot-headed young Briton had whipped out his two long navy revolvers, and was crying out:

"Forward, for Heaven's sake, and cut those red devils to pieces!"

It was difficult to say how the wild scene of confusion that followed originated.

The three *rubios*, headed by Olaf, went off at a tearing gallop down the pass, with shouts of rage, Charley Brown firing off his revolvers; and in a moment the whole Indian escort, seized with a panic, let go their prisoners, and fled down the pass, after the backs of the spearmen.

Then Olaf turned his horse, swept up to Carmelita, and called to her:

"Up! up! There is no time to lose!"

The girl understood him in a moment, caught his hand, and, setting her foot on his in the stirrup, climbed upon the horse, while big Charley Brown took up Pepita behind him almost at the same moment.

The lancers were spearing and shooting the Indian fugitives with as much zest as had the Spaniards some centuries before, and the whole pass was full of noise and confusion, when Olaf shouted to Ramirez:

"We must get back. This will not last."

Ramirez nodded.

In fact, he saw the tops of a forest of spears at the end of the pass, and saw that his own men were beginning to come back, as if they were getting frightened.

They looked down the narrow passage whence the Indian army had come, and saw that it was empty, but still hesitated to enter it.

Suddenly came the loud blast of a trumpet high over their heads, and a great rock, weighing over a thousand pounds, fell from the top of the canyon and crushed Captain Robaldo, horse and all, into a bloody mass.

Ramirez glanced up, and saw the top of the canyon lined with plumed heads.

"Into the caverns. It is our only chance," he shouted, and rode away down the narrow canyon, still unexplored, which ended in the tall arch of a cavern.

Before they could gain this shelter, a regular shower of rocks came down, and three more of the lancers were crushed to death, while the Indian spearmen at the end of the pass, raised a hideous yell and came rushing after them.

Then ensued a wild and strange running contest, in which the elements of darkness and uncertainty were added to the perils of armed enemies.

Compelled to proceed slowly, with only the knowledge that horsemen had been there before them, they rode on through winding caverns, not knowing at what moment they might come on some impassable abyss.

Luckily for them, the caverns of the hill were not totally dark, and occasionally took the form of narrow canyons, while the floor was uniformly smooth, and they could see that they were on a regularly used track of some sort.

But although their passage might have been easy enough alone, it was by no means so when they were followed and harassed by an active and vindictive enemy.

The first panic over among the followers of the procession, the regular force of spearmen came running back, and made fierce and persistent attacks on the rear of the body of Mexican lancers.

In vain did the horsemen try to drive off their foes by volleys of carbine shots; these men did not seem to fear gun-powder.

Before they cleared the caverns they had lost more than half their numbers, and the two old men, Don Ramon and Don Carlos, had been recovered from their grasp and carried away.

When they at last rode out of the cave on to the great plateau which hung like an eagle's nest over the plains of Chiapas, it was in a wild, confused mob of horse men, and to confront a steady, determined looking body of men, who stood waiting to receive them.

No undisciplined Indians were these, but a body of spearmen, ranged in just such a phalanx, as they had learned from their Spanish foes three centuries before.

The men of Iximaya, in their lonely retreat, had not changed in all those years.

Coming out as did the Mexican horsemen in confusion, their ammunition nigh spent, the sight of this new body of foes, and the cries of the men behind them, completed their demoralization.

They scattered and rode hither and thither in a mob, and the spearmen made a wild charge, butchering them almost without resistance.

Olaf, who had retained his pistols to the last, saw that all was over when Ramirez went down, struck by a stone from a sling, and he dashed away to the edge of the plateau, still carrying the girl behind him, shot down an Indian who tried to intercept him, and the next moment was flying down the steep hill into the plain below, followed by showers of stones.

How he got to the bottom, or what was the next thing that happened, passed like a dream over his mind.

When he came to his full senses, he was riding at a slow amble over an open savanna, his horse white with foam; but he was safe from pursuit, and the arms of Carmelita were round him.

The Rout

Chapter XX.

The Dead Jarocho.

The swordmaster was recalled to himself by a faint sigh from Carmelita, more like a sob; and he pulled up his horse abruptly. He saw that the girl's face was deadly pale, and a little stream of blood had trickled down from under her black hair, over her temple and into her neck.

"Did anything strike you?" he asked anxiously.

"A stone," she murmured. "I did not feel it at first; but now, how my head hurts!"

He looked back over the savanna and at the mountain-side.

No sign was to be seen of pursuers; but a single horseman was coming slowly out of the forest, half a mile off.

He took out his field-glass and uttered an exclamation of grief.

"It is poor Charley, and he is hit."

Carmelita clung to him and hid her face.

"Take me away. Let no one see me!" she murmured. "They took away my clothes, and only left me this."

But Olaf kept on looking.

"Pepita is with him."

Carmelita, uttered a cry of joy.

"Pepita! Thank Heaven; I am not alone!"

They closely watched the approaching horseman, and, as he came nearer, saw that it was indeed the young Englishman, drooping over his saddle bow, with Pepita behind him.

The girl seemed to be unhurt; for she was half supporting him and guiding the horse as it came on.

When they at last came up, it was evident that Brown had been wounded and was sick and dizzy. His head was bound up with a handkerchief, and his left arm was all dripping with blood, though it was tightly bandaged at the elbow.

Charley smiled faintly.

"We shall never see—the Lost City, old fellow," he muttered in English. "They've routed us—horse—foot and—dragoons."

"What hit your head?" asked Olaf.

"A stone—that's nothing—but my arm—one of the devils ran it through—missed my body—it'll be all right if—we can find a—house."

Olaf looked round in despair.

"There are no houses for miles. Not till we get to Chiapas. What shall we do?"

"Go into camp—next best thing—getting late—sundown soon. Trees and water—never mind grub."

The wounded man spoke faintly; but he evidently retained his senses.

Olaf took his horse by the bridle and led him on some distance, till they came to a grove of palms.

To their great joy a patch of bananas was near the palms, sure evidence of some effort at cultivation not long before.

They found a spring in the grove and made a little camp for the night, the girls, with instinctive modesty, keeping, a long way off from the men, Olaf attending to his comrade.

Bananas were plentiful and ripe, and bananas are the mainstay of the tropics; so that Charley was soon made quite comfortable and fell asleep.

Then Olaf went roaming round the grove to find the owner if possible, and was soon rewarded by coming on a small *jacal* or hut, covered with palm leaves.

But the *jacal* was deserted and silent, not a living creature within.

He struck a match to examine it and started back with a cry of horror.

In the middle of the floor lay a man's body, the throat freshly cut, while the absence of any offensive odour showed that the murder had been recent. The sight impressed him so much that he ran out and did not dare to go back for some time, till he had mastered his nerves. Then he lighted a dry stick for a torch, went in, and examined the hut closely.

It was an ordinary *jacal*, without any furniture but a low table and a few stools, with a rude pottery lamp in a corner, full of oil, with a floating wick. This he lighted, and they took another look at the dead body.

It was that of an ordinary *jarocho*[*] or peasant, dressed in a waist cloth as if at work when he was killed and otherwise naked.

On pegs in the wall, his Sunday dress of velvet, jacket and *calzoneros* or loose trousers, buttoned up the outside with silver buttons.

It was evident the man had not been robbed as well as murdered.

---

* "The name of *Jarochos* is given to those peasants who live on the sea-board round Vera Cruz. Their costume bears no resemblance whatever to that of the people around them. The inhabitants of Andalusia wear a dress very similar to theirs; and it is the general opinion, from their manners and character, that they are the descendants of the *Gitanos* of that Spanish province. Their dialect is like their attire, strange and singular. It abounds in words of the purest Castilian, interspersed with local terms disfigured by a vicious pronunciation, and cannot be understood, even by those who know Spanish, without diligent and careful study...the *machete* plays no unimportant part in all their difficulties. (continued)

How he came by this end was a mystery; but one which Olaf did not try to solve. All that he thought of was that he had found a dress for one of the girls, if she did not mind wearing male attire.

He took the poor fellow's Sunday clothes and went out into the grove, where he called:

"Carmelita! Come here! I have found clothes."

He was answered by a timid voice.

"Go away then, and leave them where we can find them."

"Here they are, then," he said; and he hung them on a banana bush, and went back to his comrade.

Ten minutes later he was startled by a little Mexican boy, in clothes a size too large for him, who swaggered up to him in the moonlight, with a saucy air that made him laugh, as he recognized Pepita.

But the girl was not in a laughing humour, though she could not help that self-conscious hectoring air, woman are apt to assume when they put on male attire.

"You must find something for Carmelita," she said, "and while you go I will take care of poor Carlos."

Much relieved to have got one girl out of an embarrassing scrape, and realizing that, the two would keep together as long as Charley was asleep, the Dane set off on another pilgrimage to the hut, which revealed nothing more. There was no other body there, though the poor *jarocho* seemed to have had a wife; for there were traces of woman's attire in the little hut, in the shape of an Indian blanket.

(cont'd) The *Jarocho* would rather want the most indispensable part of his dress than be deprived of the long sharp glittering blade which he wears in his belt. This sabre is more generally in the hand of the *Jarocho* than at his side. A small point of honour, or the most futile remark has often been the means of bringing on the most bloody and long-continued series of combats...They are strong and muscular; and nature has thrown round their persons an air of elegance in exact harmony with the devotion the Jarocho pays to three things: his horse, his sword, and his mistress." Gabriel Ferry, *Vagabond Life in Mexico*, 397-98.

After satisfying himself on this point, he blew out the lamp and was going out, when he heard the low murmur of voices somewhere near and stood still

"If I go out," he thought, "they will see I have been inside. If I stay they may come to see who it is."

Very softly he crept under the table, which stood in a corner, and waited. Presently came footsteps, and a man and woman entered the hut.

G. Doré
Tournier, sc.

Chapter XXI.

The Jacal.

THE man who entered was a dark-whiskered, half-breed ruffian, in the dress of a common peon, but the woman evidently belonged to the same class as the dead *Jarocho*; for she wore a silk petticoat, a handsome *reboso* or shawl, and black satin slippers—on feet guiltless of stockings, but very pretty and well shaped.

She had a dark Gypsy face, with laughing black eyes and abundant hair.

She seemed afraid as she came in and said:

"For the love of Heaven, Maso, don't take them. There will be a curse on them. *He* wore them last."

"I'll take the risk of that, Juanna," retorted the half-breed, with a coarse laugh. "You didn't want to come in when you saw the candle lighted, for fear his spirit had done it; but if I didn't fear him alive, I don't dead."

As he spoke he gave the body a contemptuous kick, and the woman uttered a slight cry:

"Don't do that, Maso. Remember, he was my husband this morning."

Maso uttered a foul Mexican epithet.

"He was a coward. See how easily I killed him. Where are the clothes, Juanna?"

"They *were* there," she faltered, turning away her head and pointing.

He uttered another oath.

"They're not there. You good-for nothing! If you have hidden them, I'll kill you, too."

The Dane listened and understood. It was evident that the poor *jarocho* had been murdered by his wife's lover, but what had prevented the murderer from taking the clothes before, was yet quite a mystery.

Juanna began to cry.

"Cruel Maso! When I have given up my soul for your sake, to quarrel over a few clothes! I saw them hanging there at the very moment you ran away, when the *vaqueros* came by. Very likely they came in and stole them."

Maso turned on her savagely.

"You lie, you she-devil! You've hidden them. Tell me where they are, or—"

A long knife gleamed in his hand as he spoke, and the woman started back to the door with a shriek.

In the same moment Olaf jumped up, and sent table, lamp and all, flying at Maso's head, causing the peon to utter a yell of terror and dash out, knocking down his partner in guilt.

The swordmaster followed, and saw him running like a deer across the fields, while the woman dropped senseless by the door in her terror.

The Dane laughed scornfully as he looked at the flying half-breed.

"What a people are these Mexicans! He was not afraid of a ghost, forsooth! Then it was not fear made him run. Well, if this is what I find at the first step on Mexican soil, it must be a lively country. Here is a suit of clothes for Carmelita, if the woman was dead, but she is only in a faint. What shall I do?"

The woman began to stir, and he went into the hut. An idea had struck him.

She sat up confusedly and looked round, murmuring to herself:

"*Ay de mi!* I have lost my soul. What shall I do to escape hell? The *padre* told me that all murderers were burned for ever."

Olaf spoke solemnly from the hut:

"Juanna!"

She started up with a shriek.

"It is *his* voice, *his* spirit. Oh! Save me!"

She sank on her knees, praying fervently.

"Juanna!" he called again.

"Spare me, spare me," she wailed. "I will do penance all my life, if you will only not haunt me."

"Juanna," he repeated, "Listen and obey."

"I will, I will," faltered the grossly superstitious woman, trembling. "I will do *anything*."

"Take off those fine clothes that you wear, the wages of sin, and put on only your working clothes. Never again should *you* wear finery. Your life is to be given to prayer and penance."

"I will do it all," she sobbed, and Olaf heard her, somewhat to his dismay, tearing off her clothes.

Then she dashed into the hut into a corner, snatched up something, and he saw her come out into the moonlight in the simple blanket and loin-cloth of an Indian woman.

"Now go to Maso," pursued Olaf, "and if he kills you, it will serve you right. I will wait for you in the better land. Go."

The woman slunk away, wringing her hands and moaning, and as soon as she was out of sight, Olaf came out, picked up her simple dress, and carried it away to the girls in triumph.

As he approached them he saw the slim figure of Carmelita slip away into the bushes, but the Mexican boy held his ground bravely, and graciously observed, as Olaf handed him the petticoat and *reboso:*

"You were meant for a soldier, colonel, you are such a good forager."

A few minutes later the whole party was reunited, and Carmelita, looking as pretty as a picture in the graceful dress of the *jarocho*, crept to her lover's side and whispered to him:

"A thousand thanks! Now I feel a lady once more; not a *creature*."

Olaf smiled and wondered to himself how both girls would have felt, if they knew the true history of their garments.

However, he left them to their blissful ignorance and went to the *jacal* once more, where he piled cornstacks and dry palm leaves over the body from the stores around the hut, pulled the frail tenement down into a heap on the dead man, and made everything ready to fire the pile in the morning. After that he went to sleep by his wounded friend, Charley.

MEXICAN GENTLEMEN

Chapter XXII.

The Gomez Brothers.

THE city of Chiapas†, like most Mexican towns of any size, boasts a cathedral and a plaza. Of course a cathedral implies a bishop, and bishops are plentiful in Mexico, with quite a sprinkling of archbishops, and all the other paraphernalia, of an orderly and well regulated hierarchy.

The town of Chiapas is further celebrated for its chocolate, of which the ladies are so fond that they drink it in church, and poisoned the only bishop who ever dared protest against this secular anomaly in divine service.

At least that is the legend, which has given rise to a Mexican proverb about "Chiapas chocolate."

---

† Chiapas is a province, not a city. Given various references and descriptions in the novel, Monstery is probably basing this city on Comitán (in Chiapas, near the Guatemala border), or on Chiapas's capital, Tuxtla Gutiérrez.

But Chiapas, for all its cathedral and chocolate and bishop, has a bad reputation for another thing, *pronunciamentos*[*] and revolutions, which it gets up on the smallest occasion, without reference to the central authority at the city of Mexico.

Mexico, being a confederacy of States, like the United States, *has* a central authority, but it is very seldom powerful enough to assert itself, and the different States of the confederacy have a fashion, of getting up independant revolutions on their own responsibility.

The latest *pronunciamentos* at Chiapas had been issued by Don Baldassare Ortega[†], who held the whole State, and had very strong desires to be President of Mexico itself.

Don Baldassare had no trouble to raise an army, for Mexico is always full of soldiers of fortune. He was at almost as little trouble to maintain it, for Mexico is a rich country, and has stood the exactions of three centuries of robbers without collapsing.

Don Baldassare's method of raising troops was to issue a *pronunciamento* or proclamation, calling all gallant gentlemen to his standard. After he got them there, he ordered forced loans from the towns, so much from each, and paid his troops with the proceeds.

And besides this, which was but enough to pay for horse feed and cigars, it was well understood that the officers were allowed to have *"onglas libres"*—nails free.

Inside the town, forced loans, outside, the genial presence of the too sociable bandit, who asks for purses with a bow, and kills the unwilling with a smile. Altogether a pleasant state, Chiapas; a pleasant land that of Mexico, and a great contrast to the wilder Central American republics, where the people are too fond of fighting to have much left to steal.

---

* *Pronunciamiento:* A form of military rebellion, or *coup d'état,* particularly associated with Spain, Portugal and Spanish America during the nineteenth century.

† Undoubtedly based on Monstery's nemesis in Mexico, Jesús González Ortega (1822-1881). See page liv-lvii of the Introduction.

Mexico being richer, the people are too fond of stealing to fight, except in a sort of half-hearted manner, as they did at Buena Vista and such battles.

The town of Chiapas, like most others in Mexico, has its walls and fortifications and it was from the southern gate of these that a party of six gentlemen, on very handsome horses, rode out, the evening after the destruction of Ramirez and his little band by the men of the Lost City.

They were all gentlemen, in the Mexican sense; that is, they wore handsome purple *mangas* or mantles, instead of the ordinary *serape*[*], and each man had about a thousand dollars worth of silver buttons on his jacket and trousers. They were all dressed very much alike, with broad white hats girt with silver cords an inch thick, with tassels half a foot long.

Under these broad white hats, their swarthy faces and long black hair looked doubly dark, and their figures were set off by the black velvet jackets and *calzoneros*[‡], both slashed with red or yellow silk, and loaded with silver buttons.

Each man had a voluminous silk sash of red or yellow, and a long straight sabre swung at his side, though they did not seem to be provided with firearms.

They were all stalwart, handsome men, very well mounted; and the same extravagance of silver, in the form of studs, was shown in their saddles and on the head-pieces of their bridles.

It is hardly necessary to say that they all rode well; for in Mexico that is second nature to a people that have no roads to speak of, but spend half their time in the saddle.

As they rode out, one of the gate loungers said to another:

"It's easy to see where the Gomez brothers are going to-night."

"Hush," said his comrade; "they will hear you."

---

* *Serape:* a long blanket-like shawl, often brightly colored and fringed at the ends, and worn as a cloak in Mexico, especially by men.

‡ *Calzoneros*: (Southwest). Trousers buttoned at the sides and usually slit at the bottom.

"Not they," retorted his friend—lowering his voice however—"the horses make too much clatter for us to be heard."

They watched the six horsemen till they were lost in the dust of the plain.

"Our Lady help any travellers who are coming into Chiapas from the south to-night," remarked the first lounger. "They will come in pretty light, if they come in at all."

His friend laughed.

"Serve them right. They should stay at home."

From the conversation of these gentlemen it was clear that the Gomez brothers, while to all appearance rich *haciendados*[†] were in reality professional brigands, and this was actually the case.

The fact that they could practice such a profession so openly, speaks volumes for the state of society in the Mexican republic.

Meantime the six rode along at a canter, and the youngest brother at last observed:

"I am rather tired of this humdrum life, Jose Jesus. Here we have come out three nights running and never taken a purse."

"What would you have, Jose Maria?" the next man retorted. "One cannot have luck all the time, can they?"

"For my part," interposed the third, "I am of Jose Maria's opinion. I am tired of Chiapas, and propose we shall go out into Guatemala again. It's a long time since we've heard from brother Pepe and our cousin Bragamonte, and I want to see them."

"Hear Domingo talk!" laughed the fourth. "One would think he was afraid some disaster had happened to Pepe or Tolomeo."

"And so I am, Martino," answered Domingo, seriously. "We have never before been so long without news from either. I leave it to Pedrillo if he does not agree with me."

"I certainly do," replied Pedrillo. "Ask Gil what he thinks."

† *Haciendado:* Owner of a *hacienda*. In the colonies of the Spanish Empire, a *hacienda* is an estate, similar in form to a Roman villa.

Gil Gomez was the oldest of the brothers, a grave, square-built man, rather shorter than the rest, but heavier than any. They were all strikingly alike in face and dressed their hair and beards exactly alike.

"I am of the opinion," he said, "that if we do not have some great stroke of luck to-night, we should take our mules in the morning and start for Guatemala to see our cousin Bragamonte, and find out what is the reason he or Pepe does not come or write."

"Agreed," cried Jose Maria, gaily. "And if we have luck to-night it will put us in spirits for our journey. I vote we go anyhow."

As he spoke they neared a clump of tall organ cactus, around the foot of which the broad leaves of the *maguey** made a shelter fit to conceal man and horse.

Beyond them spread on all sides a brown dusty plain, the grass withered, only the broad, fleshy leaves of the cactuses flourishing.

Here they dismounted and Gil said:

"Let us wait till the moon rises. If nothing comes to-night, nothing will come that is worth taking hereafter. Jose Ramirez has gone that way, and he leaves bare bones behind him."

They settled themselves to watch for prey like wild beasts that they were.

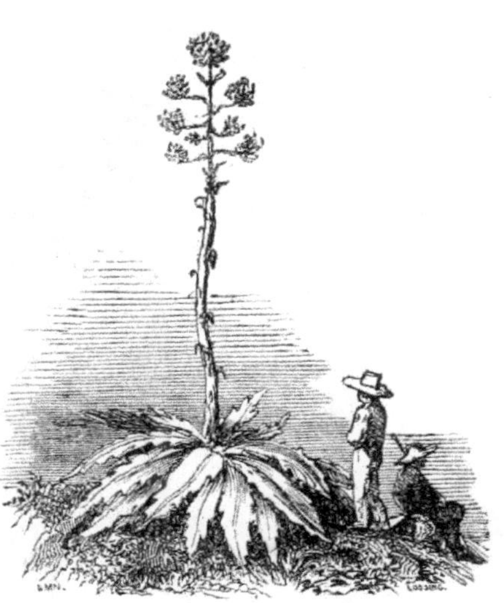

AGAVE AMERICANA.

* *Maguey:* Also known as the *agave* plant, a succulent with long, sturdy leaves bordered with sharp spines, and used to make a variety of products including *tequila*, *mezcal*, rope, clothing, roofing, and fuel.

Chapter XXIII.

The Bandits.

THE clump of cactus in which the Gomez brothers lay, was one characteristic of the republic of Mexico in the *terra caliente*, or hot belt.

In sand and dryness such as prevails there, only the cactus will grow, and without it the people would be badly off.

There are hundreds of varieties of cactus in Mexico, but the most universal and striking in appearance to the stranger, are the organ cactus and *maguey*.

The organ cactus rises in spires like the pipes of an organ, and sometimes borders the road for miles as hedges, interspersed with shorter spreading varieties.

The *maguey* has many virtues. In its centre rises a shoot, which flowers once in seven years, if allowed to.

But the people do not generally allow it to flower. Instead, they cut out the shoot and scoop a hollow, from which every day they get a pailful of juice.

And this juice, fermented, under the name of *pulque*, is the national drink of all Mexico, the substitute for lager beer, which everybody drinks.

Out of the leaves of the *maguey* they make matting, cordage, paper, and cover their houses with them; in fact Mexico would be nothing without the *maguey*.

To the Gomez brothers it had the further merit, in conjunction with the organ cactus, of hiding their horses from view while they watched the open plain.

Presently the moon rose, very near the full, and they saw a couple of moving spots, far away on the plain.

"Travellers at last!" quoth Jose Jesus Gomez, with a tone of great joy. "Only two. Who'll go out and stop them? It's not worth while for all of us to get up."

"One can never be too cautious," quoth Gil Gomez sententiously. "Let three, at least, go. They may have guns."

It was finally arranged that Jose Jesus, Jose Maria and Domingo should go, and they mounted their horses and sallied out on the plain, riding leisurely toward the two dark specks approaching so slowly.

As they rode on, the moon got higher, and the light plainer.

The dark specks were about five miles off, when they first saw them, and they resolved, as they came closer, into two horsemen.

But when they got still closer, Jose Jesus suddenly cried out:

"They're riding double, Domingo, and one has a girl behind him."

This soon became plain as the strangers came closer still.

One of them had a woman riding behind him, the other a boy in Mexican dress.

"Lassos, *hermanos*," said Domingo, as soon as they ascertained this fact.

The others understood him.

Hitherto they had been walking their horses slowly along, as had had the strangers; but now they put them to speed and rode down on the travellers, taking, the lassoes in their hands as they went.

There was no longer any disguise of their purpose, nor did they care to longer deceive the new-comers.

But just as they were almost within throwing distance, came a couple of flashes from the strangers, who had halted in silence, and down went Domingo's horse, head over heels, all in a heap, his rider leaping off in a manner that showed his consummate horsemanship, while Jose Jesus uttered a yell:

"Jesu Maria! Carajo!"

In another moment he fell off his horse which stopped dead short, while Jose Maria wheeled and galloped away as hard could go.

The three bandits had caught more than they bargained for.

As for Domingo, now unhorsed by the death of his animal, he ran for his brother's horse, and would have seized it when another flash came from one of the travellers who called out warningly:

"Cuidado! Anda!" [Take care! Go away!]

The bullet went through Domingo's hat and grazed his head with such force as to drop him to the earth senseless, when the traveller who had fired observed in English:

"We've made one horse, Charley. Drop Pepita and let her go up to the beast. He might scare at our double loads."

The Mexican boy—nothing less than Pepita Garcia, jumped off from behind Charley Brown and cautiously approached the black horse that stood mutely by its dead master. She would not have been a Spanish-American born and bred, had she not known how to ride like man, and it was no trouble to her to climb into the saddle.

Once there she cried:

"He is a beauty, but the stirrups are too long, and I have no spurs."

Olaf dismounted, took the spurs from the body of the dead robber and put them on her feet, after which he shortened the stirrups for her and asked:

"Could you take care of yourself now if they followed you?"

"I could run at least," said the girl, "and what's more, I can throw a lasso too."

Olaf nodded.

"You'll do. The lasso is better than a sword if well handled."

He returned to Charley Brown who had his left arm in a sling, and said to him:

"We are not through our troubles yet."

"Why not?" asked Charley dolefully.

"I swear I'm in no condition to do much more fighting to-night."

"You can shoot as well as ever, can't you?"

"Yes, but—"

"That's all I want you to do."

"Then load up my pistol for me. I can't do it, and I lost two charges."

Olaf took the long navy Colt, Charley's favourite, and loaded it before he returned it.

In the meantime Pepita was caracoling on her new horse in the vicinity, very much elated at their luck.

Suddenly she cried out:

"Take care. Here are four men coming at full speed, and the fifth is not dead. He is stirring again. Ah!"

She had been not far from the fallen figure of Domingo, aid as she uttered the last shriek, the brigand, who had been only shamming death, made a tiger-like leap from the ground, and caught hold of one of her stirrups.

In a moment Charley Brown, forgetting all his weakness and pain, dashed after them as Pepita's horse ran away, and the next minute there was the bandit running like a deer by the horse, Pepita trying to beat him over the head with a lasso coil, and Doctor Charley closing up, swearing voluably in English, but not daring to fire for fear of hitting Pepita.

Olaf saw it; and saw the four remaining bandits coming from the clump of cactus, and in a moment realized that they were in a bad predicament that would be very difficult to get out of.

The presence of the girls was the element of embarrassment.

He knew that he could not catch them, doubly weighted as he was, and could only watch.

Presently he saw a flash, and back came Charley and Pepita, full gallop, with four men hard after them, whirling their lassos overhead.

"Only four left," he muttered. "Now for it."

The Englishman and the girl dashed by at full speed, and Olaf began to fire at the pursuers, keeping his horse still.

He emptied his revolver, quickly, but with as good an aim as he could take in the dark, and had the satisfaction of seeing the four bandits swerve off and gallop away to the cactus clump from which they had emerged, while Brown and Pepita went on at the same wild speed to the city.

"He is right," muttered the Dane. "In love every man for his own girl. But I ought to have given that horse to Carmelita."

He rode on further without molestation to the gates of Chiapas, and entered at last the famous city of cathedrals and chocolate, where the first persons he saw were the Englishman and Pepita with a crowd of idlers round them, telling their story of assault in all probability.

As soon as Charley saw them enter, he called out:

"Hello, Olaf, who do you suppose it was set on us outside?"

"How should I know, my friend?" returned the Dane, a little testily. "You took care not to stop and inquire."

"What else could I do?" remonstrated the Englishman. "I had my girl to take care of and they were almost on us, with me not able to fight. But that's neither here nor there. What I want to say is this. Those fellows were the six Gomez brothers. That's all, old boy."

CHAPTER XXIV.

CHIAPAS.

ONE great difference between Mexico and the Central American republics, is that in Guatemala, Nicaragua, Honduras and Costa Rica they do their fighting for the most part fairly, while in Mexico assassination is the rule, battle the exception.

Even the decent members of society, so called—seem to feel no wonder when they hear of murders and highway robberies. They call it a "lucky escape" if a person gets off from such attempts on his life, but take no steps to stop the practice.

Their chief topic of consolation in Chiapas to the travellers was:

"The Gomez brothers are bad ones; but they won't come back into the town after this failure."

"I am rejoiced to hear it," answered Olaf, very politely. "There is, then, some limit to the impudence of robbers, even in Mexico."

The question then arose, being in Chiapas, how they should dispose of the girls and of themselves; for there were no hotels.

"The convent of Our Lady of Guadalupe will accommodate the *señorita*," suggested one by-stander, "and you three *señores* can go to the bishop's house. He is always hospitable."

It was impossible to tell the crowd in the streets that they were mistaken in the sex of Pepita, and not advisable either, so they rode off to the convent, where they rang at the bell, asked for the abbess, and left the two girls in safety, no questions being asked.

As they turned their horses' heads toward the plaza, Charley observed thoughtfully:

"I tell you what it is, old fellow, I was brought up the strictest kind of a Protestant, with an idea that these monks and nuns were regular heathens, but by Jove we couldn't have landed two girls in such a nice place in any Protestant country in the world."

"And now I suppose, we'd better claim the bishop's hospitality," replied his friend. "Then you'll be converted for good."

Charley laughed.

"No danger of that. But seriously, what shall we do? Have you got any money left?"

"Only what was on my horse, and my diamonds."

"The same with me."

"Did you lose much in the fight yonder?"

"A mule, a lot of clothes and about ten ounces of gold."

"Then we are not so badly off as when we entered Honduras."

"I should say not. What do you propose to do? Get married at once?"

"I would, but there is one difficulty about it."

"What is that?"

"No priest would marry us."

"Why not?"

"Carmelita is under age."

"What of that? Her father's dead and so is Pepita's father. We are their only living protectors."

"I know that; but—"

"But what? We *must* get married or else leave them. It's not proper to go on in this way. The girls would both lose all their characters."

"Yes, I know, but—"

"But what, Ole?"

"Well, it seems that they both have relatives in the city of Mexico."

"Whom they never saw."

"All the same, the abbess and the priests will insist on their joining them. You see, we are *ereticos*—heretics—and they would not let two Catholic girls marry us if they could help it."

Charley Brown pursed up his lips.

"I never thought of that. Confound their popish prejudices!"

"I thought you liked them just now," remarked Olaf, dryly.

Charley could not help smiling.

"It's confounded inconvenient. Then I suppose we shall have trouble to get them away from that convent."

"Assuredly. I never dreamed otherwise."

"And yet you let them go in there."

"Certainly."

"And why?"

"Because it was my duty."

The Dane's face was grave as he said this, and Charley stared.

"Why your duty? The girls were alone, under our protection."

"For a while, but that was only because it could not be helped. We saved their lives when they had lost all their natural protectors."

"I know that, but—"

"But as soon as we came near a town, it was our duty to put them in charge of those against whom no suspicion could exist."

"But suppose we never see them again?"

"We shall see them again."

"How do you know?"

"Because the sisters will not want to keep them. They took them in for charity, but my word on it, they will question them closely, and find out whence they came and who are their friends in Mexico."

"And will they send them there?"

"Of course they will. Even nuns cannot not keep a free hotel for all comers, and these girls come of rich families. They will be sent on to Mexico, and their friends will 'come down' to the church without asking."

"And where shall we go to-night, Ole?"

"I think we might as well bivouac on the plaza with the beggars. I don't want to go to the bishop's palace, for they would put us into the pauper's cells. It's a fine night, and we can get all we want to eat in the morning."

They rode into the plaza, watered their horses at the public fountain, and then went to sleep on the cathedral steps holding the bridles of the three horses, for they still retained the animal captured from the bandits who had attacked them.

Olaf looked at him, and when he saw how fat and in what fine order the animal was, he observed:

"I've half a mind to change horses for this brute. He looks well, and has a much finer caparison than mine."

"I'd do no such thing," said Brown dryly. "Why not?"

"Because it seems to me you'd be running your head into needless danger."

"Why?" asked the Dane sharply.

"Easily told. At present the Gomez brothers don't know you, and never saw you. If you are seen on that horse with the harness on, you will be recognized by them in broad daylight, and then good-bye to you."

Olaf snapped his fingers.

"That for the Gomez crew. I have met them all now and I can beat them all. You say they never saw me. How about to-night?"

"That was a chance meeting in the dark. It would give them no clue to you."

"How are you sure they do not know me now?"

"How should they?"

"Bragamonte may have written."

"He was too much hurt."

"Possibly; at all events I never flinched from a fight yet, and I shall not do it now."

"Then you will take that horse?"

"No; now that I look at him closer he has not the loins of my own. But I'll put the saddle on, and let them come and take it if they dare. I'm sleepy. Good night."

In another moment both men were resting on the cathedral steps, wrapped in oblivion.

Chapter XXV.

Jose Maria.

At daybreak next morning our adventurers were up, and Olaf deliberately changed the equipment of the robber's horse to his own before sunrise, and then set out to find a place where they could buy forage for the animals and food for themselves.

In this there was no difficulty; for, while hotels are scarce in the outlying towns of Mexico, *posadas* and drinking shops are plentiful, while one can buy almost anything in the markets which are held in the plazas.

They fed their horses, broke their own fast and then the question arose: "what next?"

"Let us sell the horse," suggested Olaf.

They went to the horse-market, but no one would buy the animal. It was too well known, and people feared the Gomez brothers too much.

At last came up a tall, dark man with bushy black whiskers and long hair.

"What do you want for that horse?" he asked.

Olaf looked at him narrowly. He bore so strong a resemblance to Pepe Gomez that the swordmaster answered:

"It depends on your name. What is it?"

The dark man eyed him in turn with a furtive, sullen air.

"My name is nothing to you." he said. "I will give you two *onzas* for the horse."

This was twice what the animal was worth in that land of horses.

"The animal is yours," answered Olaf. "He belonged to a dastardly thief called Gomez, whom I shot last night. If you know any of his relatives, tell them *El Rubio Bravo* has pinked their brother Pepe, their cousin Bragamonte, and that he defies them and all their clan."

The dark man had turned very pale, with a blue tinge, as Olaf spoke; but he said not a word till he had paid his money and taken the horse.

Then he said in a low voice:

"You have me now; but if you dare to meet me in the plain, in one hour, with the sword, I will show you that you have not killed all our family yet."

"I will be there, *señor*," replied the Dane politely. "By the southern gate, between the gate and the cactus clump, where you hid last night."

The stranger bowed gravely.

"I shall expect you *señor*. I am Jose Maria Gomez, at your service."

He got on the horse barebacked, and rode away across the plaza, the people staring at him but no one offering to stop him.

"A strange country," mused Olaf; "but the man is no coward."

He told Brown of the arrangement made, and the doctor announced his intention of going along to see fair play.

"I'm not good for much just now in a fight with fists, but I can shoot as well as ever," he observed, "and you don't know what sort of tricks these beggars will try on you."

They went to the convent to ask after the ladies; but were refused admittance in the most ungracious manner, and Olaf said:

"I knew it would be so. Luckily Carmelita has told me the name of her uncle in Mexico, and we can see her there. Pepita is sure to be with her."

This did not much comfort Charley, who was—to use his own words —"consumedly in love,"—but there was no help for it, so they rode away to the southern gate, and as soon as they got outside, Brown exclaimed:

"There they are! Look at the beggars! Four men on horseback and a fifth sitting on the ground by the cactus clump."

"They mean to try on the trick of which the people warned us in Tegucigalpa—four on one. The fifth must be the one you shot, Charley. Didn't you hit him badly?"

"No, confound him; the horses were going and he was going. I aimed for his body, but think I only grazed him. It was enough for me that he let go the stirrup. One thing, you potted one of them, and this fellow's horse."

"Then they wanted the horse we sold to put under the dead horse's saddle, and mount this fellow. He must be hurt or he wouldn't sit there the way he does."

They went on till they neared the clump of cactus, when Jose Maria Gomez came forward alone to meet them.

When he was within fifteen yards Brown raised his pistol and cried out:

"You're near enough! Halt!"

The Mexican pulled up and bowed.

"The *cavaliero*[*] sees I have only a sword. I can harm no one. I come only to demand the vengeance of a man on *El Rubio Bravo*, who boasts he has killed three members of my family. My brother, Jose Jesus Gomez lies on the plain, out yonder. One of you shot him. Which was it?"

---

* *Cavaliero:* A cavalier or gallant; derived from the Spanish *caballero*.

"I had that honour," answered Olaf blandly, "and I will shoot you and your brothers too if you attempt any foul play."

Jose Maria bowed again.

"There is no need of boasting," he said. "You are in no danger of foul play. We did not know it was you last night, or we should not have assaulted you in the way we did. Our quarrel is a solemn one."

Indeed, there was a certain dignity in this dark outlaw's manner as he spoke, that almost compelled respect, and Olaf answered:

"Be it so. What would you?"

"To fight you on foot with the sword, to the death," replied Jose Maria gravely.

"That is the thing I never did yet," said the Dane, as gravely. "I am satisfied as soon as blood is shed in a duel. Death is not a necessity in every affair."

Jose Maria shook his head, frowning.

"*Our* affairs are different. *We* fight to the death only, after one of our number is hurt, and here you have already killed one."

"That was no a duel. In short, I will not fight a duel with you unless it is well understood that first blood ends the affair," returned the sword-master.

Jose Maria shrugged his shoulders.

"Since you are afraid, I have done all I care to make this meeting honourable. Now look to yourself."

He wheeled his horse and galloped off to his brothers, who had been watching with the most eager interest.

He said something to them, and in a moment they pulled out from under the trappings of their horses four carbines, and fired a regular volley at the Dane and his friend.

But in a contest with firearms the two blondes were more than their match, and the next moment they were peppering the brigands with pistol-shots, and going at full gallop for the gate of the city.

Indeed it was hardly prudent to stay out there any longer.

The suddenness and confusion of the attack caused all the shots to miss, except one of Charley Brown's, which struck Jose Maria's horse, in the shoulder, making a flesh-wound.

The bandits galloped after them loading as they went, and chased them to the gate of the city, where Olaf turned and made a charge with his sword in one hand and a pistol in the other, his lance swinging at his back.

He fired five shots, missing every one, and cursing his luck and the lance swinging at his right arm.

Finally, full of rage, he caught up the lance and cast it like a spear, transfixing Jose Maria, and uttering a shout of triumph.

"One more of your Terrible Seven gone," cried the Dane, tauntingly, and just at that moment he heard shouts behind him.

The next moment, out of the gate, led by Charley Brown, came a party of young Mexican gentlemen, in all their bravery of velveteen and silver buttons, flourishing their long *machetes*, or broadswords, and yelling valoriously:

"Muerta a los guerrilleros! Muerta a Gomez!"

[Death to the robbers! Death to Gomez!]

Six men had terrorized the town; but now that the citizens saw two men fight them, the cowardly Mexicans took heart and came on, twenty to one, to finish the battle.

As for the Gomez brothers, they did not wait to be overwhelmed; but, firing a parting volley in revenge, they turned and fled, and Chiapas was at peace for a time, as El Rubio Bravo rode in at the gate.

Mexico City.

Chapter XXVI.

Mexico.

THERE is no city on the continent of North America that has so many elements of beauty as Mexico the magnificent. Situated on a grand table-land, with just enough elevation above the sea to make the climate delightful all the year round, it is surrounded by the grandest mountains to be seen near any city of the world.

Popocatépetl and Iztaccíhuatl raise their snow-crowned summits to the skies, forty miles away, and between them lies the pass of Otumba, whence Cortez and Scott advanced to their victories.*

---

* *Cortez and Scott:* The first name is a reference to conquistador Hernán Cortés, who commanded Spanish forces in the march on Tenochtitlan in 1519. The second name is a reference to General Winfield Scott, who led American forces to victory during the Mexican-American War (1846-1848).

The city boasts of broad streets, generous, plazas, the *Alameda*—a grand park with rides and drives called *paseos* in all directions—and crowds of picturesque costumes in every street and on all the corners.

Rancheros and *jarochos* from the country around, in their dashing velveteen and silver, prance about on their blooded horses and bow to the ladies driving on the *paseo*, in the cool of the evening.

The great cathedral, with its flat roof, looks down over the plaza and its crowds, and the bells are clanging for a festival.

Out on the *paseo*, among the horsemen, two men were especially noticeable as being *rubios*, in that land of swart men. They wore the Mexican dress and rode fine horses with silver studded harness, but they did not look like Mexicans, and there was a difference in the way they sat their animals.

Mexicans always ride with a straight leg, by the balance alone, but these men had shortened their stirrups to a position more like that used in Europe, with knees slightly bent.

They rode well enough, however, to show that there are more styles of equitation than one, and more than a dozen of the fair occupants of the carriages cast admiring glances at them; for a *rubio* is generally a favourite with Mexican ladies.

The two friends, however, did not seem inclined to respond to the advances of the ladies, and one of them said to the other in English:

"It's no use, colonel. You were so sure we should find them here, but I don't see anything that looks like them."

"Don't be impatient, my friend," retorted the Dane lightly. "I have not lived among these people for nothing. We shall see them here."

They rode slowly along scrutinizing all the carriages, for they were of course searching for the ladies of their respective affections who—as they knew—had been sent to the city of Mexico from the convent of Chiapas.

The *paseo* on which they were riding ran out past the Alameda toward the castle of Chepultepec about three miles off, but as they went on they noticed all the water-carts had stopped and turned round about without any apparent reason.

The road was as good as ever further on, but the carriages and horsemen kept in the track of the water carts and like them turned round and came back.

Not a horseman or vehicle ventured beyond this intangible boundary till our two friends rode up there and passed outside.

Their conduct excited immediate remark, and a moment later they heard a voice calling:

"Señores, señores, un momento!" [Gentlemen, Gentlemen, a moment!]

Charley turned his head to look.

"What's the matter, I wonder? By Jove, it's one of those good-for-nothing Greasers after us."

Good-for-nothing or not, he was a very nice, grey-bearded old gentleman, well dressed and on a fine horse, and he doffed his hat with the true Spanish grace as he came up, saying:

"I crave a thousand pardons of the honourable gentlemen, but I take the privilege of age and our common Christianity to excuse the liberty of addressing you without previous acquaintance."

Olaf's hat was off before the other had finished speaking, and he answered sweetly:

"*Señor*, you have no need of any excuse to those who can see in your benevolent face the sure index of a Christian gentleman's disposition. What may be your honourable pleasure?"

Charley Brown, who began by this time to understand Spanish pretty well, grumbled to himself in his native British:

"Too blessed polite by half. I hate these greasers."

But the old gentleman had come on a friendly errand, for he went on:

"I presume from your riding on here, that you are strangers in this city."

"We arrived here this morning," answered Olaf promptly. What about this road, *señor*?"

"Simply that if you ride a quarter of a mile further on, now that it is getting dark, you will be robbed and murdered. That is all. It is only safe to go to Chepultepec in the morning, when the robbers have gone home."

Olaf bowed low and answered:

"We are very grateful for your warning, but my friend and I are armed and used to taking care of ourselves. For all that we are exceedingly thankful to you, *señor*. May I offer my card and request the pleasure of knowing your honourable name ?"

The old Mexican took the card with a bow.

"The cavalier will excuse my inability to read his card in this light. I am Don Lerdo de Ximenes, and my residence is at No. 357 Calle de San Francisco, where I shall be happy to place my house at the disposition of such noble Americans as yourselves."

Olaf started slightly as the other announced himself and then replied:

"Then you are the cousin of my old friend Don Carlos de Ximenes of Havana, and you will know me better when I say I am Don Olavo Svenson, commonly known as—"

"El Rubio Bravo" exclaimed Don Lerdo in a tone of delight. "Is it possible? My niece Dona Carmelita, who arrived three days ago, has told me what a favourite you were of my cousin Carlos, and I am very much charmed to see you. You will come to see us to-morrow?"

He looked nervously down the road as he spoke, for the evening was drawing on, and the carriages and horses were growing less and less frequent, even on the frequented part of the *paseo*.

"You must excuse me if I leave you," he went on, hurriedly, "but I am a family man, not a king of the sword, like you, Don Olavo. You will call to-morrow? *Buenos noches*."

He galloped away as hard as he could go, and Olaf perceived in the dusk of the road, toward Chapultepec, several horsemen coming down toward them, the cause of Don Lerdo's too evident terror.

"There are the gentlemen of the road[†], Charley," he said, carelessly. "Are you for a little adventure to-night? For my part, I am tired of doing nothing but eating and riding. I thought this Mexico was full of fights, but they seem to have nothing but night work."

Charley yawned.

"Those fellows down the road are not worth an adventure; there are too many to make it profitable. See, there are one three, seven, ten, fifteen to be counted, and Heaven knows how many hiding in the bushes. They'll have to rob each other to-night, for I don't care to run the gauntlet of that crowd without a better excuse."

He turned his horse back as he spoke, but Olaf looked longingly down the road.

"I'd like one little dash," he muttered.

"I have a kind of impression that I should meet the last of the Gomez brothers there, and I want to close my accounts with them."

Charley Brown shrugged his shoulders.

"You seem to have a great love for running your head into danger. What is there to gain down there? Thieves don't carry much in the way of plunder, and you don't want to turn robber on your own account."

"All the same," returned Olaf, obstinately, "I have made up my mind to take a ride to Chepultepec to-night, let who will come on the road. I never let pickpockets scare me in American or English cities. I am fond of seeing all that is to be seen, and I want to find what sort of people are these gentlemen of the Mexican road. Will you come with me, or shall I go alone, my friend?"

Charley growled:

"You're a fool, and I'm another. Come on. We'll try it, anyway."

† *Gentlemen of the road:* slang of the period for highwaymen or *bandidos.*

A mexican outlaw, from an old broadside.

Chapter XXVII.

A Strange Ride.

BOTH men were well armed in the modern American fashion; that is to say each had a pair of revolvers.

Behind them the *paseo* was rapidly emptying as the last rays of twilight reddened the top of Popocatépetl; before them stretched the broad and beautifully level *paseo* to the foot of the hill of Chepultepec, for several miles, bordered with trees, and clothed with occasional horsemen coming lazily on.

Our two friends loosened their pistols in the holsters and cantered gently on, the best point of the Mexican horses they rode.

In about five minutes they came to the first horseman, a dashing cavalier in velvet and silver, who looked like any other Mexican gentleman and saluted them with a polite "*Buenos noches, señores*."

"Not much like a robber," was the comment of Charley Brown. "Perhaps he's only coming home from the Castle."

As they swept past him Olaf took a sly glance over his shoulder, and saw that the cavalier was also looking back, and had slackened his pace to a walk.

"He's a robber sure enough," said the Dane; "but it seems to me I saw him only this morning on the plaza, smoking a cigarette."

"Shouldn't wonder. These Greasers are all alike," commented Brown.

The people they met were two in number of the same dashing appearance, and Olaf said to his companion:

"Draw your pistol, but keep it down by your leg."

They rode on and the new-comers opened to either side of the road and halted.

"Good evening, cavaliers," said one. "You seem in a hurry."

His tone was jeering, but Olaf did not notice it as he swept passed.

Neither offered to pursue the *rubios*, but as the Dane looked back he saw that the first man was coming to join the other two.

"I see their plan," was his only comment.

Ahead of them were three more men on horseback, and these halted in the road as they came.

"Take out your other revolver and be ready to charge," quoth Olaf, coolly. "I know these fellows to a dot. They're used to having fools give in like lambs."

They rode on a little faster, and as they came up, one of the three men shouted:

"Stop! You're on the wrong road!"

Olaf laughed and galloped on, raising his pistol so as to be seen, while Charley, who had recovered from his wound—for it was six weeks since they had left Chiapas—followed his example.

Crack! Crack!

The three Mexicans wheeled their horses and fled. They were evidently not used to being the passive parties in an affair of this kind.

As they went, one of them uttered a cry of pain, and they noticed him reeling on his horse.

A little further on were about a dozen more in groups of two or three at a time strung along the road, and the first three galloped up to them, when they all clustered together, prepared to dispute the passage, about a quarter of a mile further

"They're too strong for us," observed the Englishman, "We'd better turn back."

"Not from Mexicans," replied the Dane in a tone of determination. "I'm going to give these fellows a lesson and show them that two good men can ride to Chepultepec in spite of them."

On they went now at a stretching gallop, and as they came near, the bandits began to fire pistols at them with an uncertain aim, for the bullets whistled wide.

"Just what I thought," quoth Olaf coolly. "Firearms are not natural to these people. The knife is their national weapon. Don't fire till you are sure."

In a few moments more, they were close on the Mexicans, who showed signs of wavering, all but one man.

He rode out in front, and fired a pistol with such good aim that Charley Brown ducked his head to avoid the bullet.

Then the two men began firing, and the whole crowd of bandits fled, crying:

"Los diablos Yanquis!" [The Yankee devils!]

All but the man who had so near shot Brown.

He flashed out a sword and rode at Olaf, who wore his own battle-blade, Mexican fashion, and in a moment more the two swords were clashing in a regular duel, the swordmaster laughing and taunting his opponent as he parried his savage cuts.

"Not quite enough, my friend. Very well meant, but that was a false cut. Try again. Why you have good notion! Aha! Did you think you had me then? Take that!"

He made a rapid slash at the other's face, but to his surprise it was parried and the bandit cut back with such skill and force that it almost reached his sword-arm.

"Halt! One moment!" cried the Dane, as he wheeled his horse out of distance. "You are too good a swordsman to be a thief. Who are you? I don't want to kill you. I am a professional, you an amateur."

The strange horseman uttered a cry of amazement:

"I know that voice. Are you not El Rubio Bravo?"

"The same, *señor.*"

The stranger threw down his sword.

"And we were fighting together," he cried. "Ah, my friend, do you not know me? In my fallen fortunes I am still your friend, Jose Ramirez."

Chapter XXVIII.

The General Bandit.

FOR several seconds Olaf was too much amazed to do more than repeat:

"Jose Ramirez! Here!"

"Yes, my friend," said the ex-general, "Jose Ramirez, here. Once a general at the head of a gallant troop, now fallen to seeking purses on the road, but always your friend."

He turned in his saddle, and shouted out:

"It is a friend. It is all a mistake. Come up again."

"No closer, if you please, my friend," said Olaf, abruptly. "I have had enough of your comrades, for the present. Tell me how you came here, before I know if you are fit to be the friend of an honourable soldier."

Ramirez laughed.

"You thought I was dead."

"Of course I did. I saw you struck down in the battle. Had I been alone, I should have tried to rescue you; but I had lady in charge, and—"

"That is all right, my Norse friend. I do not blame you one bit. It is true I went down. One of those confounded Indians hit me with a stone and I was stunned; but I came to myself while the confusion was still wild, found myself alone in a heap of dead with my horse standing by me and saw the men of that confounded Lost City—which I wish we'd never gone near—busily cutting out the hearts of the last of my poor devils. Not wishing to have that cheerful operation performed on myself, I made a spring to my horse and galloped away with a whole *posse* after me, down the mountain into the plain, and, by Jove! they followed one half-way to Tabasco, where I finally arrived more dead than alive."

"Then that was the reason they did not chase us," said Olaf, thoughtfully. "I have often wondered how they came to let us escape."

"Oh, they are liable to make mistakes as well as any one else," answered Ramirez lightly. "I tell you I had quite a little time of it, and still worse when I got to Tabasco."

"Why?"

"Why! Simply because I was too well known there. The Ortega party had been beaten, and I was one of Ortega's principal followers. To make a long story short, they clapped me into prison there and I only escaped ten days ago."

"How did you escape?"

"A woman, of course. There always is a woman in the case. The jailer's wife, a pretty, kind-hearted creature, took pity on the *rubio*, and thanks to a jealous husband who used to beat her, and a few looks of languishment on my part, she let me out one night and insisted on running away with me. What could a man do? I took the gifts of Heaven, got back my horse and arms, left the lady at one of her friends, and made for Mexico, the only place short of the United States where I am not well known by sight."

"And what made you adopt this life?"

"This life? It is only a change of names. We gentlemen of the road make war just as our soldiers of fortune did—*onglas libres*—nails free. It is a fine life, my friend. You would do well to join us. My friend Ortega is sure to succeed, and I have here the nucleus of a very pretty little band to join him as soon as he has taken Tabasco. You can have any situation under the new government you wish."

"Thanks," was the dry reply. "I have seen all I wish to see of this delightful country. As soon as I have done some business which I intend to do to-morrow, I shall take the first steamer for New Orleans."

Ramirez sighed as if he felt grieved.

He looked around up and down the road, where the bandits, to the number of twenty, were clustered as if hesitating.

"I am so sorry," he observed. "We could make such a fine troop of these fellows, and Ortega is certain to succeed."

The Dane smiled a little scornfully.

"These fellows! You know well enough that they are not worth half their numbers of your old men. They let us two drive them like sheep."

"That is true," replied Ramirez, in a tone of confidential regret, "but what is a man to do? All they need is teaching, and you and I together might make our fortunes with them, Olavo. I have a scheme to take them all into the city some evening and make a sweep of the Bank of Mexico. It could be done easy enough with the right men, and we could put Ortega in funds at once to raise a hundred thousand men. Just think of what might be done with a hundred thousand men."

"Yes, if the bank were in our hands: but in the meantime, my friend, from being a general and a cavalier, you have become what the world calls a common robber."

"And what would you have?" asked Ramirez, with some bitterness. "In our unhappy land the robber is the only gentleman who lives at his ease and is feared and respected. I have tried to make war like a gentleman, but it is no use. The men would not follow me without liberty to plunder. Now I am chief of this little band simply because I am the boldest man and the best shot among them. You think I am only a common robber now. I will show you that I can walk into Mexico on the plaza before all the world and no one dare touch me."

"Oh, come, my friend, you are joking. True you hold this road; but the police must know you, and in the city—"

Ramirez laid his hand on the Dane's knee.

"I tell you what I will do," he said. "I will wager you two gold *onzas* [forty dollars], that I can meet you on the Plaza at noon under the shadow of the cathedral, and have all my men in plain view armed and mounted as they now are, and that not a single officer or man dare molest us."

Olaf looked incredulous.

"I'll not make the bet. True, your present mode of life is one I hate; but you have been my friend, and I do not want to see you taken. Don't try it."

"On the contrary, Colonel Don Olavo," answered Ramirez sharply: "I will show you that I am as much respected as any man in Mexico and that if you hate—as you call it—my present mode of life, you hate what is the profession of half the gentlemen of Mexico."

"Well, well, let us turn the conversation," was the good-humoured reply. "Your notions are not the same as mine. Have you any objection to my going to Chepultepec and returning to show people it can be done?"

"None whatever," was the cordial answer, "and how prospers your love affair my friend?"

Olaf told him as they rode along to the grim castle on the heights of Chepultepec, and the ex-general observed:

"All the more reason we should go to the city to-morrow to see you. You do not know our people yet, Olavo. That old fox Ximenes will cheat you out of your eyes. He will never let you see your Carmelita again if he can help it, because you are a heretic. But leave it to me, I know how to manage these fellows. Meet me on the Plaza at ten to-morrow morning and we will pay a call to Don Lerdo de Ximenes. You shall have your Carmelita and our friend Carlos his Pepita, or my name is not Jose Ramirez."

Then they rode on again and finally parted like old friends, when the Dane and his British comrade returned to the city.

Chapter XXIX.

Don Lerdo's Letter.

DON LERDO DE XIMENES sat in a hammock on one of the balconies of his *patio*, and he looked worried and anxious though he was trying to calm his nerves by the infallible and consoling recipe of a Mexican husk cigarette.

Father Geromino had just left him after giving him a long lecture, and the Don did not know what to do.

He was naturally a good-natured man, but he was dreadfully afraid of his father confessor, and the latter had just told him it was his duty at any hazard to keep his wards from seeing any heretics, more especially since they were admittedly in love with two of the accursed tribe.

Don Lerdo was a rich, easy-going old gentleman who owned a coffee *hacienda* on the road to Vera Cruz, and had but one object in life—to be allowed to live in peace and quietness as they do in other countries not so given to revolutions.

He had seen the Americans enter Mexico in Santa Anna's time, and was one of those not few Mexicans who regretted ever after that the country had not then been annexed by "*Los Yanquis*."†

"For when they were here," soliloquized Don Lerdo, "one could ride to Chepultepec and anywhere else in safety, and ever since it has been a carnival of robbers."

Which was all very true, and a good many other people in Mexico think it, if they dare not all say it.

"And what in the world am I to do with these two girls?" went on Don Lerdo mournfully. "My cousin Carlos and his friend Garcia are both dead, and these girls would be dead too had not these heretics saved them. And now they are both bent on marrying the *rubios*, and father Geromino says that if I consent to it I shall run the risk of ten or twelve thousand years of purgatory. I wish they had carried them off and not given them in charge of the abbess at Chiapas. It was, of course, strictly honourable, but it is exceedingly inconvenient to me to have to decide a question of this sort. And then, too, no one will marry them here, for they have no dowry. What fools my cousin and Don Ramon were to put their money into gold and get killed."

The good Don gave a jump here and dropped his cigarette.

A thundering knock had just come at the outer door of the house and it echoed through the *patio* like an answer to his thoughts.

Houses in the city of Mexico are all built round an inner court called the *patio*, for it is against the law to have windows overlooking a neighbour, and one must have air and light somehow.

Don Lerdo's *patio* was surrounded by tall colonnades with several stories of balcony having polished brass railings. The front on the street had windows and balconies, and the old gentleman hurried to one of these to see who was at the door.

He beheld a hoppled* horse standing and lashing away the flies with his tail, while a Mexican gentleman with a purple *manga* draped over his

† During the Mexican-American War, the United States army captured Mexico City and occupied it from September 14, 1847, to June 12, 1848.

velvet and silver, stood at the door. The hopples of the horse were little silver chains round the fetlocks of his forelegs in the usual fashion.

"Thank goodness it is not the heretics," muttered the old gentleman and then he saw the door open, heard a few words with his servant, saw the gentleman give a note to the man and then turn away, unhopple his horse, mount and ride off.

Don Lerdo returned to the patio and his cigarette, when he was approached by his majordomo, who handed him the letter.

The old Mexican took it, and as he read his face grew as pale as ashes, so pale that the man noticed it and asked:

"Is the *señor* ill? Shall I fetch anything?"

"No, no, Tonto, it is nothing. Go and get my horse ready at once. I am called away on business."

The man departed, mystified, and Don Lerdo with shaking fingers re-opened the note he had crushed, and read in it the cause of his sudden exhibition of fear.

It was written in a bold hand, and ran in the following fashion:

"*To the Señor Don Lerdo de Ximenes.*

"MY VERY DEAR SIR:—A friend of mine, Don Olavo de Sovensone, lately saved the life and honour of one of your relatives, Donna Carmelita de Ximenes, who loves him, and whom he wishes to marry. I learn from other sources that you are unwilling to permit this match to take place, because Don Olavo does not belong to the ranks of the faithful. You will do well, *señor*, to remember that, in these times, no man's property is safe from the ravages of war, and that the *patriots of our party hold all the roads between here and Vera Cruz, on which lies your own hacienda*. Don Olavo is a friend of mine, and I will answer for his good standing in the faith we both have the honour to profess. He is now lodging at the Posada de San Trinidad, and you will do well to call on him at once, and give your legal and full consent to his marriage with the lady who has become your ward

* *Hopple:* a leg harness, usually of leather, to control the gait of trotting or pacing horses.

by Mexican law. If you fail to do this, *you will receive no more returns from your estates this year, where the coffee crop is just growing ripe, but you will have instead a visit from*

"Your humble servant,

"At the disposition of your worship,

"JOSE RAMIREZ.

"*General of Cavalry, in the service of the Chiapas Republic.*"

Don Lerdo nearly cried when he read this letter, and groaned to himself:

"Yes, what he says is true. The coffee is nearly ripe and they could sweep it in a single night. Father Geromino is a good man, but I must take care of my own while I have it. Purgatory is a bad thing, but poverty is worse while one is alive. These patriots are all the same, and they say this Ramirez is a devil as bad as the *guerrilla* Cortina."[†]

He was hunting about for his spurs and hat while he was talking, and when he had found them sent up word that he "wished to see the *señoritas* at once!"

Presently down came Carmelita and Pepita, with eyes red with crying:

They had both been lectured by Father Geromino on the enormity of wishing to marry *"ereticos"* but were evidently quite unconvinced of the sin though they knew that they could not get married without the consent of this their nearest relative and guardian.

Don Lerdo amazed and confounded them with the brusque salutation:

"How soon think you can you get ready to be married, both of you, to those *rubios?*"

Carmelita turned crimson and Pepita blue at the question.

Camelita faltered:

"Cousin, are you crazy?"

† Juan Cortina (1824–1894), known as the "Red Robber of the Rio Grande" and the "Rio Grande Robin Hood", was a Mexican rancher, politician, paramilitary leader, outlaw, and folk hero.

Pepita, giggled nervously and made no answer at all.

Don Lerdo stamped his foot testily.

"You fools, as long as I said no, you were at me all the time, begging and praying. Now I say yes, you are dumb. How soon can you get ready, I ask? In an hour?"

"In an hour! The idea!"

Both were indignant in a moment. The fact was that Don Lerdo was an old bachelor and did not understand women.

"Very well, then; when? To-morrow? Next day? Next week? I have changed my mind, and Father Geromino can go to the devil. After all, I am master in my own house."

The girls had recovered their colour, and it was with a faint smile mantling her lips that Carmelita, asked:

"Are you in earnest? Do you give your free consent to our marriage?"

"Yes, yes, I tell you. When can you get ready? Tell me quickly."

Camellia threw her arms round him and hugged him coaxingly.

"And can we have all we need for dressing?"

"Yes, yes, anything."

The old bachelor had vague ideas on the subject, or he would not have been so liberal. Carmelita pursed up her lips as if in a fit of deep consideration ere she said:

"Very well, then, I think that—if—we hurry very much—we can be ready in—one week from to-morrow."

The old man nodded absently.

"It is a bargain. Go and get ready as soon as you can. I am about to call on your lovers. They are, I find, honourable cavaliers and *excellent Catholics*."

He left the *patio* and they saw him mount his horse and ride off down the street toward the Plaza. Carmelita turned to Pepita:

"Do you know I can hardly believe it? I wonder what has changed him so suddenly."

They would not have wondered so much had they heard the tone in which this rich and respectable Mexican was addressed by a man whom he knew to be a robber, in broad daylight and in the plaza of Mexico city.

Don Jose Ramirez, his purple *manga* thrown gracefully over one shoulder, stood chatting with two other *rubios* as the old man approached, and the Mexican heard him say as he came up:

"There is our man. You see, in this country it is necessary to be on the right side of the soldier of fortune, no matter what you call him at other times."

He took Don Lerdo aside, and asked in a low, menacing tone:

"Well, have you consented, or do you want a visit from our people?"

"I consent most heartily. Which are the two honourable cavaliers?" answered the old Mexican, nervously.

"I will introduce you," was the polite reply, and the brigand turned to his two friends with the assurance of a man of the world introducing them formally.

Don Lerdo's Letter

Chapter XXX.

Conclusion.

A STIFF norther[*] was blowing over the waves of the Gulf of Mexico, and blowing the yellow fever out of Vera Cruz.

It was the first norther of the season, and turned the town from an oven into an ice-house. But as we said before, it drove out the yellow fever and therefore was welcome, though it killed all those who were already sick. Out in the bay off the mole, lay a steamer pitching at her anchor, and on the deck was a trio of men talking to each other and eyeing the land.

"You cannot go back, Ramirez, in this norther. You'd better come with us," said Olaf Svenson, kindly. "No boat could live in that sea and the steamer won't wait till it's over. It will last three days, and till it's over you are a prisoner."

---

* *Norther:* a cold gale from the north, common to the Gulf of Mexico, formed during the winter by a vigorous outbreak of continental polar air behind a cold front.

Ramirez looked back longingly.

"I don't like to go," he muttered. "Everything is ripe for a change and I shall miss my chance. Ortega has offered me the chief command of all his cavalry, and he is bound to succeed."

"Or be shot," observed Charley Brown in a dry tone. "You forget that."

"Well, shot or victorious it will all be over," said Ramirez, with a half sigh. "I do not like to leave him in his peril."

"You'll have to this time," said Olaf. "See, they are getting up the anchor now."

In fact the funnel of the steamer was sending forth clouds of black smoke and the sailors were winding up the windlass. The wind was increasing every moment, and it was clearly impossible for any boat to reach the shore, for the waves were dashing showers of spray over the top of the mole.

Ramirez had come on board to see his friends and their brides off to the United States, and while they were drinking parting healths in the cabin, the vessel began to pitch and they felt a cold gust come down the cabin hatchway.

When they went down below half an hour before, it had been suffocatingly hot without a cloud in the heavens.

They came up to find a dark cloud full of hail and snow, bearing down on them with a furious wind before it, and when the cloud passed, the thermometer had sunk from ninety-eight to forty, with a gale blowing thirty miles an hour.

Such are the pleasant contrasts of Mexican climate in the autumn and winter, and such the conditions under which Don Jose Ramirez, patriot general and brigand chief, was carried off to the United States whether he would or no.

The three *rubios* arrived in New Orleans together and there separated to their future lives, whither we can only follow them for a little space to tell what became of them.

Doctor Charley Brown having put his savings of Honduras into diamonds and and gold, had quite a snug little sum on which to found a practice for himself. He settled in the city of New Orleans and earned a great reputation in the treatment of yellow fever, on which he wrote a book in years long after.

His wife, the pretty and coquettish Pepita of old, was as devoted as Spanish-American wives generally are, which is saying a good deal, and ceased to flirt from the day in which she was married.

Jose Ramirez also remained in the United States, where he served in the civil war and found what a difference there is between fighting in Mexico, and in countries where Anglo Saxons are the combatants. He had his fill of it, lost a leg, and finally retired into the tobacco and cotton business in Texas, where he still loves to tell stories of his old *guerrilla* days.

His friend Ortega, always on the point of succeeding, nevertheless failed, just about the time Ramirez landed in New Orleans. In consequence, he was shot, which was the main reason why Jose never went back to Mexico.

Don Lerdo, mild and inoffensive, managed to please both sides during the subsequent troubles in Mexico, and kept his coffee estates, under Maximillian, Juarez, Lerdo de Trejada and Diaz in succession, earning the title of "the Weathercock," by his facility in changing his politics.

The Gomez brothers, failing in killing the Danish swordmaster, ended in losing their valuable lives one after the other in duels with *espadachíns*.

The "Terrible Seven," once broken by the Dane, ceased to excite terror and ended by being exterminated.

As for Olaf Svenson, he went to the city of San Francisco, where he made a great name as a professor of the noble art of swordsmanship, and had the satisfaction of establishing a school of fencers who could beat the best French pupils that came that way.

He still lives and is still an enthusiast on the subject of the sword, holding the idea that no exercise can be compared with that of fencing, in that it makes weak men strong, timid men brave, sick men well, and all men gentlemen.

When asked how his theory works among the Spanish-Americans, who are all fond of the sword and yet low in the scale of civilization, he answers proudly:

"What you call civilization is not all you think. It covers much cowardice, selfishness and dishonesty. Yet I will say that in all my travels I have never met grander men—polite, brave, generous—than I have seen in the mountains of the Spanish-American countries. The race is dying out, but another is coming to take its place. The Yankee nation will, in time, absorb all the continent. When it does, you will find that of lands in the world none is more favoured than that bright clime which saw the valour of Cortez, Pizarro, Alvarado and all the brave, indomitable *conquistadores* who carved an empire with their swords, that will always be grand and wonderful."

THE END.

Conclusion

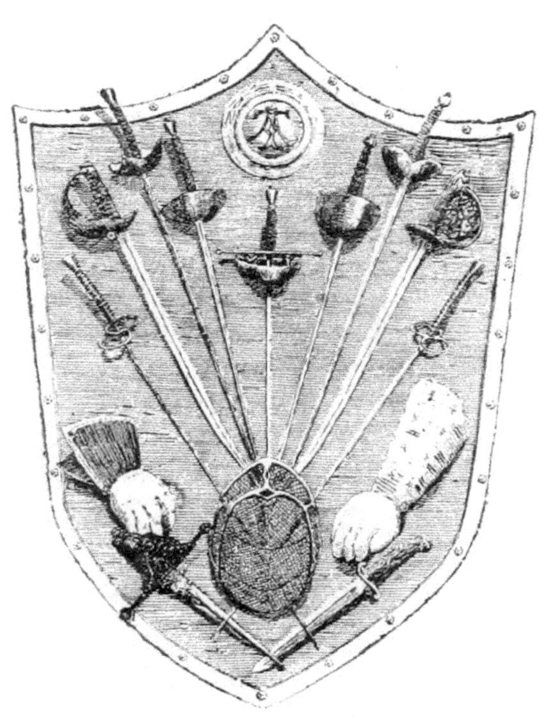

APPENDIX

Spanish American Documents Relating to Col. Monstery

CONTEST BETWEEN MONSTERY AND PROF. POUPARD.

(English translation on pages lxviii-lxx of the Introduction)

ASALTO DE ARMAS ENTRE PROFESORES.

Durante la semann, antes del domingo 1 del presente, se decia, que por deseoc de ciertas autoridades, iba á tener lugar un asalto de las armas, entre el coronel Monstery, el famoso profesor y tirador de los Estados Unidos, y M. Poupard, el profesor de mas fama en México.

El domingo 1 de Marzo, por invitacion, asistimos á la sala de coronel Monstery, calle de San José del real núm. 1. Al entrar encontramos la sala llena de señores, y entre ellos á muchos de distincion. A las once y media ilegó Mr. Poupard, y fué cordialmente recibido por el coronel, y convidado á empezar el asalto.

El coronel estonces dijo: que el principal objeto de su venida á México, era para resteblecer su sa lud, que aun no estaba en buena condicion. Pero que sin embargo, deseaba dar un asalto con las armas siguientes:

1. Florete.
2. Sable de infatería.
3. Espada.
4. Sable como montado
5. Juego de puñal
6. Puñal contra florete y sable.
7. Esgrima de bayoneta.
8. Sable á pié contra bayoneta.
9. Sable como montado contra bayonet.
10. Boxear.

Despues de esta esplicacion, el coronel saludó á su adversario y á la concurriencia, y empezaron con la muralla o las posturas (que es la introduccion de esgrima.) Despues poniéndo e as caretas, empezaron el asalto, cuyo resultado fué la victoria para el coronel, como que las primeras cuatro estocadas con dos desarmes fueron en favor el coronel.

Lo que estrañaron los que conocen al Sr. Poupard fué, los dos desarmes, por la much fama de la fuerza de su muñeca.

El coronel despues invitó al Sr. Poupard á alistarse para el asalto de sable; pero el profesor rehusó como los demas profesores, que eran cinco, y entre elles el Sr Martel, el mas antiguo de México, tal vez por consideracion á no fatigar al coronel, y como el asalto principalmente debia ser con el Sr. Poupard, el Sr. Becker, antes capitan al servicio de los Estado-Mayor del general Leyva, aceptó y mostró considerable destreza en el manejo del sable; pero el coronel por su destreza superior lo venció. Como tambien en el 3, con la espada. En el 4, sable como montado. En el 5, juego de puñal, el coronel dijo que se sentia muy bien, y con deseos de probar la destreza del Sr. Poupard 6 de cualquiera otra persona en el juego de puñal, pues que nunca habia encontrado una persona competente para dicha arma. Pero como no hubo quien obsequiase su deseo, pasó desapercibido y sin efecto.

Sin embargo, el, coronel tenia, deseos de probar su destreza contra el Sr. Poupard en dicha arma, y ofreció al Sr. Poupard su puñal contra su florete, lo que tambien rehusó, como las otras veces que fué invitado.

El capitan Becker aceptó tirar, y fué conquistado con puñal contra florete, y puñal contra espada, pero el capitan logró tocar al coronel dos veces en el brazo en el último juego, difícil para el coronel.

Llegó el 7. combate; el coronel anunció al Sr. Poupard que era el tiempo para esgrima del bajoneta, y que siendo el arma con la cual los franceses habian alcanzado tanta gloria, esperaba que él se distinguiera lo misno; pero el Sr. Poupard no se sintió deseoso de conquistar estos laureles. El capitan Becker mostró su conocimiento en esta arma; pero el coronel in nejó la referida arma con la misma habilidad que el florete; pues sus rápidos ataques y repuestas contra la coraza, no daban oportunidad al contrario para haberlo tocado, i no deja duda de la fama que el coronel tiene en los Estados-Unidos por la sencillez y efectividad de su sistema en dicho arte.

8. El coronel propuso oposicion de bayoneta contra su sable, pero no habiendo quien aceptara, se pasó.

9. Defensa de sable como montada por el coronel, contra bayoneta, en cuyo difícil juego se defendió en una elevacion. Demostró que sin embargo de ser muy difícil, vencer al infante por ser el arma demasiado corta, aun se defendió y mostró que el de caballería tenia defensa contra la bayonet, siendo el arma mas temible.

10. Boxear. El Sr. Valdez, discípulo del coronel, dió tanto crédito á su profesor como a si mismo, y se cree que tomando el Sr. Valdez otras diez lecciones ademas de las que ya ha tomado, será un formidable tirador en ese arte.

– *El Monitor Republicano*, Mexico City, March 17, 1868.

MONSTERY VS. MEXICO, 1870-1871. (EXCERPTS)

COMISION MIXTA DE RECLAMACIONES ENTRE LA REPÚBLICA MEXICANA Y LOS ESTADOS-UNIDOS DE AMÉRICA.

Ministerio de relaciones exteriores.—Seccion de América.—Núm. 376.

Reclamacion de Thomas H. Monstery contra la República de México.

El reclamante solicita que se le satisfaga el valor de las joyas y dinero que perdió en México, en Pichucalco, en los dias 4 y 5 de Agosto de 1860, en consecuencia del robo que le hizo Francisco Flores, comandante de la guarnicion mexicana de aquel lugar; y sostiene ademas que en la fecha de este suceso tenia el carácter de ciudadano americano.

La exposicion de los he mante, aunque contradicha por la prueba & lo ménos en un importantísimo particular, es la siguiente:

En 1859 el reclamante emigró á México en compañía del general José María Melo, que poco despues fué nombrado comandante militar del Estado de Chiapas, recibiendo tambien el reclamante el nombramiento de instructor general militar, con el grado y consideracion de coronel de caballería en el mismo Estado. En el año de 1860 ocurrió en Chiapas una de esas frecuentes insurrecciones, que tanto deploran los amigos de la libertad y del progreso, en este continente, y de ello resultó la captura y ejecucion del general Melo, y que el memorialista saliese del Estado con su «dinero, joyas y diamantes». Dice el reclamante que *se preparaba para dejar el país, y que marchó para Veracruz*, deteniéndose en su camino para este puerto, en el pueblo de Pichucalco, en el mes de Julio de 1860. Esto lo hizo por invitacion de Flores, que le instó para que asistiese á la feria que entónces so celebraba en aquella localidad; y con el objeto al mismo tiempo de dar al dicho Flores y á algunos de sus oficiales unas cuantas lecciones de esgrima, y ejercicios de espada.

Flores, segun dice, le dió alojamiento en una de las habitaciones del edificio ocupado por las tropas que estaban á su mando; y como sabia que en poder del reclamante se encontraba una gran suma de dinero, joyas, &c., le concedió una guardia especial para sus cuartos, en los que se pusieron centinelas así de dia como de no che.

En la noche del 4 de Agosto de 1860, el reclamante comió con el prefecto Sr. Castillo; y cuando volvió & su casa en la mañana del 5, encontró que su baul, con joyas y dinero, había desaparecido.

Un soldado llamado Martinez confiesa el robo hecho por Flores, con ayuda suya, aunque muy contra su voluntad; y esta declaracion ocupa una gran parte del memorial. De ella aparece que no había tal guardia ni tales centinelas en las habitaciones del reclamante, y que Flores no tuvo para efectuar el robo á las doce de la noche, mas inconvenientes que los que pudieron proporcionarle el peso y la cantidad de lo robado.

Flores fué preso y encausado con este motivo; pero lo único que se sabe sobre el resultado definitivo de este asunto, es la manifestacion general hecha por el reclamante, de que le fué imposible obtener justicia por razon de la posicion, rango militar é influencia, &c., del encausado.

Pero por mas justos que estos fundamentos pudieran ser en otras circunstancias para establecer reclamaciones, y por mas detestables que pudieran parecer los hechos mencionados, en caso de ser ciertos, habrá de verse, ain embargo, que segun nuestro dictámen, carecen de importancia en el presente asunto.

Son varias las cuestiones, interesantes todas, que se desprenden de los hechos explicados en este coso; y entre ellas, la que los abogados de ambas partes han discutido con alguna extension, á saber: si los gobiernos son responsables de los robes privados cometidos por oficiales y empleados que están á su servicio. Hay tambien otra cuestion que no se ha tratado, relativa á la responsabilidad por razon de pérdidas de bienes que estaban puestos bajo la custodia y proteccion de una guardia militar, y fueron robados por la misma. Pero deseosos, como lo estamos sinceramente, de abstenernos de toda averiguacion innecesaria, nos limitarémos única y exclusivamente á examinar y decidir aquellos puntos, que relativos al caso particular de que se trata, sean necesarios para su debida resolucion.

Y aquí, *in limine judicii*, nos encontramos desde luego con una cuestion, cuyos resultados son vitales. ¿Cuál era la nacionalidad del reclamante en la época en que sufrió la pérdida de que se trata?

***

Es por consiguiente muy importante considerar los hechos y las alegaciones del memorial á la luz de las misnias pruebas dol reclamante.

¿Qué hacia él en Pichucalco? ¿Estaba en marcha hácia los Estados-Un idos?

Su ocupacion era entóneos dar instruccion militar á Flores y & sus oficiales, jugar al monte en la feria, y comer con el prefecto; pero ¿cuáles eran sus intencione respecto á lo futuro?

LEYES.—TOMO X.—2.

El 15 de Agosto, diez dias despues del robo, se procura de Policarpo Hernandez, alcalde 10 constitucional interino del departamento de Pichucalco, Estado de Chiapas, una certificacion en que se califica de «coronel de caballería de este Estado,» es decir, de Chiapas, de donde segun su memorial había partido el reclamante para volver á su país.

Mas tarde, el 17 del mismo mes, obtuvo tambien el reclamante, del mismo funcionario, y en el mismo estado de Chiapas, otra certificacion en que se le caracteriza como «coronel 6 instructor general de armas en eso Estado,» es decir, en Chiapas.

Esta prueba documental obtenida á su propia instancia, y presentada por él, es concluyente, faltando, como así sucede de una manera absoluta, toda otra demostracion de que el reclamante hubiese abandonado su empleo militar, y tambien de las pretensiones que tenia en aquel tiempo;

y de ella se deduce que la circunstancia de la ciudadanía mexicana permaneció adherida al reclamante, dado caso que en efecto la hubiera tenido anteriormente.

Ademas, la prueba recibida, y producida en apoyo de la accion del reclamante es de todo punto decisiva, en cuanto al particular de que se trata, y & las intenciones que él mismo tenia en la época del robo.

Ignacio Quiroga dice que en la fecha de este suceso «se habia comprometido con el reclamante para ir con él á Veracruz á unirse con el ejército liberal de México, bajo el mando del presidente Juarez.»

Pedro Pacheco dice, «que vió al reclamante en el pueblo de Pichucalco, Estado de Chiapas, México, á fines de Julio de 1860: que se comprometió á ir con él y otros varios á Veracruz para unirse con el ejército mexicano á las órdenes del general Juarez.»

El reclamante no ha producido prueba alguna, ni dicho nada en oposicion & esta prueba, respecto de su ocupacion y sus designios, y por lo tonto no podemos dudar que despues de la muerte del general Melo, así como ha, bia acontecido ántes de este suceso, el reclamante estaba en el servicio militar de México; y que habiendo desempeñado funciones activas como coronel de caballería, se encontraba en aquellos momentos en que ocurrió el robo, solicitando empleo militar mas reciente é inmediato, y domiciliado en México.

Por lo tanto, si la ley de 1854 comprendía al reclamante, y pudo naturalizarlo por razon de su empleo de coronel de ejército, esta ciudadanía la conservaba el redamante en la fecha del robo.

Los términos de la ley mexicana de 1854 son bien explícitos...

***

¿Puede quejarse nadie que se encuentre en tales casos, si se le deja solo, abandonado ála consideracion y ála justicia de la potencia extraña, cuya proteccion buscó él voluntariamente, y en cuyo servicio ofreció su vida?

¿Qué cosa mejor puede desear quien encuentra dulce morir por todo otro país que no sea el suyo?

Pero aunque pudiera haber equivocacion en nuestro juicio, respecto á la sabiduría y á la justicia de que segun las leyes de México se trasfiera la ciudadanía mexicana á los que voluntariamente aceptan dichas leyes, sostenemos, sin embargo, que nos hallamos en el caso de aplicarlas en el presente asunto, y que no queda para nosotros mas arbitrio, que declarar sin lugar la reclamacion.

Así se ordena por lo tanto.—*William H. Wadsworth.—Francisco G. Palacio.*

Traducido por órden de la comision. Washington, D.C., Octubre 3 de 1870.—*J. I. Rodríguez.*

Concuerda con su original.—Lo certifico.—*J. Cárlos Mejía*, secretario.

Es copia. México, Marzo 10 de 1871.

«Diario Oficial.»—Num. 69, del 10 de Marzo de 1871.

- *Recopilación de leyes, decretos y providencias de los poderes legislative y ejecutivo de las union. Vol. 8-9, Jan.-June 1871.* (Mexico: Imprenta Del Gobierno, En Palacio, 1872).

WORKS CITED

Baltimore Sun.

Beezley, William H. *Judas at the Jockey Club and Other Episodes of Porfirian Mexico.* Lincoln: University of Nebraska Press, 2018.

Bleiler, Everett Franklin. *Science-fiction, the Early Years: A Full Description of More Than 3,000 Science-fiction Stories from Earliest Times to the Appearance of the Genre Magazines in 1930: with Author, Title, and Motif Indexes.* Kent, Ohio: Kent State University Press, 1990.

Broecker, Randy. *Fantasy of the 20th Century: An Illustrated History.* New York: Barnes & Noble Books, 2001.

Canfield, H. S. "Soldier of Fortune," in *Everybody's Magazine,* October, 1902.

Carreño, Alberto María. *Archivo del General Porfirio Díaz, Memorias y documentos. Tomo IV.* México: Universidad Nacional Autónoma de México, Instituto de Historia/Elede, 1947.

Chicago Daily News.

Chicago Daily Tribune.

Claim of Thos. H. Monstery vs. Mexican Government, Memorial, filed November 1869.

Claims on the Part of Citizens of the United States and Mexico, 44th Congress, 2d Session. Washington: Goverment Printing Office, 1877.

Daily Alta California.

Daily Inter Ocean.

Dallas Morning News.

Doubleday, Charles William. *Reminiscences of the Filibuster War in Nicaragua.* New York: G. P. Putnam's Sons, 1886.

El Monitor Republicano.

Elkhart Daily Review.

Escudero, Angel. *El Duelo en México.* Mexico City: Imprenta Mundial, 1936.

Estatutos de la sociedad de recreo titulada Circulo de la Habana. Habana: "El Iris," 1861.

Ferry, Gabriel. *Vagabond Life in Mexico.* New York: Harper & Brothers, 1856.

Gomez-Martinez, Arturo. "L'Escrime au Mexique" in *L'Escrime Francaise,* February 1959.

Guardia, Ricardo Fernández. *Cuentos Ticos: Short Stories of Costa Rica.* Cleveland: Burrows Brothers, 1904.

Haggard, H. Rider. *King Solomon's Mines.* Pleasantville, N.Y.: The Reader's Digest, 1993.

Haggard, H. Rider. *The People of the Mist.* New York: Ballantine, 1973.

Hanson, Carter F. "Lost Among White Others: Late-Victorian Lost Race Novels for Boys" in *Nineteenth-Century Contexts: An Interdisciplinary Journal*, Volume 23, Issue 4. Abingdon: Routledge, 2002.

Jersey Journal.

Jump, Edward. *San Francisco at the Fair.* California: 1864.

Kernan, J. Frank. *Reminiscences of the Old Fire Laddies and Volunteer Fire Departments of New York and Brooklyn: Together with a Complete History of the Paid Departments of Both Cities.* New York: M. Crane, 1885.

"La Esgrima en la Habana," *El Sport*, June 13, 1888.

"La Esgrima en la Habana," *El Sport*, May 27, 1888.

La Sociedad.

Lauria-Santiago, Aldo. *An Agrarian Republic: Commercial Agriculture and the Politics of Peasant Communities in El Salvador, 1823–1914.* Pittsburgh: University of Pittsburgh Press, 1999.

Mexican Herald.

Mexican War Pension, Act of January 29, A.D. 1887, Declaration of Survivor for Pension. Mexican War Pension, Act of January 29, 1887, Survivor's Brief. Partial transcription by Diane Hayes. Pension, Illinois, NARA microfilm publication T317 (Washington D.C.: National Archives and Records Administration, n.d.); FHL microfilm 537,007.

Miller, Ben. "A Grand Assault-of-Arms in Old New York, directed by Col. Thomas Monstery" (https://outofthiscentury.wordpress.com/2015/04/09/a-grand-assault-of-arms-in-old-new-york-directed-by-col-thomas-monstery/ last accessed on 7/24/2018).

Monstery, Col. Thomas H. *El Rubio Bravo, King of the Swordsmen: Or, the Terrible Brothers of Tabasco.* New York: Beadle & Adams, 1881.

[Monstery, Col. Thomas H.]. *El Rubio Bravo, King of the Swordsmen: Or, the Terrible Brothers of Tabasco*. London: Aldine Publishing Co., [1893].

Monstery, Col. Thomas H. *Fighting Tom, the Terror of the Toughs*. New York: Beadle & Adams, 1883.

Monstery, Col. Thomas H. *Iron Wrist: the Swordmaster. A Tale of Court and Camp*. New York: Beadle & Adams, 1879.

Monstery, Col. Thomas H. *Self-Defense for Gentlemen and Ladies.* Berkely: North Atlantic Books, 2015.

Monstery, Col. Thomas H. *The Demon Duelist, or, The League of Steel: a Story of German Student Life*. New York: Beadle & Adams, 1881.

Necrópolis de La Habana: historia de los cementerios de esta ciudad: con multitud de noticías interesantes. Habana: Imprenta El Trabajo, 1875.

New York Clipper.

New York Daily Graphic.

New York Herald.

New York Sun.

New York Telegraph.

New York World.

New York, Passenger Lists, 1820-1957, Year: 1867; Arrival: New York, New York; Microfilm Serial: M237, 1820-1897; Microfilm Roll: Roll 287; Line: 1; List Number: 1058.

"Notes on the Life of Thomas Hoyer Monstery," ca. 1870s, MS copy, courtesy of Thomas Monstery's great great granddaughter Diane Hayes.

Quisenberry, Anderson C. *Lopez's Expeditions to Cuba, 1850 and 1851.* Louisville: John P. Morton and Co., 1906.

Recopilación de leyes, decretos y providencias de los poderes legislative y ejecutivo de las union. Vol. 8-9, Jan.-June 1871. (Mexico: Imprenta Del Gobierno, En Palacio, 1872).

Revista bimestre cubana, July-October, 1910.

Reyes, Rafael. *Nociones de historia del Salvador: precedidas de un resúmen de historia universal.* Barcelona, España: Talleres Gráficos de José Casamelo, 1910.

Roche, James Jeffrey. *The Story of the Filibusters.* London: T. F. Unwin, 1891.

San Francisco Newsletter.

Semana literaria, ó, Compañero de las damas, Volume 1. Habana: M. Soler, 1847.

Squier, Ephraim George. *Honduras and Guatemala.* [New York: 1854].

Temas, Issues 49-52. Habana: Departamento de Ciencia y Técnica del Ministerio de Cultura, 2007.

The House of Beadle and Adams and its Dime and Nickel Novels, Vol. 2. Norman: University of Oklahoma Press, 1962.

Topeka State Journal.

Turf, Field, and Farm.

The Two Republics.

Utica Saturday Globe.

Von Scherzer, Karl Ritter. *Travels in the Free States of Central America: Nicaragua, Honduras, Volume* 2. London: Longman, Brown, Green, Longmans, & Roberts, 1857.

Weekly Alta California.

Whittaker, Capt. Frederick. *The Sword Prince: The Romantic Life of Col. Monstery, American Champion-at-Arms.* New York: M. J. Ivers & Co., 1884.

ILLUSTRATION CREDITS

Frontispiece: John Joseph Flinn, *The Hand-Book of Chicago Biography* (Chicago: The Standard Guide Company, 1893).

Contents, i: H. S. Canfield, "Monstery: Soldier of Fortune" *Everybody's Magazine,* October, 1902.

Contents, ii: "Statue from Palenque." Desire Charnay, *Ancient Cities of the New World: Being Travels and Explorations in Mexico and Central America from 1857-1882* (London: Chapman and Hall, 1887).

Contents, iii: "Statue from Copan." Charnay, *Ancient Cities of the New World.*

Contents, iv: Tavernier, Adolphe Eugène, *Amateurs et salles d'armes de Paris* (Paris: C. Marpon et E. Flammarion, [1886]).

Page v: "Monstery: Soldier of Fortune", *Everybody's Magazine,* October, 1902.

Page x: Col. Thomas H. Monstery, *El Rubio Bravo* (New York: Beadle & Adams, 1881).

Page xi: [Col. Thomas H. Monstery], *El Rubio Bravo* (London: Aldine Publishing Co., [1893])

Page xvii: *Frank Leslie's Illustrated Newspaper*, May 3, 1856..

Page xix: The Miriam and Ira D. Wallach Division of Art, Prints and Photographs: Print Collection, The New York Public Library. "General Narciso López." New York Public Library Digital Collections.

Page xxiii: Photograph courtesy of Diane Hayes.

Page xxix: Mathew B. Brady, [William Walker, three-quarter length studio portrait, standing, left arm resting on pedestal, facing slightly right]. Photographic print courtesy of the Library of Congress.

Page xxx: R.M. Devens, *Our First Century* (Springfield, Mass.: C.A. Nichols & Co., 1876).

Page xxxiv: "Santos Guardiola." William V. Wells, *Explorations and adventures in Honduras: comprising sketches of travel in the gold regions of Olancho, and a review of the history and general resources of Central America; with maps and numerous illustrations* (New York: Harper & Brothers, 1857).

Page xl: William Miller, *Health, exercise and amusement: athletic sports and how to train for them* (Melbourne: Massina, 1895).

Page xliii: "Jose Maria Melo." Jesús María Henao, *Historia de Colombia para la enseñanza secundaria* (Bogota: Librería Colombiana, C. Roldán & Tamayo, 1920).

Page xlv: "Gen. Gerardo Barrios, Ex-President of San Salvador, Central America, Assassinated August 28, 1865." *Frank Leslie's Illustrated Newspaper*, Oct 21, 1865.

Page xlix: Photograph courtesy of J. Makali Bruton of Mexico.

Page liii: [Miguel Miramón, half-length portrait, seated, facing front]. Photographic print courtesy of the Library of Congress.

Page lv: [Jesús González Ortega, half-length portrait, facing front]. Photographic print courtesy of the Library of Congress.

Page lvii: *La Sociedad,* July 15, 1860

Page lxv: *El Monitor Republicano* February 15, 1868

Page lxvii: Angel Escudero, *El duelo en México* (México: Impr. Mundial, 1936).

Page lxxvi: [The execution of Emperor Maximilian and General Miramon by firing squad]. Photographic print courtesy of the Library of Congress.

Page lxxvii: *Daily Alta California*, February 14, 1869.

Page lxxviii: "Francisco V. Aguilera." Manuel F. Alfonso and T. Valero Martinez, *Cuba before the world: a comprehensive and descriptive account of the Republic of Cuba from the earliest times to the present day* (San Francisco, Calif.: Souvenir Guide of Cuba Co., publisher, 1915).

Page lxxxi: Francis Wilson, *Francis Wilson's Life of Himself* (Boston, New York: Houghton Mifflin Company, 1924).

Page lxxxiii: *Chicago Daily Tribune*, February 2, 1896.

Page lxxxv: Image courtesy of Diane Hayes.

Page lxxxvi: "Salvador Cisneros." Alfonso and Martinez, *Cuba before the world.*

Page lxxxix: The Miriam and Ira D. Wallach Division of Art, Prints and Photographs: Photography Collection, The New York Public Library. "The old monastery at Cuernavaca" New York Public Library Digital Collections.

Page xci: Photograph courtesy of Diane Hayes.

Page cvi: Honduras: *Harper's New Monthly Magazine*, May, 1856.

Page cvii: Frederick Catherwood, *Incidents of travel in Central America, Chiapas, and Yucatan* (London: Arthur Hall, Virtue & Co., Paternoster Row, 1854).

Page cviii: Tabasco/Chiapas: William Byam, *A Sketch of the State of Chiapas, Mexico* ([Los Angeles, Cal.]: Press of G. Rice & sons, 1897).

Page cix: Mexico City Environs: Thomas Wallace Knox, *The Boy Travellers in Mexico: Adventures of Two Youths in a Journey to Northern and Central Mexico, Campeachy, and Yucatan, with a Description of the Republics of Central America and of the Nicaragua Canal* (New York: Harper & Brothers, 1890).

Page cxii: *Chicago of Today: The Metropolis of the West* (Chicago, Ill.: Acme Publishing and Engraving Co., 1891).

Page 1: Truxillo, 1671. Ogilby, John, *America: being the latest, and most accurate description of the Nevv vvorld; containing the original of the inhabitants, and the remarkable voyages thither* (London, Printed by the author, and are to be had at his house, 1671).

Page 9: "Monstery: Soldier of Fortune", *Everybody's Magazine,* October, 1902.

Page 10: "City of Tegucigalpa." Thomas Wallace Knox, *The Boy Travellers in Mexico: Adventures of Two Youths in a Journey to Northern and Central Mexico, Campeachy, and Yucatan, with a Description of the Republics of Central America and of the Nicaragua Canal* (New York: Harper & Brothers, 1890).

Page 17: "City of Tegucigalpa." *Harper's New Monthly Magazine*, May, 1856.

Page 18: Simón de Frías, *Tratado elemental de la destreza del sable* (Mexico: En la imprenta de Arizpe, 1809).

Page 25: "Of Spanish Blood." Knox, *The Boy Travellers in Mexico.*

Page 26: "Moeurs et Costumes de Mexico. - Les combats de coqs au Parral, etat de Chihuahua" in *Le Monde Illustré,* August 10, 1867.

Page 35: "Code Signaling With the Fan." Knox, *The Boy Travellers in Mexico.*

Page 36: "Occasional Patrons of the Monte de Piedad." Knox, *The Boy Travellers in Mexico.*

Page 43: Knox, *The Boy Travellers in Mexico.*

Page 44: Francisco Goya, *Pepe Romero matando á toro parado*, 1815. Courtesy of the New York Public Library.

Page 49: Knox, *The Boy Travellers in Mexico.*

Page 50: "Scenes de la Vie Mexicaine" in *Musée Des Familles: Lectures du Soir, XXXI année.* Paris: Rue St. Roch, 1863-1864.

Page 61: "Scenes de la Vie Mexicaine" in *Musée Des Familles.*

Page 62: "Bull-Fight in Jutecalpa." *Harper's New Monthly Magazine*, May, 1856.

Page 68: "The Matador's Triumph." Knox, *The Boy Travellers in Mexico.*

Page 70: Friedrich August Wilhelm Ludwig Roux, *Die Kreussler'sche Stoßfechtschule. Zum Gebrauch für Academieen und Militärschulen nach mathematischen Grundsätzen bearbeitet* (Jena: Druck und Verlag von Friedrich Mauke, 1849). (Source: https://fencingclassics.wordpress.com)

Page 76: "Battle of Rivas" [Nicaragua]. *Frank Leslie's Illustrated Newspaper*, May 7, 1856. Source: Anne S. K. Brown Military Collection.

Page 83: "Road to Olancho." *Harper's New Monthly Magazine*, May, 1856.

Page 84: "Mexican Guerrilleros in 1848". Courtesy of the Library of Congress.

Page 90: Th. Armin, *Das alte Mexiko und die Eroberung Neuspaniens durch Ferdinand Cortez. (*Leipzig: Berlag von Otto Spamer, 1865).

Page 93: "Scenes de la Vie Mexicaine" in *Musée Des Familles.*

Page 94: "San Franciscan Mission." Knox, *The Boy Travellers in Mexico.*

Page 101: "A Member of the Church Party." Knox, *The Boy Travellers in Mexico.*

Page 102: Armin, *Das alte Mexiko.*

Page 108: Armin, *Das alte Mexiko.*

Page 109: "Human Sacrifices." Charnay, *Ancient Cities of the New World.*

Page 110: Charnay, *Ancient Cities of the New World.*

Page 117: "Riding in a Silla." Catherwood, *Incidents of Travel.*

Page 118: "General View of Palenque." Catherwood, *Incidents of Travel.*

Page 123: "A Servant at the Hacienda." Knox, *The Boy Travellers in Mexico.*

Page 124: Aztec Warriors, from Folio 67 of the *Codex Mendoza,* MS.

Page 129: Armin, *Das alte Mexiko.*

Page 131: Catherwood, *Incidents of Travel.*

Page 132: *Harper's New Monthly Magazine, May, 1856.*

Page 138: "In the Forest." Knox, *The Boy Travellers in Mexico.*

Page 140: "Seeking the Mysterious City." Knox, *The Boy Travellers in Mexico.*

Page 147: Catherwood, *Incidents of travel.*

Page 148: "Indian King, Drawn from Clavigaro, Ramirez MS., and Father Duran." Charnay, *Ancient Cities of the New World.*

Page 155: Armin, *Das alte Mexiko.*

Page 156: Catherwood, *Incidents of travel.*

Page 161: "Wants a Souvenir. A Stage Brigand." Knox, *The Boy Travellers in Mexico.*

Page 162: "L'escrime à la Navaja: La *desjarreiazo*." Gustav Doré et Le Baron Davillier, "Voyage en Espagne", *Le Tour du Monde: Nouveau Journal des Voyages, Vol. 12* (Paris: Librairie Hachette Et Cie, 1865).

Page 167: "Joaquin, the Mountain Robber", *Sacramento Union Steamer,* April 22, 1853.

Page 168: The Miriam and Ira D. Wallach Division of Art, Prints and Photographs: Photography Collection, The New York Public Library. "Mexican Gentlemen." New York Public Library Digital Collections.

Page 173: "Agave Americana." Benjamin Moore Norman, *Rambles in Yucatan; or, Notes of Travel through the Peninsula* (New York: J. & H. G. Langley, 1843).

Page 174: "Mexican Troops in Sonora." *Harper's Weekly,* August 7, 1886.

Page 180: Armin, *Das alte Mexiko.*

Page 185: "A City Gate." Frederick A. Ober, *Travels in Mexico and life among the Mexicans* (Boston: Estes & Lauriat, 1885).

Page 186: Armin, *Das alte Mexiko.*

Page 192: Ober, *Travels in Mexico.*

Page 198: "Echo ya la autoridad garra al malvado Ignacio Parra." Broadside courtesy of the Library of Congress.

Page 203: Armin, *Das alte Mexiko.*

Page 204: "Scenes de la Vie Mexicaine" in *Musée Des Familles.*

Page 210: "Ancient House." Ober, *Travels in Mexico.*

Page 216: "Bells of San Blas." William Henry Bishop, *Mexico, California and Arizona; being a new and revised edition of Old Mexico and her lost provinces* (New York, Harper & Brothers, 1900).

Page 217: "A Mexican Gateway." Barrett, Robert South, *Modern Mexico's standard guide to the city of Mexico and vicinity,* City of Mexico, Mexico; New York: Modern Mexico, [1903].

Page 218: *Harper's Weekly,* March, 1859.

Page 222: "Monstery: Soldier of Fortune", *Everybody's Magazine,* October, 1902.

Page 223: "Idol at Quirigua." Catherwood, *Incidents of travel in Central America, Chiapas, and Yucatan.*

Page 224: Tavernier, *Amateurs et salles d'armes de Paris.*

Page 242: Tavernier, *Amateurs et salles d'armes de Paris.*

About the Author

COL. THOMAS H. MONSTERY

Thomas H. Monstery was born on April 21, 1824, in Copenhagen, Denmark. As a youth he joined the Danish navy, and completed his military training at the Royal Military Institute of Gymnastics and Arms in Copenhagen. He later went on to study at the Central Institute of Physical Culture in Stockholm, Sweden, from which he graduated a master of arms. As a soldier, he fought under twelve flags in Europe and the Americas, took part in numerous revolutions, ascended to the rank of colonel, and participated in more than fifty duels with the sword, knife, and pistol. After immigrating to the United States, he embarked upon a distinguished career as a fencing master and instructor of pugilism, opening schools in Baltimore, Oakland, San Francisco, New York, and Chicago, and became recognized as one of the greatest fencing masters in America. During this time, he authored a number of classic articles on the art and science of self-defense, republished under the title *Self-Defense for Gentlemen and Ladies: A Nineteenth-Century Treatise on Boxing, Kicking, Grappling, and Fencing with the Cane and Quarterstaff* (Berkeley: North Atlantic Books, 2015).

About the Editor

BEN MILLER

Ben Miller is an American filmmaker and author. He is a graduate of New York University's Tisch School of the Arts, was the winner of the Alfred P. Sloan Foundation Grant for screenwriting, and has worked for notable personages such as Martin Scorsese and Roger Corman. For the last fourteen years, Miller has studied fencing at the Martinez Academy of Arms, one of the last places in the world still teaching an authentic living tradition of classical fencing. He has served as the Academy's *chef de salle*, and has authored articles for the Association of Historical Fencing, focusing on the fencing and dueling of the American colonial period. He is the author of *Irish Swordsmanship: Fencing and Dueling in Eighteenth Century Ireland* (New York: Hudson Society Press, 2017); a contributor to *Scottish Fencing: Five 18th Century Texts on the Use of the Small-sword, Broadsword, Spadroon, Cavalry Sword, and Highland Battle-field Tactics* (Hollywood: Hudson Society Press, 2018); and the editor of Colonel Monstery's *Self-Defense for Gentlemen and Ladies: A Nineteenth-Century Treatise on Boxing, Kicking, Grappling, and Fencing with the Cane and Quarterstaff* (Berkeley: North Atlantic Books, 2015). He also wrote the foreword to the republication of Donald McBane's classic martial arts treatise, *The Expert Sword-Man's Companion: Or the True Art of Self-Defence* (New York: Jared Kirby Rare Books, 2017). Miller's articles about fencing and martial arts history can be found on the websites *martialartsnewyork.org* and *outofthiscentury.wordpress.com*.

www.ingramcontent.com/pod-product-compliance
Lightning Source LLC
Chambersburg PA
CBHW021829090426
42811CB00032B/2080/J

* 9 7 8 0 9 9 9 0 5 6 7 5 2 *